WEIRD CANADIAN LAWS

Strange, Bizarre, Wacky & Absurd

Lisa Wojna

BLUE
BIKE
BOOKS

The Publisher: Blue Bike Books

Library and Archives Canada Cataloguing in Publication

Wojna, Lisa, 1962–
  Weird Canadian laws : strange, bizarre, wacky & absurd / Lisa Wojna;
  Roger Garcia, illustrator.

ISBN-13: 978-1-897278-12-3
ISBN-10: 1-897278-12-8

  1. Law—Canada—Humor. 2. Law—Canada—Popular works.
I. Title.

K184.7.C2W67 2006   349.7102'07   C2006-904511-9

Project Director: Nicholle Carrière
Project Editor: Bridget Stirling
Cover Image: Roger Garcia
Illustrations: Roger Garcia

PC: P1

DEDICATION

To all the new friends I met—through snail mail, e-mail and over the phone—while working on this project. Meeting so many people so willing to help reinforced my belief that ours is the best country in the world.

To Helen and Delilah, who proved the meaning of true friendship a little closer to home.

To my mother, Mary—reading her poems and listening to her play the piano instilled in me a love for all things creative.

And to my dad, Mitch, who always told me to "open my eyes" and "look it up"—two lessons I haven't forgotten.

ACKNOWLEDGEMENTS

Without the kind assistance of a great number of people working at libraries, archives, and city halls across the country, this book simply wouldn't have seen the light of day. Every community mentioned in these pages had a hard-working staff person (with more than enough to keep him or her busy) who gave up a lunch hour or break to pass something of interest my way. Add to that the individuals who agreed to research specific items on my behalf, and I am deeply indebted indeed. My sincerest thanks go out to you all.

I'd like to thank a few people who went beyond all expectations, putting themselves out considerably to help with this project:

☛ Stuart McLean, archivist with the Yarmouth County Museum and Archives in Yarmouth, Nova Scotia. He not only supplied me with laws from his community, but he also dug deep to provide information on some unique laws from his home province as well.

☞ Edmonton, Alberta's Mayor Stephen Mandel. Many of the blanket e-mails I sent went out to mayors, city clerks, chief administrative officers and other city officials. I decided that if I duplicated my contacts to each community, I'd hopefully hit one person with the time to return my e-mail. I was stunned to have Mayor Mandel personally write me back to tell me he'd passed my request to the appropriate person. Thank you so much for thinking my request important enough for a big city mayor to respond.

☞ Mayor Jim Sheasgreen of Fort Saskatchewan is another example of the man at the top taking time for what some would see as a troublesome request.

☞ To Carolina Roemmich of the Prince of Wales Armouries Heritage Centre, City of Edmonton Archives. In record time, she dug up the original versions of a handful of specific repealed laws I'd requested.

☞ Helen Lowen, librarian with the Law Society Library branch in Wetaskiwin, Alberta. Helen spent hours of her own free time researching items, finding me books, showing me how to use the Canadian Criminal Code and answering countless other questions. Without her invaluable assistance, I would have floundered endlessly in an ocean of legalese.

☞ As always, to the staff of the Wetaskiwin Public Library.

☞ Thank you to my editor, Bridget Stirling, and to Nicholle Carrière, the publisher of Blue Bike Books. With so many sections and subsections and overlapping topics, it takes a keen eye to ensure the biggest blooper of all isn't mine!

☞ And last, but most certainly not least, to my long-suffering family—my husband Garry, children Peter, Melissa, Matthew and Nathan, and my dearest granddaughter Jada. This project has been a particularly time-consuming one, and your support was essential to its completion.

CONTENTS

INTRODUCTION

Odd, unique, unusual, and just plain strange—but not necessarily unnecessary. At every level of government, one fact that came across loud and clear as I was researching this collection of interesting laws was that something as simple (yet as complicated) as common sense sometimes needs to be legislated. Behind many of the laws in this collection are some gems of tales. After all, who would have thought Yellowknife city council would have to pass a bylaw prohibiting residents there from owning a pet lion? Yup, there's a whopper of a story behind that one.

Most of the laws in this collection made sense in their day. Likely, they were instituted because someone somewhere did something so out of the ordinary that prosecuting him or her was more difficult than it would have been had a law against the action in question been in place. In other circumstances, bylaws were passed to ensure peace and order for communities and their residents. Still other situations saw laws developed to protect society as a whole—from disease, for example. Hence the "no spitting on public property" bylaws.

Whether they were able to provide an item for this collection or not, most communities I was successful in contacting acknowledged they'd had a strange law—or at least a law that was unique to that community—in their history. Some communities, on the other hand, responded to my request for information by saying they'd never had a strange law on the books, at the present time or in the past. In an email message, Special Constable Rob Ridley of Carstairs, Alberta, explained that the community where he serves was: "Established on May 15, 1903 and recorded in the North-West Territories Gazette on Monday, June 15, 1903, as Order in Council 176/03. Since that time we have attracted such outstanding local governance that no odd or strange law has ever been passed here. Perhaps that is, in itself, unique."

Hmmm. Reflecting a little more on human nature being what it is, nothing strange is very strange indeed!

Then again, another contributor pointed out that what makes sense today may not make sense tomorrow. Ronald M. Swiddle, solicitor for the city of Sudbury, Ontario, said in his written correspondence: "Although we may be accused of having many odd laws now, I am certain that they are not as odd as they will appear in the future. It is the passage of time that makes us realize items that were major concerns in the past. Indeed, there was a time when most rooms contained a spittoon. There was a time when smoking was permitted everywhere. I am certain other of our current activities will seem equally odd through the future's mirror."

Debrah A. Rabbitts, assistant to the mayor and council of the city of Orillia, Ontario, had this anonymous quote attached to the bottom of her email: "Most good judgment comes from experience...most experience comes from bad judgment." It's an apt phrase for the contents of this book.

Some correspondents shared other interesting tidbits from days gone by. For example, J. Harry Beuker, municipal law enforcement officer for the town of Innisfail, Alberta, added this morsel of information. He noted that in the early 1900s, the town's only constable earned $320 per year, plus 10 percent of revenue collected from fines issued. It's hard to imagine that being a sufficient wage to raise a family.

The town of Wilkie, Saskatchewan, contributed this 1922 bylaw setting the town's water rates that, more than pointing to what people could and couldn't do in that community, provides a snapshot of the economics of the day:

- ☛ hotels, schools, livery and dray barns: $6.00 per month
- ☛ restaurants, laundries, and apartment blocks: $5.00 per month
- ☛ dwellings and all other buildings (except the creamery): $3.00 per month

☞ all householders using public connections: $1.00 per month

The communities in this book often change status from one entry to another. I've chosen to refer to them with the status they had at the time they enacted the particular law being mentioned.

Unless otherwise noted and with the exception of the Canadian Criminal Code violations listed, many of the laws in this collection have been repealed.

Sections of the laws that are in quotations are portions taken directly from a law. In these cases, the wording has been kept, either because it adds to the unique flavour of the law or, in some cases, because it is so convoluted as to make the rule unclear altogether.

Most importantly, I'm eternally grateful for the vast amount of information I received from communities across this wonderful country we call home. To know that many busy people took time out of their day to come up with a selection or two for this book is humbling indeed.

It's important to note that while the majority of the information contained in this book was found in primary sources, such as the laws themselves, the snippets entered here are simplified portions of those laws and not a detailed legal assessment. Any error in the interpretation of these laws is entirely mine.

So with all that in mind, kick off your shoes, lean back, and get ready for a good chuckle at the expense of your forefathers. And do so without an ounce of guilt. After all, chances are the youngsters of tomorrow will have a good laugh looking back on the choices we've made today.

Crime
in Canada

*From "serious wrong doings" to actions that are
"deemed injurious to the public welfare," committing
a crime in Canada can mean anything from melting
money to murder.*

*While committing a crime is never funny, there are
some odd situations provided for in the Canadian
Criminal Code.*

NO THANKS, WE'RE CANADIAN

Television Regulations

It makes perfect sense that the Canadian Broadcasting Corporation's mandate is to pack its primary viewing hours, from 6:00 AM to midnight, with a minimum of 60 percent Canadian content. But it might surprise you to know that privately owned television stations and networks in Canada face similar requirements. They, too, must meet 60 percent Canadian content requirements from 6:00 AM to midnight, and 50 percent of the airtime between 6:00 PM and midnight must be similarly padded with Canadian-based entertainment.

Radio Regulations

Laws about what can or can not be broadcast on Canadian radio and television because of censorship issues don't appear nearly as stringent as rules about Canadian content. Federal laws stipulate Canadian radio stations must maintain a minimum of 35 percent Canadian content when it comes to weekly music selections. Although their quota is much smaller, ethnic radio stations aren't completely exempt from Canadian content rules either. They must ensure that at least seven percent of the music they air weekly is of Canadian origin.

Their French language counterparts, on the other hand, follow a slightly different set of rules, with a minimum of 65 percent of their weekly music selections required to be in French.

LIFE OR DEATH MATTERS

Prohibiting Provocation

Take 10 paces, turn and shoot. You might be unlucky enough to drop dead, but chances are the guy who shot you might wish he could switch places. That's because inciting someone to fight is against the law in Canada, punishable by two years in prison.

All Murders Are not Created Equal

Shoot to kill and you might still escape incarceration, especially if you feared for your life. According to the Canadian Criminal Code, an individual "made to commit a crime under duress or fear for their safety" is forgiven for his or her actions.

Scared to Death

Technically, you're not in trouble if you frighten someone to death. There is, of course, an exception to every rule. In this case, if you frighten a sick person or a child and they die, you've committed "culpable homicide" and can face criminal charges.

FAIR-MARKET VALUE

And the Winner Is?

By Canadian law, if you enter your name in a free draw, you must still earn what you've just won. No easy come here. Nope, if you want to take home that backyard barbecue you just had your name pulled for, you'd better hope you've read the fine print. Chances are, there was a mathematical question somewhere on the entry form near where you filled out your name and telephone number. Often these questions are simple enough that an elementary school student could answer them, but they need to be answered nonetheless. It appears that it's the idea of getting something for nothing that the Canadian government has a problem with, not the mathematical ability of its residents. Some retailers are more forgiving than the federal government when it comes to giving away free stuff. To help their customers along, they often provide an answer to the "skill-testing question" on the draw box for all to see.

The Value of Money

It's an old trick played by many a youngster—place a penny on a railway track and watch it transform into a flattened piece of copper after a train passes by. But should the proper authorities catch you doing it, the stunt could cost you a $250 fine or a year in jail. That's because in Canada, it is against the law to "melt down, break up or use otherwise than as currency any coin that is current and legal tender in Canada."

CRIMINAL OFFENSIVENESS

That's No Bull!

Livestock can be quite the challenge in Canada. For example, if your prize bull gets it in his head to escape from his pen and wander about, you're likely to face a $25 fine should the right person notice. Now, if that bull decides to have his way with the neighbour's purebred herd and manages to impregnate any (or all) of the cows, you could find yourself in even deeper trouble. Your neighbour could fine you for any and all damages—and keep the resulting offspring as well.

Stinky?

It is against the Canadian Criminal Code for anyone to cause a stink in public—literally. Section 178 of the Criminal Code "makes it a summary conviction offense to do certain things with an offensive volatile substance or a stink or stench bomb."

Sacred Servant

Nothing other than divine intervention can obstruct or prevent a clergy person from conducting a service or performing any other clerical duty. Break the law, and you're guilty of an "indictable offence," and you could face up to two years in jail.

That's Not Funny

Caped crusaders beware! You might soon find yourselves out of work, because it's a breach of the Canadian Criminal Code for illegal acts to be depicted in comic books. As defined in Section C-46 of the 2005 Canadian Criminal Code, a "crime comic" is a picture or image showing the "commission of crimes, real or fictitious" or "events connected with the commission of crimes, real or fictitious, whether occurring before or after the commission of the crime." I'll bet that's news to the creators of Superman!

BE HONEST, NOW

What's In a Name?

It's been said that imitation is the greatest form of flattery. But if you think the Canadian government will be thrilled to learn you've used the words "Parliament Hill" to name your business or to identify the items you sell, you're sadly mistaken. Using "Parliament Hill" to describe anything other than the official site in Ottawa, Ontario, is against the law.

No Fooling

Anyone who fraudulently "pretends to exercise or to use any kind of witchcraft, sorcery, enchantment or conjuration," or claims to tell fortunes or have other paranormal abilities, is guilty of "pretending to practice witchcraft." As with many laws, an intensely obvious question remains. How do you go about discerning whether someone is guilty of pretending or if he or she is, indeed, a gifted psychic?

Truth or Dare

Tell a tale you know is false and have it end up in the pages of your local paper, and you could be charged with spreading false news. If you're guilty, you could face up to two years in jail.

No Questions Asked

Use the words above when advertising a reward for the return of a lost item, and you're guilty of breaking a federal law.

Simply Treasonous!

You'd better practise your manners before taking in a royal visit. That's because it is a crime to startle the Queen in any way. Should you commit the dirty deed, you could spend up to 14 years in jail. Knowingly selling her or any of her representatives defective merchandise is another no-no. The same penalty applies.

Building
Regulations

*Building regulations were most likely initially
enforced for citizens' safety.*

*While some of the following entries seem like nothing
more than common sense, and it boggles the mind how
enacting a law was necessary, still others remind us
of a time and place long forgotten.*

CONSTRUCTIVE BEHAVIOUR

Moving Along

In 1897, if you planned on moving a house in Summerside, PEI, and you had to take a break for a while, you'd better make sure you assigned someone watchman duty. It was against the law to have any "house or building so being removed stand on any street or square without a watchman being in attendance."

Strictly Forbidden

Mud huts and homes with straw roofs were banned in the town of Ponoka, Alberta, in 1914. In the name of fire prevention, residents had to avoid the use of manure, hay, straw and any other "inflammable materials" in the construction of their homes. It appears, however, that wood was not considered an inflammable material.

Building Code

While the use of coal for heating is nearly obsolete, and there are few trucks delivering coal these days, the city of Sault Ste. Marie, Ontario, still has a regulation on the books regarding the construction of coal chutes. Any business constructing a coal chute is required to submit a detailed drawing to the city engineer. The homeowner must also

- ☛ pay for the construction,
- ☛ pay the city any taxes, and an annual area rental, resulting from the existence of the chute,
- ☛ keep everything in good repair,
- ☛ maintain neighbouring sidewalks and repair any damages resulting from the construction of and delivery of coal,
- ☛ allow the city access, should they require it, for the installation of "pipes, cables, wires, poles and other appliances in or through" the area of the chute" and
- ☛ last, but not least, not even think about holding the city liable should a burglar enter the premises through the coal chute.

Building Permit Required

It cost real estate moguls 50 cents for a building permit in the town of Wilkie, Saskatchewan, in 1913. Failure to comply with this bylaw before building your dream home could cost you $25 or 30 days in jail. The law was repealed in 1923.

Icy Stakes

Cutting ice on lakes, ponds and rivers around Yarmouth, Nova Scotia, was no simple matter in 1916. Town bylaws of that day required anyone cutting ice for home use to identify the area by floating softwood pieces of 4 feet (1.2 metres) or more in length and 3 inches (7.5 centimetres) in diameter. That way (it was hoped), anyone passing by would see the hole in the ice and therefore be protected from an unexpected fall into the frigid waters. Noncompliance, as well as removing stakes from the water, could land you a $20 fine or up to three months in jail.

Paying the Tax Man

It has long been said that the only two guarantees in life
are death and taxes, but developing a personal income
tax system in Canada was a long, arduous and somewhat
unstructured process. Some communities in the country
initiated a type of personal income tax system of their
own, but they seemed to tax only men of a certain age.

In 1917, the federal government first imposed an annual
tax on both people and corporations under the Income
War Tax Act. In all provinces except Québec, the federal
government took the responsibility for collecting personal
taxes away from the municipalities. They also collected
corporate taxes for most of Canada, with the exception of
Québec, Alberta and Ontario. Of course, the municipalities wouldn't be robbed of their due—they just started
collecting taxes of a different sort.

PAYING YOUR DUES

Warfage of Vessels

In 1897, the town of Summerside, PEI, not only charged vessels a parking fee of sorts for docking in their bay, but they also charged a tax on the goods on board. A bylaw dated that year enabled the wharfinger (the keeper of the wharf) the ability to "ask, demand, take and receive of" fees as outlined by the town. For example, ships landing with cedar posts were charged 15 cents per 100 posts. Coal brought in 5 cents a ton and cordwood brought 16 cents a cord. Transported goods not included in the list were charged at a rate of "2 cents per barrel, bulk of 5 cubic feet, or 10 cents per ton, at option of wharfinger."

Tax Time

Businesses, income earners, landowners and "special franchises" in the town of Daysland, Alberta, were first faced with paying municipal and school taxes in 1908. Men aged 21 and older who didn't fit into any of the aforementioned tax categories wouldn't get off scot-free. They had to pay an annual $2.00 poll tax.

A similar poll tax was instituted in the village of Terrace, BC, in 1928. Every male was expected to pay a $5.00 annual tax. The money was used to help support local hospitals and schools.

Work and Taxes

Men aged 21 to 60 living in the town of Cochrane, Alberta, in 1914 were out-of-pocket after the town council passed a bylaw requiring them to pay a $1.00 labour tax, due on May 1 each year. The police chief was responsible for collecting the tax and was authorized to "use all necessary means" to do so.

Income Tax

As of 1925, if you lived in Sault Ste. Marie, Ontario, and earned any money at all, you were required to file a statement of income by May of each year, have your income assessed and possibly pay a tax. Since municipalities no longer have the authority to collect an income tax, the law is no longer in effect.

Property
Laws

Private property doesn't mean you can do whatever you want on your land. There are countless building bylaws regulating what you can and can not do with and on your property in every municipality across the country.

And, of course, what the general public can and can't do on public land is just as restricted. As always, there are rules and regulations for everything.

GOOD NEIGHBOURS

Mend Your Fences

If your dog wandered into the neighbour's wheat field, trampling his way through to the watering hole on the other side, you might have been let off with just a slap on the wrist in 1898. At that time, the law in the North-West Territories, which took up most of Canada west of Neepawa, Manitoba, stated if your property wasn't completely surrounded by a "lawful fence," then the problem was all yours. What constituted a lawful fence varied depending on exactly where you lived. Some areas required a height of 4'6" (1.4 metres), while others required barbed or plain wire secured to posts. So if you wanted to protect yourself, you'd have to be sure of your legal location and the applicable fencing requirements.

Measure Up!

Fences are strictly regulated in London, Ontario. If your neighbour builds a fence, it can't be less than 3'6" (1.07 metres) or more than 4'6" (1.37 metres) in height. And barbed wire is absolutely forbidden within city limits.

Dim Those Lights!

A front yard light might make you feel safe at night, but if its glow flows beyond your property line, you could find yourself face to face with a bylaw officer. That's the law in the city of Regina, Saskatchewan.

Pristine Property
Property owners in the town of Morden, Manitoba, are expected to follow strict guidelines when it comes to upkeep. Along with the obvious expectations of cleanliness and safety, the town council restricts the number of vehicles parked or stored on a person's land, and it's against a 2001 bylaw for residents to store household appliances in a location "visible from any public street, road or lane." The town also monitors excessive weed growth and unkempt lawns. So if your dandelions are growing out of control, you'd better get your weed whacker out. Breaking any portion of the bylaw could result in town workers taking the matters into their own hands—and charging you for it!

Hot and Cold

Air conditioners and heat exchangers must be strategically placed in Regina homes. A bylaw in that Saskatchewan city states they can't be "closer to the front lot line than the front wall" of the building they are attached to and "closer than 3 metres (10 feet) to a door or window of a dwelling on an adjoining lot."

A LITTLE RESPECT

Looking After Our Elders

The city of Whitehorse, Yukon, takes the responsibility of caring for its elders seriously. In an effort to compensate for seniors' growing utility bills, a 2002 bylaw gives everyone aged 65 and older an annual grant of up to $500.

A Grave Situation

It's been said you know the quality of a society by the way they treat their dead. And it seems to be an apt adage for the people of Bowden, Alberta. In 1954, the village council enacted a bylaw outlining specific regulations for cemeteries. In particular, they went to great lengths to explain how excess earth is to be removed from the site immediately after the grave is filled in. They then required that "gravel, stone, paper or boxes or any-thing of a similar nature...be removed within 48 hours after the burial," even being so particular as to rule that "nothing of a size greater than one square inch be left in the vicinity of the grave."

DON'T MAKE A MESS!

Art, No Art

City officials in Regina, Saskatchewan, don't look kindly on graffiti. Though some would beg to differ, in that city, it's not art—it's a crime. To put an end to vandalism, city officials passed a bylaw providing residents with some hints on how to combat the problem. They suggest property owners

- grow plants along the exterior walls of buildings,
- use "anti-graffiti coatings on surfaces previously covered by graffiti" or
- pay artists to paint murals on areas attracting graffiti.

The image that comes to mind, should everyone follow these rules to the letter, is an aerial view of nothing but greenery and an occasional mural.

Snow Littering
An old bylaw in Parkdale, PEI, prohibited people from littering town streets and sidewalks—with snow! It was one of many outdated bylaws in the Charlottetown Area Municipalities Act repealed between 1997 and 2002.

Trim Those Trees

Out-of-control greenery encroaching on town sidewalks or on public roadways is against the law in Oak Bay, BC. In 1994, council made it law for residents to control their foliage with a Hazardous Tree and Shrub Bylaw.

Safety Conscious

For the sake of public safety, in 1914, the town of Ponoka, Alberta, enacted a lengthy bylaw restricting a number of potentially dangerous behaviours. You couldn't break, train or breed your horse in town. You couldn't fasten your horse to any "tree, shrub or sapling." Sidewalks were made for people, not for bikes, horses or carriages. Even wheelbarrows and tricycles were forbidden on town sidewalks. It was illegal to use barbed wire when building a fence that bordered any highway, street, road lane, alley or byway in town limits. In fact, any errant nail protruding through the fence post could get you into trouble as well.

And business owners weren't allowed to sweep their way out their store doors and onto town sidewalks. They were expected to collect their rubbish in a dustpan and dispose of it in a properly enclosed garbage can.

Nothing but a Nuisance
A bylaw passed by the city of Kelowna, BC, in 1932 made it illegal to "excavate a hole or pit on any property by removing soil, sand or gravel unless erecting a building." The reason was simple—holes and pits were a nuisance. The penalty for breaking this bylaw was $100, and it wasn't repealed until 1990.

GREENING UP

Saving Water

The laws of supply and demand are strictly adhered to in the city of Guelph, Ontario. So much so that in 2003, the city council enacted a bylaw stating it was against the law to water your lawn during a rainstorm. Allowing tap water to pool around plants and trees or to run off you lawn and onto the street in front of your home also could be cause for a visit from the city's bylaw officer. The same bylaw states that hosing down your driveway rather than sweeping up any dry dirt or debris is another no-no. Break the law, and the city could decide to reduce the amount of water supplied to your home.

Two Will Do

The town of Cochrane, Alberta, has taken its commitment to environmental consciousness seriously after the council in that community passed a new waste management bylaw in December 2005. In Cochrane, it doesn't matter if you have a family of two or twelve. Residents now have a "two unit limit" when it comes to having their garbage picked up at the curb. And what constitutes a single unit is not just any size of garbage bag. A bag larger than 66 by 91 centimetres is now treated as two units— no exceptions! If, on special occasions, you have an extra bag to add to your curbside pickup, that garbage must be placed in a special "Town of Cochrane Excess Waste Bag" for an additional $2.00 fee.

Collection of Compost

The town council in Stavely, Alberta, may have yet to pass a bylaw on the matter, but they have distributed a notice to all town residents explaining how compost garbage "must be bagged in clear bags." The council-sanctioned bags can be purchased at the Stavely Grocery Store and, for residents choosing this option, the compost drop-off is only open on Fridays from 8:00 AM to 3:00 PM.

Curfews

"What can't you do during the day that you have to be out of doors after dark?" Many of us can recall having one parent or another ask this question at some point during our youth. And it appears youngsters staying outside after dark were of concern to the general population throughout the ages.

Although curfew laws are still on the books in several communities, and rumblings about enacting curfew bylaws in towns and cities across the country are a topic of frequent news reports, this kind of bylaw is rarely enforced.

DO YOU KNOW WHERE YOUR CHILDREN ARE?

Curfew Bell

In 1895, the Women's Christian Temperance Union played its part when it came to regulating the whereabouts of youngsters in the town of Dresden, Ontario. The ladies did this by ringing the town bell daily at 9:00 PM to remind residents it was curfew time. The bell was the signal for all youths age 16 and younger to be off public streets and in their homes or suffer the wrath of the on-duty constable. If youngsters weren't safe in the loving arms of their families after the curfew bell sounded, they would get a free ride, courtesy of the constable, and their parents or guardians could be fined as much as $5.00. The fine increased depending on the frequency of the youngster's rebellion.

Curfew Time

In Sault Ste. Marie, Ontario, a curfew for youth 16 and under was established by enacting a bylaw "in accordance with the provisions of the Children's Protection Act of Ontario." Parents or guardians permitting their youngsters to wander the streets after

9:00 PM would be fined $1.00 for a first offence and $2.00 for a second offence. Break the law three or more times, and they were fined $5.00 each time. While this bylaw was passed in 1921 and is still on the books, it hasn't been enforced, since according to city officials, it wouldn't likely survive a Canadian Charter of Rights and Freedoms challenge based on age discrimination.

Still the Law

A currently active curfew bylaw in Churchill, Manitoba, provides youth there with a stepping-stone of sorts to obtaining the rights of adulthood. Youth aged 11 and younger have to be off the streets and at home by 10:00 PM. Youth 12 to 16 have an extra hour before they're in trouble for roaming about unaccompanied by a parent, and youth over 16 but not yet the "age of majority," (which in Manitoba is 18) have to be safe and sound behind closed doors by midnight. This curfew bylaw also applies to being in a "public place" without a parent or adult guardian.

Police escort young lawbreakers home. If there is no adult available to meet the officer escort, and one can't be found in short order, the teen could find him or herself "delivered to the appropriate child care agency."

Churchill has a rather unique way of doling out punishment to fit this crime as well. For youth involved, a first offence warrants a warning, and any second and subsequent offense will cost as much as $100 and assigned community service hours.

Parents and guardians who don't take the curfew laws seriously could find themselves back in school: "Any guardian that is found in contravention of this bylaw a second time shall be sent to community services to receive parenting classes."

NO TIME FOR FUN

Dance With Me

You may like to swing your partner 'round and 'round the dance floor, but there were strict guidelines on how far into the wee hours you could party in the village of Smithers, BC, in 1934. The council enacted a curfew bylaw of a unique sort, stating that the last tune played at any dance had to end by midnight on Saturday and by 2:00 AM on any other night of the week. It seems the reasoning behind this was to ensure partiers had a relatively early night on Saturday, giving them no excuses for not filling the pews at Sunday morning worship.

Early to Bed

In 1947, the village of Smithers, BC, agreed to amend their curfew bylaw of 1930. The original curfew mandated that children age 15 and younger had to be indoors by 9:00 PM during the winter months of October to March and by 10:00 PM from April to September. The court could fine people who allowed their youngsters out past curfew unaccompanied by a parent or guardian. But the situation caused a whole lot of problems for peace officers on days the "Moving Picture Theatre of the Village of Smithers" was operating, since the movies didn't typically end until 10:00 PM or later. To accommodate the situation and keep parents and their youngsters happy—not to mention the owner of the movie theatre and the peace officers on duty those nights—village council agreed to extend the curfew, on movie nights only, to 10:30 PM.

Hunting
Regulations

Hunters beware!

While you might think you have the corner on the market when it comes to knowing all there is to know about hunting, think again. We may all be Canadian, but hunting regulations differ from province to province and are continually evolving throughout.

See what I mean…

TRACKING DOWN THE RULES

Laws of Yesteryear

In 1909, Alberta's Minister of Agriculture paid a bounty of $10 for each timber wolf pelt, $1.00 for each prairie wolf pelt and $1.00 for each wolf pup pelt. But if the wolves you claimed that you killed in Alberta actually came from outside the province, you could face a $100 fine.

Laws of Today

☞ Animals may pose a nuisance as they wander through town streets, but you still can't hunt or trap wild prey in Canmore, Alberta. A 1991 bylaw makes it clear, stating that a hunter could be fined as much as $2500 for his efforts.

☛ It is against the law to use a pistol, revolver or "any firearm that is capable of firing more than one bullet during one pressure of the trigger" while hunting in Alberta.

☛ Hunters going after big game in Saskatchewan must be completely outfitted with an "outer suit of scarlet, bright yellow, blaze orange or white or any combination of these colors." Head gear of one of these colours, except white, must also be worn.

☛ Brightly coloured clothing is not required for hunters in Alberta. The only exception to this rule is for those hunting on Camp Wainwright, but bow hunters hunting in the bow-only portion of Camp Wainwright are exempt from clothing rules.

The Lord's Day

From the founding of this country until well into the 20th century, Sunday was considered a sacred day of rest. All but the most essential services stopped for this 24-hour period, and people were expected to do just that—rest.

But what form that "rest" took was almost as controversial as later decisions to open retail businesses and liquor stores on Sundays.

NO-FUN DAY

Batter Up!

Throughout most of Canada's early history, keeping the Lord's Day holy meant regulating what events could and could not occur on Sunday. But in 1968, the town of Blenheim, Ontario, did bend the rules slightly. They decided that public sports, previously banned on the day of rest, could be played after 1:30 PM. And they were very specific as to which sports would get the reprieve. Approved athletic activities included "baseball, softball, fast ball, football, rugby, rugger, soccer, hockey, lacrosse, tennis, badminton, swimming and aquatic sports events, tract [track] and field, bowling and curling, public skating and figure skating."

The town of Cochrane, Alberta, was a step ahead of Blenheim, having passed a similar law in 1950. Cochrane, too, listed those sports allowed, and the town's list, for the most part, mirrored Blenheim's. Looks like if you played basketball, volleyball or ping pong, you were out of luck—at least in these two communities.

Let the Show Begin!

Laws surrounding Sunday activities loosened slightly in 1967 in the town of Trenton, Ontario, after a referendum of sorts was held and the majority of the public agreed that a little entertainment on Sunday afternoons wasn't any great sin. The council members of the day agreed, and on January 15, 1968, it was deemed lawful for movies, theatrical performances, concerts and lectures to be held after 1:30 PM.

Clean Fun Only

While restrictions on participating in or attending events such as air and car shows or taking part in certain sporting events on Sundays were loosened in the town of Fahler, Alberta, in 1968, some activities were still taboo. It was still against the law to engage in or attend "horse races, or horse race meetings, dog races, boxing contests or exhibitions of wrestling or other like contests or exhibitions" on Sundays.

Still Revered

The year is 2002. The Yukon has revised its statutes, and the Lord's Day Act is still on the books. Residents there can take part in sporting events and other recreational activities, provided the event begins after 1:30 PM. Sunday movies, concerts and other performances are okay as well, as long as they also follow the time stipulation. There is a provision to repeal the statute, but it would take a vote by the electorate saying they are "in favour of the repeal of the bylaw passed under the authority of the Lord's Day Act that regulates public games and sports for gain after 1:30 o'clock in the afternoon of the Lord's Day." To date, a public vote has not been held.

YOU CAN'T SELL THAT TODAY!

Got Gas?

If you ran out of gas on a Sunday in the village of Fahler, Alberta, in 1954, you couldn't fill up at just any gas station. The village passed a bylaw stating that all but one gas station in the community had to remain closed on Sunday. Each gas station would take a turn at being the lucky station open each week, and all other stations were responsible for posting a notice in a prominent place directing needy customers to the open station. Any gas station owner opening for business on a Sunday when it wasn't his or her turn would have the station closed by the village constable. The fine for a first offence was $5, $25 for the second offence and as much as $100 for a third or subsequent offence.

Open for Business

Depending on the type of wares they pedalled, shop owners in the village of Smithers, BC, had to abide by strict "Lord's Day" guidelines as early as 1934. Other than "Automobile Repair Shops or Gasoline Service Stations," all shops were to be closed on Sundays and all statutory holidays. Regular shop hours of 8:45 AM to 6:00 PM were kept from Monday to Wednesday and on Friday. Thursday, however, was subject to the "Weekly Half Holiday Act," and closing time was moved back to 1:00 PM. Shop owners were allowed to compensate for some of the closed hours on Thursday by staying open to 9:00 PM on Saturday. And just because you might be selling your goods as a street vendor instead of an actual store, the law still applied. "Hawkers and Peddlers" weren't allowed to sell goods when stores were closed. The fine for breaking any portion of this bylaw could cost you $100—a pretty penny in the Dirty Thirties.

Garbage
and Gunk

*Public sanitation and the health of residents go hand
in hand, and from the earliest days, newly founded communities across the country were quick to formulate laws
in this regard.*

*While all were logical (after a fashion), it seems bizarre
that some needed to be mentioned at all.*

OUTDOOR PLUMBING

The Throne

Construction of an outhouse at every home or public place was mandatory in the town of Ponoka, Alberta, in 1929. And not just any old outhouse would do. A seat must be securely attached to the framework of the outhouse "in such a manner that same may be easily and expeditiously lifted up and left standing open when required." A 5-gallon (19-litre) galvanized bucket was to be used as a receptacle, and any previously dug pit-style outhouse was to be dismantled and covered in. The bucket had to be dumped twice a month in the appropriate corner of the town's nuisance grounds. Refuse to comply with this bylaw, and the town could take it on itself to build your personal throne for you, charge you for materials and labour and then hit you with a fine of up to $50 or 60 days in jail, "with or without hard labour."

Public Record

A sanitary bylaw in Terrace, BC, required the staff person responsible for removing "night soil" to follow a set of stringent guidelines. He had to maintain a record of all toilets in the municipality and provide a monthly report to the village clerk, complete with each owner's name and the dates of cleaning. Talk about airing your dirty laundry in public! Residents interfering with the cleaning of their toilet faced a fine of up to $25.

No-fly Zone

Outhouse regulations were a little less stringent in the village of Quesnel, BC. In 1950, a bylaw regulated the style of an outhouse but still allowed a dugout pit. However, the bylaw did stipulate that this outdoor privy should be "so banked and eased as to be absolutely fly tight."

Keep Your Distance

A 1946 bylaw in the village of Westlock, Alberta, outlined a list of specific distances an outhouse could be located from different buildings. They had to be within 5 feet (1.5 metres) of the rear property line of any lot, at least 2 feet (60 centimetres) from a lane or adjoining lot, a minimum of 50 feet (15 metres) from any well site and at least 20 feet (6 metres) from any "dwelling, store, restaurant or any other place where food is stored or consumed."

Price Per Pail

A 1910 bylaw in the town of Okotoks, Alberta, also required residents to outfit their outhouses with metal pails, rather than just dirt pits. According to Lucy Rowed, historical assistant with the town of Okotoks Museum and Archives, "The 'Scavenger' was duly appointed to empty unmaintained, overflowing or stinky closets at a cost to the owner of 25 cents per pail."

Bucket Brigade

Weyburn, Saskatchewan, was strict about the disposal of the contents of the family waste bucket. In 1913, the town enacted a bylaw outlining all the particulars of waste management in that community. First, residents not connected with the city sewer system were required to purchase (at cost) a specially regulated "galvanized iron pail" measuring about 2 ft² (0.05 m³). The homeowner was then expected to build an outhouse of sorts, following specific regulations outlined by the city, to house the pail.

Pail Provided

In Wilkie, Saskatchewan, the sanitation system for personal waste was subject to yet another set of unique regulations. In a 1930 town bylaw, the council legislated that every homeowner had to provide an "outside pail closet" that was completely "fly-proof" and had "self-closing covers." No additional garbage of any kind, such as kitchen waste or used wash water, could be added to the contents of closet pails. For the convenience of having town officials dispose of the contents of these pails on a regular basis, each homeowner was charged an annual fee of $8.00 per pail. And not just anyone had the privilege of collecting the contents of these pails. In fact, any unauthorized person removing or disposing of any night soil could face a fine of his or her own.

Water Closet Etiquette

In 1924, the town of Cochrane, Alberta, passed a bylaw making it illegal to plug the town's sewer system by putting "garbage, offal, dead animals, vegetable parings, ashes, cinders, rags, strings, hair combings, matches or any other matter or thing that would tend to obstruct any pipe or sewer in any water closet, bathtub, wash bowl, kitchen sink or any other fixture connected with the sewer system of the town of Cochrane." To ensure no one—residents and their guests alike—broke this law, it was also stipulated that each householder post a complete copy of the bylaw in a clearly visible place in any bathroom or washing area so that no one could use the excuse he or she wasn't aware of the restrictions. Failure to follow the bylaw could cost the offender $50 or up to 21 days in jail—that was, once the jails were finally built!

TOILETS GO INDOORS

Indoor Plumbing

In 1950, indoor washrooms, or water closets, were coming into fashion in the village of Quesnel, BC, necessitating the institution of a bylaw regulating their construction in that community. Should a homeowner install a water closet in his or her dwelling, a window measuring 3 ft^2 (0.9 m^2) and able to open to at least half its height was required.

Bathroom Rules

A 1975 bylaw in the city of Kelowna, BC, states: "every dwelling house, hotel, boarding house, rooming house, restaurant, store, factory and manufactory or whatsoever kind, erected within the city shall have a water-closet, toilet or lavatory accommodation in connection therewith." While the idea seems like a no-brainer, this law is still in effect.

Privy Patrol

When you gotta go, you gotta go—or so the saying goes. But in the town of Barrhead, Alberta, finding a pit stop for the purpose of relieving yourself became a little more difficult after the town council passed a bylaw in 1970 ordering privies removed from some private properties. According to the bylaw, homes on land bordering town streets where sewer and water mains were located had to be connected with town service. Water closets or privies not connected to the town's system had to be removed from the property within 30 days of notice from the town. Failure to do so meant the town could send their people in to do the dirty work and add the cost of the effort to the property owner's taxes.

TAKE OUT THE TRASH

Ashes to Ashes

The disposal of ashes must have posed a significant challenge in years past, since bylaws managing their disposal were enacted in many communities across the country. No one—householder or servant—was allowed to deposit ashes in any street, lane, road or public property of any sort in the town of Lloydminster, Alberta. The 1913 bylaw went on to specify that ashes were to be placed in a metal container not less than 27 inches in height and 3 inches in diameter. They were to remain in the container until cool, but the bylaw doesn't go on to explain where they should be deposited at that point. Still, dare to defy what was written and you could face a $10 fine or 20 days in jail.

Careful With That

Disposing of ashes in the town of Carman, Manitoba, was no simple matter in December 1955. That's when town council passed a law outlining the appropriate manner of getting rid of the potentially flyaway garbage. According to the new bylaw, ashes simply couldn't be dumped in the street or on any town property, and anyone caught dumping ashes would face a $2.00 fine for each offense. Strangely enough, the law was repealed just a few months later.

In the Can

In 1929, Ponoka, Alberta, definitely had a say in how you dis-
posed of your household waste. The town enacted a law that
garbage not able to be burned must be placed in a tightly sealed
zinc or galvanized "refuse bucket." This garbage can was to be
located at the rear of each home and business property, and
town employees collected the contents once a week. Homes and
businesses not providing a garbage bucket for themselves would
be provided with one—and subsequently charged for the item—
by the town and could face a $50 fine or up to 60 days in jail
for non-compliance.

Planes, Trains, Automobiles and More

Keeping people safe on roads, lanes, streets and highways has been a major concern for communities everywhere from the days of the first horse-drawn carts. Developing rules of the road makes good sense. After all, you can't have traffic moving in all directions without causing some sort of disaster. Just try driving the wrong way on a one-way street!

What is interesting, however, is how some communities regulated everything from when and where you could push your wheelbarrow to common-sense pedestrian protocol.

SLOW DOWN!

No Speed Freaks Here

In the town of Peace River, Alberta, anyone driving a vehicle of
any description—horse-drawn buggy, automobile or even unicy-
cle—couldn't exceed a speed of 6 miles per hour (9.7 kilometres
per hour) "while in the act of crossing over the Harmon River
Bridge." Considering that a brisk power walker likely exceeds
the 6 mile per hour limit, one is hard-pressed to understand
why anyone would bother driving their vehicle into town at all.
Still, break the law, and you could face a fine of $100. And if
you were unable to pay, you could face a prison sentence of up
to 60 days, "with or without hard labour." Also known as Heart
River Bridge, the structure was located within town limits. The
1925 bylaw doesn't mention if the same speed was enforced
throughout the rest of the town.

Slow-moving Vehicles

Motorized vehicles of any kind were kept restrained in the town of Lloydminster, Alberta, in 1919. That's when the town fathers enacted a speed limit of 12 miles per hour. If you dared to speed through that community, a hefty fine of up to $50 was charged for a first offense. And if you didn't control that heavy foot of yours, second and subsequent fines were double that. If you couldn't pay the piper, you had to pack your bags and spend the next 30 days in jail.

Back Lane Safety

The city of Winnipeg, Manitoba, eliminated one speeding loophole in 1978. Anyone driving down a back lane must keep his speed to a maximum of 30 kilometres per hour. The law was updated in 2002 and is still in effect.

Easy Does It

The town of Okotoks didn't adhere to rushing about, especially when it came to motor vehicle traffic. A 1910 bylaw restricted the speed in town to 10 miles per hour (16 kilometres per hour), and reduced that further to 5 miles per hour (8 kilometres per hour) when approaching another car. An article in the *Okotoks Review* stated: "Every precaution must be taken to avoid accident, even to stopping car altogether."

Tough on Traffic

The town of Wilkie, Saskatchewan, was pretty tough on all types of traffic using town streets and sidewalks in 1922. An extensive bylaw developed that year regulated everything from speed limits to parking. For example, slow traffic, including horses and motor vehicles travelling less than 4 miles per hour (6.5 kilometres per hour), had to hug the curb when travelling through town. Vehicles were considered "fast traffic" when they were travelling more than 4 miles per hour (6.5 kilometres per hour).

Most rules of the road were similar to those of today. What was unique was how horses and Fords were treated alike. Both were expected to pass to the left of slow traffic. When meeting at a stop sign, the horse or motor vehicle to the right had the right of way. However, the bylaw does get a little muddy when referring to parking regulations. For example, it stipulates "No vehicle shall stop with its left to the curb." One would assume this didn't apply to a solitary horse and saddle operation, since it's pretty hard to get a horse to stand still at its tether while you do your shopping!

Pace Yourself
A 1910 amendment to a 1901 bylaw added a few restrictions to the speed of horse travel in the town of Rat Portage (now Kenora), Ontario. Your equine-powered transportation—with or without carriage—couldn't pass across bridges in the town "at any rate of speed greater or faster than a walk."

Whoa, Nellie!

The first cars might not have made their appearance yet on the streets of North Battleford, Saskatchewan, in 1906, but speed limits were still strictly enforced. Horses couldn't gallop, carriage drivers needed to slow down through town and racing of any kind was strictly prohibited. Slow-moving traffic travelling less than 4 miles per hour (6.5 kilometres per hour) had to pull over as close to the right curb as possible to allow other traffic to pass by. And if you decided to stop by the local market and pick up a few things, you'd better make sure your horse was secured to something strong enough to prevent him from getting loose.

In 1917, another traffic bylaw in the same community defined the term "vehicle" as including "equestrians, led horses and everything on wheels or runners, drawn or driven by animal or mechanical power of every description, except baby carriages." In that same bylaw, the word "horse" included "horses, mules, oxen or other beasts of burden."

TRAFFIC FLOW

Keep the Streets Clear

"No person" was allowed to tie his horse or horses to "any ring or hook in any other way across the sidewalk, path or crossing" in the village of Standard, Alberta. The 1923 bylaw prevented the gathering of any group of people as well, so it's safe to say a protest rally of any kind wasn't in the cards.

Well, Duh!

According to a 1965 traffic bylaw in the village of Quesnel, BC, you were absolutely prohibited from building any "structure, object, substance, or thing" in the middle of any street. After all, you could block the flow of traffic!

Don't Play in Traffic

There is a time and place for athletic amusement, and the middle of the street is simply not the right place at any time, according to a 1965 traffic bylaw in Quesnel, BC. Council deemed it against the law to do anything on city streets that might be "likely or calculated to frighten horses or embarrass or delay the passage of vehicles."

Safe Parking

At one time it was against the law to park any closer than 10 feet (3 metres) from a house in Calgary, and that included a car, carriage or wagon.

Safe Streets

Wilkie, Saskatchewan's town council went all out making sure their town streets were safe in 1922. They passed a bylaw making it illegal to throw stones, balls of ice or snow, hard balls of any kind or any other "dangerous missile or use any bow and arrow in the street."

Parking Prohibited

It was against the law in 1922 in the town of Wilkie, Saskatchewan, to park a carriage on town streets and unhitch your horse. While parked on town streets, carriage and horse had to remain as one unit.

City Streets

A bylaw passed in the city of St. John's, Newfoundland, in 1970 made it illegal to dig a hole, ditch, drain or sewer in city streets without first getting a permit from the city engineer.

First-class Delivery

Anyone dropping a package of any kind on the streets or sidewalks of St. John's, Newfoundland, is guilty of obstructing free passage and could face a $25 fine.

Comfortable Passage

Since 1970, sidewalks in the city of St. John's, Newfoundland, have to be a minimum of 3.048 metres wide on streets that are 18.288 metres in width and larger—and yes, the bylaw is that precise! Sidewalk width on narrow streets was to be determined by a meeting of council.

Keep It Moving

The Grand Parade, an area in downtown Halifax, Nova Scotia, holds special significance to the residents of that city. So much so that the council enacted a bylaw in 1950 making it illegal for residents to leave a vehicle standing stationary and abandoned without written permission from the public works department. You also couldn't skateboard in the area. Either offense was punishable by a $20 fine or 10 days in jail.

Foot Traffic

Pedestrians had their rules and regulations drawn out in detail for them after the town of Yarmouth, Nova Scotia, passed a bylaw in 1923. Just like vehicles driving on the road, people on foot had to pass oncoming pedestrians to the right. When passing a person walking in the same direction as yourself, you had to pass them on their left. If you happened to be walking side by side with a friend, you'd have to move to a single-file formation when meeting oncoming pedestrians. And it was absolutely against the law for two or more baby carriages to be wheeled side by side on any sidewalk.

No Parking

In the early 1900s, the town of Innisfail, Alberta, passed a bylaw requiring all horses and horse-powered vehicles be parked on the south side of Main Street. Because Main Street runs east and west in Innisfail, the south side of the street gave some shade to horses on hot summer days.

Clear the Sidewalks

It is illegal to "lead, ride or drive a horse or cattle" on the sidewalks of Digby, Nova Scotia. The "Horses and Cattle Bylaw" was enacted in 1975. Residents insisting on walking their livestock on the sidewalk were slapped with a $100 fine or two months in the nearest jail. This law wasn't repealed until 2000.

SNOW MESSING AROUND

Snow Exceptions

It is against the law to operate a snowmobile within town limits in Morden, Manitoba—unless, of course, a snowstorm has shut down highways to regular vehicle traffic.

Off Limits

The town of Beausejour, Manitoba, accepts snowmobile traffic between October 15 and April 15 as a regular part of life. Snowmobile operators there are expected to "share the roadways with other vehicular traffic." Of course, they're expected to obey all Criminal Code, Highway Traffic Act and off-road regulations. Oh, and one more thing. They are absolutely prohibited from travelling the streets of Park Avenue and First Street North.

Snow Sailing

In 1971, the village of Airdrie, Alberta, passed a bylaw allowing "Ski-Doos to use the east and west lanes" for travel in and out of the community but only between the hours of 10:00 AM and 10:00 PM. The bylaw was repealed in 1982.

Insurance Please

A 1994 bylaw okayed riding a snowmobile in Whitehorse, Yukon. But if the local authorities stop you, you'd better have read the small print. While the use of "motor toboggans" is fine, you must have valid insurance. Every snowmobiler must also have a set of identification numbers "placed upon the hood of his motor, toboggan or some other conspicuous place thereon."

Sleigh Bells Ring!

Even the horse-drawn sleighs of yesteryear had horns—of sorts.
To warn pedestrians of their approach, the town of Lloydminster,
Alberta, made it law in 1916 that any horse, mule or other animal
pulling a sleigh through city streets must be equipped with bells.

STOP, THIEF!

Take Your Keys!

In a concerted effort to reduce auto theft in 1955, the town of Fahler, Alberta, passed a bylaw permitting the town constable to remove the keys from cars parked within town limits during the evening and night. Apparently it was fairly common practice at the time for motorists to leave their doors unlocked and their keys in the ignition. Drivers who'd had their keys confiscated only had to "apply" to the constable to have them returned. This "service" was provided "free of charge."

Lock the Doors

Leaving your car unattended and unlocked wasn't just a potential lure to thieves, it was also against the law in the town of Cochrane, Alberta, in 1948. The rationale behind the rule was to prevent an unauthorized person from jumping in the driver's seat and taking the vehicle for a spin. Unfortunately, if the car was stolen, the owner wasn't just missing his vehicle. Reporting it could cost him as much as $10 or 21 days in jail!

TWO-WHEELED TERRORS

Do You Have a Licence for That Thing?

If you were found riding your bicycle through the streets of Fort Saskatchewan, Alberta, without a licence in 1945, you could find yourself facing a fine. That year, council passed a bylaw making bicycle licences mandatory.

Measure Those Wheels
Westlock, Alberta, enacted a bylaw in 1946 stating that no one could ride a bicycle with wheels larger than 46 centimetres (18 inches) on village sidewalks or boulevards. Smaller wheels appear to have been okay, though.

Don't Lose Control

Riding a bicycle might be good for your health, but let go of those handlebars, and you might find your face planted in a roadside hedge. This could be why the city of Vernon, BC, used a portion of an old bylaw and incorporated it into their current traffic bylaw. Section 805 states: "No rider of a bicycle shall remove both hands from the handle bars or feet from the pedals, or practice any acrobatic or fancy riding on any street." The earlier bylaw contributing this remnant dated back to 1949.

Bicycles Beware
As early as 1916, the village of Lloydminster, Alberta, enacted a bylaw stating bicycles of any size were not allowed on village sidewalks. They had to share the roads with all other vehicle traffic of the day.

Blow That Horn

Bicycles in Wilkie, Saskatchewan, had to have a "proper alarm bell, gong or horn," and bike riders were expected to blow their horn to signal their approach to pedestrians and other road traffic. The same 1922 bylaw also legislated that, similar to other vehicle traffic, bicycles were required to "carry in front...a lighted lamp from one hour after sunset to one hour before sunrise."

SAFE MOTORING

Eyes On the Road

Newfoundland and Labrador leads the country when it comes to legislating cell phone use. As of April 1, 2003, that province made it illegal to "use a handheld cellular phone while driving." A motorist caught talking on the phone while driving can be charged under a "number of provincial, territorial or federal laws including, but not limited to, those related to dangerous driving, careless driving and (in the case of an accident) criminal negligence causing death or injury."

Red Means Stop

It may be clear sailing for miles around, but you still can't turn right on a red light in Québec. Although the law has been repeatedly disputed, it's still in effect.

10 and 2

A 1965 traffic bylaw in the town of Quesnel, BC, made it illegal to drive a car or a bicycle without keeping at least one hand on the steering wheel. Youngsters on bikes, trikes, roller skates or sleighs were forbidden from catching rides by grabbing on to moving vehicles. And it was against the law for the driver of any vehicle to "permit any part of his body or any part of a passenger's body to extend outside the vehicle." The only exception to the rule was when the driver needed to perform a turning signal.

Imagine That?

A law passed in 1918 in the town of Yarmouth, Nova Scotia, made it illegal to drive any type of vehicle the wrong way down a one-way street. The same traffic bylaw made it mandatory for drivers to use signals when stopping or turning. They were to do so by "raising a whip or hand vertically."

KEEPING ON TRACK

Whistling Softly

What was initially seen as a safety measure has fast become an urban nuisance, and for some communities across the country, that nuisance had to be dealt with. The city of Winnipeg, Manitoba, first silenced train whistles going through town in 1979. But the engineer travelling through the city had better stay sharp, since other than the 20 crossings listed in the bylaw where sounding the engine whistle is prohibited, he can blow to his heart's content everywhere else.

Right of Way

In Cornerbrook, Newfoundland, it is illegal to change gears when crossing a railway track. This restriction is part of Newfoundland's Highway Traffic Act of 1990. What's strange about this law is that since the provincial government shut down and disassembled the railroad in the 1980s, there are no longer any trains operating in that province.

More Powerful than a Speeding Locomotive?

Cross a set of railway tracks in front of an oncoming train, and it doesn't matter how large your vehicle is—there's no doubt who will win. Still, the Newfoundland Act of 1892 made it illegal to cause any injury to railway trains. Anyone caught damaging any railway property could be sentenced to a jail term of up to 12 months hard labour.

AND THEN THERE ARE SOME OTHER VEHICLES...

Wheelbarrow Regulations

If you're planning to transport a wheelbarrow load of dirt from your home to your neighbour's, don't even think about using the sidewalk. That's because St. John's, Newfoundland, banned this form of traffic on city sidewalks many years ago, and the bylaw is still on the books.

Harness Those Hobbies!

Boys will be boys, and often, the bigger the boys, the bigger the toys—or the more dangerous, anyway. According to a bylaw enacted in the town of Morden, Manitoba, in 2003, some toys require regulating or else someone might get hurt. Council in that community decided operating a "gas-powered model vehicle within 300 metres of a residence" is potentially dangerous and therefore outlawed. And people with a passion for flying have to replace their powered airplanes and helicopters with safer and more sedate kites—at least if they want to fly in town. Operating a model aircraft within Morden town limits is now strictly prohibited.

Cool, Clear Waters

And in an effort to keep them that way, the city of Nanaimo, BC, passed a bylaw that is particularly unique to their community. Since March 1995, it has been illegal for anyone to venture into the surrounding waterway in a motorboat whose engine is not equipped with an "exhaust system that permits the exhaust gases from the engine of the motorboat to be expelled directly in to the air without first passing through water." Your motorboat is also required to have a muffler to cool those exhaust fumes and expel them with minimum noise.

Ride 'Em in Safely

Curiously enough, you can still ride your horse into Canmore, as long as you use the public highway and conform to the Traffic Bylaw and Vehicles Act.

Take a Walk on the Right Side

According to a 1922 bylaw, pedestrians in the town of Wilkie, Saskatchewan, had to follow the example of road traffic. They, too, had to pass to the right of any oncoming pedestrians. And anyone willfully breaking this law could face a fine of $25 or 30 days in jail "with or without hard labour."

Not on My Sidewalk

According to a 1922 bylaw, you could not "run, draw or push" a handcart or any other vehicle on sidewalks in the town of Wilkie, Saskatchewan, unless you were repairing it.

Reinforced Bridges

In 1913, it was law in the town of Wilkie, Saskatchewan, for anyone crossing a bridge or culvert with any "traction engine or threshing machine" to reinforce the area with planks 2 inches (5 centimetres) or more in thickness before crossing. Failure to comply with this bylaw could cost you $50 or 30 days in jail.

IT'S NOT EASY BEING GREEN

Environmental Consciousness

It is against the law for motorists in the city of Guelph, Ontario, to allow their vehicle to idle for more than 10 minutes in any 60-minute period. The city bylaw, which was established in 1998, is still in effect.

The city of London, Ontario, is even stricter with their 1999 idling bylaw. Unless you are an on-duty emergency worker or police officer, you have a maximum of five minutes of idling time before you get a ticket.

While the environmental consciousness is admirable, it is unclear how officials manage to monitor vehicle idle time.

Guns and Ammo

*"Ride 'em cowboy and away we go!" The words
trigger thoughts of guns firing off into a clear blue
prairie horizon while riders on horseback gallop off to
an unknown destination.*

*While guns and other weapons are historically all about
survival, in an untrained hand they can also be deadly.
Thus, the development of firearms laws that to this day
cause heated debates across the country.*

*The following laws are just a few examples of how these
regulations developed over the years.*

READY, AIM, FIRE!

Keep a Lid on Your Explosives

You couldn't keep more than 50 pounds of gunpowder or other explosives on your property in the town of Ponoka, Alberta, in 1914. The council enacted a bylaw saying that amount of fire-power had to be kept a minimum of 100 feet (30.5 metres) from any buildings. You couldn't have more than three barrels of gasoline or kerosene on hand either unless they were located at least 60 feet (18 metres) from any building or stored in iron tanks.

Bombs Away!

In 1964, the town council passed a bylaw making it illegal for anyone to make, distribute or sell a stink bomb in Trenton, Ontario. Break the law and you're fined $25 for the first offence. If you're foolish enough to try it again, the second and subsequent offences will cost you $50. And if you don't pay up your fines after that, you'll be thrown into the clink for up to one month.

Don't Flex That Bow!

Another bylaw enacted in 1956 in Trenton, Ontario, made it illegal to "sell, barter, give, lend, transfer or deliver any bows and arrows to minors within the town of Trenton," unless, of course, the arrow had a rubber-covered tip. And don't plan on setting up for a little target practice either. Minors and adults alike were also forbidden from letting an arrow fly anywhere within the "Corporation of the Town of Trenton." Those caught breaking the bylaw were subject to a $25 fine.

Permit Required

Since 1965, it has been against the law to indiscriminately set explosives to blast rock in the district of Squamish, BC. That's when the council there enacted a bylaw mandating that anyone who wants to blast away at the corner of a mountain must first obtain an explosives permit, complete with a minimum of $150,000 in liability insurance!

Butt Out

In 1914, in the town of Ponoka, Alberta, carrying an open flame into a barn or walking in with a lit cigarette or burning pipe could cost you more than a disastrous fire. Should the town fathers learn of your indiscretion, you could face a $25 fine or up to 30 days in jail, with or without hard labour. While portions of this extensive bylaw were repealed and replaced with updated versions throughout the years, the entire bylaw wasn't repealed until 1998.

You Can't Do That
In Public

*Some behaviours are just plain rude, while others
are simply inconsiderate.*

*Strangely enough, what appears to be common sense
to the general public must be made law for the few that
just don't get it.*

DON'T DISTURB THE PEACE

Silence Your Power Saws

Power saws are a noisy tool, and ongoing use is just plain disruptive. In the district of Oak Bay, BC, a 1976 bylaw made it illegal to operate a power saw earlier than 8:00 AM and later than 7:00 PM, Monday to Saturday. But if you found yourself wanting to finish up a few odds and ends requiring the use of a power saw on Sunday, you were out of luck altogether, no matter what the time of day. Sunday was a day of rest, and power saws simply disturbed the peace and quiet of the day. If, on the other hand, you decided to use a good old-fashioned hand saw, that was just fine.

Keep It Down, Would Ya?

An Edmonton, Alberta noise bylaw passed in 1925 made it clear residents couldn't bother their neighbours with any "unusual or unnecessary noise or noise likely to disturb persons in his neighbourhood." Fair enough, you might say. But the same bylaw makes it illegal for any person to "blow or sound or cause to be blown or sounded within the limits of the city of Edmonton, the steam whistle of any locomotive." Since there were exceptions that allowed for train whistles to be blown for safety, based on Alberta statutes of the day, one has to wonder if just anyone was wandering railway yards and blowing steam whistles willy-nilly?

Good Vibrations?

In 2005, council members in Squamish, BC, made a unique addition to their noise bylaw. It is not only illegal to make noise that might "disturb or is liable to disturb the quiet, peace, rest, enjoyment, comfort or convenience of individuals or the public," unnecessary "vibrations" are against the law too. Generally speaking, it's pretty much hush-hush in that community between the hours of 8:00 PM and 8:00 AM.

YOU CAN'T HANG OUT THERE!

No Loitering

Take care of your business and move along. In order to eliminate loitering in the town of Rat Portage (Kenora), Ontario, a bylaw was passed in 1901 making it illegal to park your "horse, cart, carriage, wagon, sleigh or other vehicle" on town streets any longer than absolutely necessary to conduct your business.

In 1976, the county of Halifax, Nova Scotia, passed a similar loitering bylaw, making it illegal for folks to idle about in the halls, washrooms, parking lots or any other common areas of a shopping mall.

Street Sense

Retired gents who enjoyed lounging on benches and watching the world go by had to come up with another pastime. The streets of North Battleford, Saskatchewan, were made for walking—not running, racing or loitering—and town council made these restrictions law in 1906.

IT'S ALL FUN AND GAMES...

Boys Will Be Boys

From the beginning of time, young lads, full of vim and vigour, have always found something to do in what precious spare time they have. If they aren't out capturing frogs or snagging a string of fish, they're likely building forts or planning a treasure hunt. But in 1811, the province of Nova Scotia clamped down on the shenanigans of young boys. That year, it passed an act preventing "boys and others from coasting and sliding down the hills in the streets of Halifax."

More than a century later, in 1916, Yarmouth, Nova Scotia, enacted a bylaw restricting tomfoolery in that community. Throwing snowballs, stones or any other item was against the law. And people swimming in the nearby water hole must either be properly clothed or, if wading without swimwear, not visible to any neighbouring house or street.

KEEP YOUR SHIRT ON

Cover Up!

A municipal bylaw enacted in 1985 in the town of D'Outremont, Québec, made it illegal to appear in public places wearing only your bathing suit. But when one resident heard of the new bylaw, he charged the town with discrimination, saying it "denied him certain fundamental rights that were guaranteed by the Canadian Charter of Rights and Freedoms." The plaintiff, who regularly jogged in nothing more than a bathing suit and routinely sunbathed with his family in public parks, had his claim heard. The end result saw the bylaw declared *ultra vires* (void), based on the Constitution Acts of 1867 and 1982.

Birthday Suit

According to a portion of a 1905 public morals bylaw, it was just fine to bathe in the nude "in any public waters" around the city of Kelowna, BC—just so long as you did so after 9:00 PM and before 6:00 AM. During peak hours, you were required to wear a little more than just your birthday suit or face a fine of up to $100. The entire public morals bylaw was repealed in 1990, but dare to bare your nude body on one of Kelowna's public beaches today and you might still find yourself in hot water with the local officials.

SPLISH SPLASH

No Swimming

In an effort to keep people safe, the city of Kelowna, BC, passed a bylaw in 1944 restricting residents and visitors from bathing and wading in certain parts of Okanagan Lake. The problem is that it isn't always clear which parts of the lake are restricted areas. For example, one portion of the bylaw reads:

"...that part of the said Okanagan Lake between the wire fence on the west side of the Bathing Pool in front of the Grandstand on that Part of District Lot Fourteen (14) in Group One (1) in the City of Kelowna in the Province of British Columbia covered by Certificate of Title No. 35714F leased to The Kelowna Aquatic Association, and a line extending due West into the said Okanagan Lake from a point Six Hundred feet (600') north from the right bank of Mill Creek where the said Mill Creek runs into the said Okanagan Lake..."

To say it's difficult to know where to draw the line (so to speak) is an understatement. And according to one city official, it's not certain if anyone's ever been fined under this bylaw, but people "violate it all the time."

Cleaning Up
Those Acts

It's been said cleanliness is next to godliness.

*Canada's founders took this saying to heart, enforcing
polite behaviour and outlawing nuisance behaviour
like spitting in public.*

NO SPITTING!

Keeping City Streets Disease Free

In Yarmouth, Nova Scotia, it was against the law in 1909 for anyone to "expectorate, spit or otherwise deposit saliva" on city streets, sidewalks, stairways, building entrances or any other location where the general public might travel. The goal of the bylaw was to "prevent the spread of disease." Breaking the law could cost $50 in fines or 10 days in jail.

Don't Spit—Anywhere!

In 1917, it was against the law to spit on the sidewalks or in any public place in the town of Trenton, Ontario. And in case you were in any doubt over what that all included, the town fathers were specific. The bylaw clearly states that spitting is not permitted on any "sidewalk or upon the floor of any public building or buildings hall or church."

In 1909, the town council in Yarmouth, Nova Scotia, passed a similar law, making it illegal to spit on the sidewalk or on the floor of any public building "in which 10 or more persons are accustomed to be employed or to congregate or frequent."

Swallow That!
Although a river runs through the sleepy prairie city of Saskatoon, Saskatchewan, no steamship line has ever used the port as its home base. Still, should one set up shop, the city is prepared. In 1910, they passed the Bylaw Prohibiting Spitting in Public Places, and one of the public places cited was the office of any steamship line. Although the law is no longer in the books in its original format, it hasn't been repealed completely. Instead, the Public Spitting, Urination and Defecation Prohibition Bylaw replaced it in 2004.

CLEAN AND DRY

The Common Towel

The year was 1936 and a disease called trachoma had reared its ugly head in the small BC village of Williams Lake. In an effort to snuff out the spread of this and other infections, Williams Lake enacted a bylaw making it illegal for restaurants, schools, hotels and other public areas with a shared bathroom to use a common "roller towel." Anyone not adhering to the bylaw could face a $100 fine—a substantial amount even today, but considerably more so in the dusty, dirty days of the Great Depression.

Business Etiquette

It's a dog-eat-dog world when it comes to succeeding in business, and municipalities across the country pull the strings when it comes to making sure local ventures benefit the community as a whole.

When it comes to best business practices, location—and the governing body regulating commercial etiquette in that location—can spell success or disaster.

THAT'S SHOW BUSINESS!

Licencing Laws

Any actor, singer, circus rider, tightrope walker, acrobat, gymnast, menagerie, hippodrome, dog or pony show or any other such production had to pay for the privilege of stimulating your imagination in the town of Ponoka, Alberta. In 1914, a bylaw made it mandatory for all sorts of entertainers to obtain a performer's licence that, depending on the event, could cost upwards of $50 per day before they even had the privilege of hoisting a tent or holding a show.

Travelling stationary exhibits weren't exempt from the performance licence law either. If you made your livelihood charging people for the chance to see a stuffed two-headed calf, you needed to cough up $10 first.

Everyone Loves a Circus

Entertainers have awed audiences since the beginning of time, and a visiting circus is sure to draw crowds from far and wide. But at least one community made sure any "showmen, circus siders, mountebanks or jugulars [jugglers]" had their paperwork in order before the first tent was pitched in town. The town of Chatham, Ontario, updated their Bylaw Regulating Exhibitions of Waxwork in 1858 to include the above performers, making it unlawful for anyone to strut their stuff before first procuring a licence from the town clerk. If they neglected to do so, it could cost them as much as $20 in fines.

DRIVING
THE RULES HOME

Rules of the Road for Taxicabs

Modest dress is not even a question for taxicab drivers in Halifax, Nova Scotia. According to a 1999 bylaw in that city, wearing socks is a must for cabbies.

But if you think Halifax council is tough, they've got nothing on taxicab regulations passed by the city of Prince George, BC, in 1955. Cabbies there were expressly forbidden from:

☛ allowing any person to "stand on any part of the exterior of the taxicab or sit on the sides or doors" when the cab is "in motion,"

☛ permitting fares jumping into the car when the cab is still "in motion" or

☛ collecting fares while the cab is still moving.

Cabbies also had to have class when it came to attracting passengers. They couldn't hoot and holler at pedestrians. The couldn't "seek employment by repeatedly and persistently driving the taxicab to and fro upon any street...or by hovering in front of any theatre, hall, hotel, public resort, railway or ferry station, or other place of public gathering." Taxi drivers couldn't "loiter or cruise about the street...for the purpose of obtaining passengers," nor could they accept anyone behaving in an "unseemly, disorderly or riotous" manner in their cars.

And speaking of the cab itself, the operator was responsible for disinfecting it weekly—at the very least!

FALSE ADVERTISING

By Any Other Name

Everybody loves a sale. But the name a business gives to its sale is almost as important as what is being sold. In 1960, the city of Halifax, Nova Scotia, enacted a bylaw regulating all "Going Out of Business, Removal of Business, and Fire and Other Altered Goods Sales," and it's still in effect to this day. First and foremost, regardless whether it's being called a "Final Days Sale," a "Lease Expires Sale," a "Liquidation Sale" or any other turn of phrase, if a business advertises it is having a sale because it is going out of business, it must, indeed, be going out of business. A "Removal of Business" sale means that the business is liquidating its stock and will then move to another location. And if a business is having a "Fire and Other Altered Goods Sale," it is only reasonable to expect the items on sale have been damaged in some way. Business owners holding any of these sales are required to obtain a special licence from the city. With the licence, the city provides the business owner with a badge that he or she must then wear in plain sight for the duration of the sale.

You have to be in business for a minimum of six months before the city will sell you the $385 licence for any of these sales. If, on the other hand, you die before your six months is up, the city is lenient on your heirs. They are then allowed to apply for a licence for an out-of-business sale to clear up your estate.

This bylaw has been revisited several times over the years, but even with nine amendments, it's still alive and kicking!

UNDERCOVER SALES

Out of Sight, Out of Mind?

An Edmonton, Alberta bylaw dated August 10, 1931, put a new spin on what might be offensive to the general public. That year council made it illegal for shop owners to display any "pistol, revolver, dirk, dagger, bowie knife, stiletto, metal knuckles, skull cracker, slug shot or other offensive weapon of a like character" in shop windows. The law was repealed in 1996.

Strategic Placement

You can't use sandwich boards to attract folks a few blocks down to your business in Regina, Saskatchewan. A city bylaw states that sidewalk signs must be located "directly in front of the premises being advertised and must not interfere with movement of pedestrians."

Working from Home

Home-based businesses aren't discouraged from setting up shop in the city of Winkler, Manitoba—as long as they do so quietly. The city's home occupations policy states there is to be "no exterior display, no exterior storage of materials, and no exterior indication of the home occupation or variation of the residential character of the principal or accessory building."

SELLING IN THE STREETS

Hawkers and Peddlers

Watch out Watkins. Red alert Amway! Enterprising folk trying to make an extra buck or two in the town of Neepawa better make sure they have a valid business licence before selling door to door or setting up a table at the local farmer's market in Neepawa, Manitoba. Since 1993, a proper licence has been required in that community. There are (as always) some exceptions to the rule. Farmers selling their own fresh produce are exempt from the rule, as are people selling subscriptions for newspapers, magazines or other items approved by the Public Libraries Act and the Municipal Act. If, on the other hand, you're selling fresh Okanagan cherries from a roadside fruit truck, and the farm fresh produce isn't your own, you'll have to make that trip to city hall.

Extra, Extra!

Say goodbye to the days of the street-corner newspaper vendor. In 1950, the town of Carman, Manitoba, made it illegal to sell newspapers, magazines or any other type of publication on town streets or the surrounding highways. Breaking the law could cost you $50. And if you didn't have the money to make good your fine, you could find yourself in jail for a maximum of six months. Needless to say, selling subscriptions didn't pay!

Transient Photographers Must Sign In

While it's perfectly legal for freelance photographers to travel through the city of Cornwall, Ontario, and take photographs for the purpose of someday selling the images to one publication or another, other shutterbugs passing through aren't so lucky.

Transient photographers coming to town for the purpose of shooting school pictures or those promising to capture your baby's most precious moments, for example, need a licence, according to a 2006 bylaw.

Business Etiquette

A public market might typically be a little chaotic, but that doesn't mean there are no rules. The city of Windsor, Ontario, made sure vendors didn't add to the noise level by "calling out their wares," as it were. In 1942, the council of the day passed a bylaw making it illegal for sales folk to stand in the aisles of the public market and advertise their daily specials by calling out to patrons walking by.

FOOD AND DRINK

A Sober Thought

It wasn't until 2002 that the province of British Columbia revamped what some residents in that province felt were some seriously outdated liquor laws. Some of the previous regulations were:

- ☛ a patron had to eat if he wanted to order a beer in a restaurant
- ☛ a patron had to remain seated while drinking in a restaurant
- ☛ a restaurant couldn't call itself a "bar and grill"
- ☛ games such as "name that tune" or video trivia games were prohibited in restaurants

Even restaurant decor, such as the height and width of a dance floor, was regulated

After December 2, 2002, these and other regulations were terminated, and restaurants became far more user friendly. Today, if you are dining out and can't finish that nice bottle of wine you ordered, the restaurant is allowed to reseal the bottle for you to take home.

Butchering Bylaws

A 1943 bylaw in the city of Windsor, Ontario, made it illegal for anyone to slaughter an animal or bird of any kind in city streets. And if you were hauling manure or other farm refuse through town, you'd better make sure your load was properly secured. Leaving a trail of leftovers as you passed through could cost you $50.

Original Packing

Butter sold in retail stores in the village of Quesnel, BC, in 1950 had to be sold in its original wrapping. Should a store-owner want to divide the butter into smaller amounts, he had to follow explicit directions approved by the local "Medical Officer of Health."

True Weight

The town constable in Yorkton, Saskatchewan, in 1903 had a rather out-of-the-ordinary annual responsibility. A now obsolete bylaw stated, "It shall be the duty of the Town Constable, at least once in every year, to enter the premises of any baker or vendor of bread, within the said town and weigh the bread found therein." According to the bylaw, each loaf of bread had to weigh a minimum of 2 pounds (907 grams), and the town constable could just drop by unannounced to check if the bread in any local bakery was up to snuff. And while bread was cooling on the rack, its succulent aroma tempting each pedestrian walking by to come in and buy a loaf, patrons who kept their wits about them could ask to have their loaf weighed in front of them—just to be doubly sure they weren't getting cheated out of a slice or two—and the bakery had to have a scale on hand just for that purpose.

The same bylaw also required bakers to follow a strict set of guidelines as far as bread making went. Most importantly, bakers had to make sure their bread was safe. Bakers were forbidden from using any "deleterious material in the making of bread sold or offered or exposed for sale within the said town."

Measuring Up to the Neighbours

In 1996, Edmonton, Alberta, repealed 3884 bylaws that had become obsolete in that city. One of those laws also revolved around the sale of fresh bread. In 1913, Edmonton had two weight restrictions for the bakeries in their community. Loaves were to weigh either 1½ pounds (680 grams) or 3 pounds (1.36 kilograms). Fancy breads could weigh in at 21 ounces (595 grams). The city inspector who made his way through every bakery in that city annually could grant a little leeway, depending on how long the bread was out of the oven. Delivery, on the other hand, was more strictly regulated. The baker planning to deliver his bread must "furnish baskets for the handling of bread, and shall instruct all employees to do the same."

Check That Clock

Butchers in the town of Melville, Saskatchewan, had to check their clocks before slaughtering any animals for human consumption. A bylaw dated 1927 made it illegal to butcher any animal on a weekend. When the dirty deed did occur, it had to take place between the hours of 6:00 PM and 10:00 PM from April 1 to September 30. The rest of the year, butchering had to occur between 1:00 PM and 5:00 PM. The town's meat inspector could issue a special permit from time to time to accommodate exceptional circumstances. Interestingly enough, the bylaw lists no concrete fine for breaking the law.

Got Milk?

Don't plan on selling milk or cream between the hours of 10:00 PM and 7:00 AM in the city of Kingston, Ontario. A 1940 bylaw makes it illegal to do so.

Speaking of Milk...

The last time you could buy farm-fresh milk from a dairy farmer around the city of Grande Prairie, Alberta, was in 1989. That year, city council enacted a bylaw stating it was against the law to sell unpasteurized milk for family consumption.

Something Smells Fishy

Entrepreneurs peddling perch or bartering bass in Trenton, Ontario, had to follow restrictions as early as 1917. That's when the town passed a bylaw restricting anyone from "exposing" or selling fish from their wagon or any other conveyance. The only exception to the bylaw was if a peddler was selling fish at the public market or if he or she was delivering to retail dealers. The fine for breaking the law? $50.

Get Your Fruitcake Here!

Enterprising business folk in the town of Clifton, Alberta, couldn't just go about willy-nilly selling fruitcake, lemon pops, ginger beer or other refreshments. A bylaw deeming it necessary for independent vendors to obtain a business licence was first enacted in 1859, and a licence was even required for a lemonade stand. The town charged the vendor one dollar for the permit, but failure to obtain such a licence could result in prosecution and a $20 fine.

Stock Your Cupboards

Run out of milk on Mondays in the town of Trenton, Ontario, and there was a time when you would have to make do with water until Tuesday morning. In 1960, the town made it law that all grocery stores were to remain closed on Monday.

WHO, WHERE, WHEN?

Location, Location, Location

An entrepreneur wanting to establish an automobile junkyard in Prince Edward Island will have to take several things into consideration when choosing a location. A provincial law states that this type of business can't be located "within a radius of 500 feet (152 metres) of any public park, public playground, public bathing beach, school, church, hospital, cemetery or public hall; within 100 feet (30 metres) of any highway; or within 1000 feet (305 metres) of any residential premises other than those of the applicant for a permit..."

Shop Closing

As recent as the 1990 version of the St. John's, Newfoundland Act, the city council could determine the hours of operation for city retail shops and other businesses as well as what days they must be closed for holidays.

Who Makes the Rules?

The city of Vancouver, BC, initially enacted a bylaw in 1987 called the Shops Closing Bylaw. In a nutshell, any retail outlet can stay open 24 hours a day from Monday to Saturday. The only exception to the rule is if the Licence Bylaw restricts hours of operation. Hmmmm?

Don't Offend the Neighbours

The pioneers who founded this great country of ours survived by making use of everything they came in contact with. An animal was killed for meat, its hide used for warmth, its bones crushed for fertilizer and its tallow boiled for making candles and soap. But when thrifty entrepreneurs began setting up shop and boiling tallow and crushing bones on a large scale, the village of Quesnel, BC, had to step in. What started out as the smell of money turned into an offensive odour for anyone unfortunate enough to live close by. So in 1950, Quesnel council made it law for anyone setting up such a business or any other such "obnoxious or offensive trade" must obtain consent of council first. Likely, this type of stinky enterprise was relegated to the outskirts of town.

Child Labour

In 1916, in the town of Yarmouth, Nova Scotia, a person had to be 16 years old to enter or work in billiard rooms and bowling alleys. The exception to this rule applied to the pin setters in bowling alleys—they could be 12 years old. Of course, only boys were allowed these jobs, and regulations for girls didn't even exist.

Buyer Beware

Palm readers and fortune tellers would have found themselves doing a lot of charity work in 1901 in the town of Rat Portage (Kenora), Ontario, should they have chosen to give residents there a reading. A town bylaw passed that year made it illegal to charge for such services.

No Soliciting

Residents in the city of Beaconsfield, Ontario, are likely thrilled with their council. It is against the law in that city for any "peddler, book agent, canvasser, vendor or public crier [to] at any time do business door to door in any residential zone of the municipality except on behalf of a Beaconsfield nonprofit community organization." And even if you are one of the few exceptions, you still need to pay an annual licencing fee of $30.

DINING OUT

Summer Dining

There's no doubt that restaurant owners have several issues to consider when expanding their business to include sidewalk cafés. Furnishings have to be weatherproof. Pedestrians have to make their way down the street without resorting to walking on the road. Emergency vehicles still have to get by if necessary. For the most part, these considerations are typically a matter of common sense. At the same time, there are always a few unexpected restrictions whenever you deal with your local government.

In the town of Kentville, Nova Scotia, a 2003 bylaw agreed that businesses landscaping around their summer sidewalk café was a good idea, but decided that the landscaping must be of a "temporary nature" unless a business owner had prior written consent from the town. Restaurant owners there were also required to pay a rental charge of 50 cents per ft^2 (0.1 m^2) to run a sidewalk café from May to September.

Fast-food Foreshadowing
Businesses in the city of Windsor, Ontario, are promptly fined if they don't prevent wrappers, containers or even a foul odor from escaping the confines of their operations onto city streets. This bylaw was first passed in 1965.

Open for Business
Restaurant owners in the town of Yarmouth, Nova Scotia, were allowed to open for business on Sundays in 1916, providing they followed a few rules set out by council. They could not sell tobacco, cigars, cigarettes, candy, confectionery, fruit or drinks except tea, coffee, cocoa, chocolate or milk. Breaking the law could cost you $50 or 50 days in jail.

DIRTY BUSINESS

Butt Out

The town fathers in Melville, Saskatchewan, seemed to have
a somewhat advanced sense of awareness where the health of
their youngsters was concerned. In 1955, a bylaw was passed to
"limit and regulate the number of tobacco advertising signs in
the ice stadium." Only one company was allowed to advertise
its brand of tobacco at any one time, and for the privilege, they
were responsible for supplying and maintaining the stadium
time clock.

Coal, Hard Facts

Heating your home with coal was no easy feat in 1936. That
year, the town of Carman, Manitoba, enacted a bylaw requiring
coal-sellers to sell their product by weight. To avoid any discrep-
ancy, all loads of coal were to be weighed on the town scales
before delivery, and the town weigh-master would collect the
princely sum of 10 cents per load to add to the town's coffers.
The coal seller would receive a ticket certifying the load's true
weight from the weigh-master, and that ticket would in turn be
given to the end user on delivery. Try to break free of the red
tape, and the town could slap you with a $50 fine.

In 1943, another bylaw added restrictions to the amount dray-
men could charge for delivering coal or wood within Carman's
town limits. If they were delivering wood they couldn't charge
more than 50 cents per cord. Coal would be delivered for not
less than 50 cents and not more than 80 cents per ton or portion thereof. Talk about complicated!

Made to Shop

Shopping carts in the town of Kenora, Ontario, became such an unsightly nuisance in 1992 that town council had no choice but to take clear and decisive action. A bylaw passed that prohibited anyone from abandoning shopping carts on private property without the consent of the property owners. It was also against the law to abandon shopping carts on town property. Unfortunately, the owner of the shopping cart, and not the patron who abandoned it, would face a $15 fine should they want the cart returned.

Mind Your
Manners

Proper etiquette was an important consideration to the courageous men and women who pioneered this vast and wild country. To be well mannered was a sign of civilization—like the difference between using a fork and using your fingers to eat your dinner.

Today, it's a generally accepted fact that you're likely to hear "foul language" while walking city streets, so there's no need for a bylaw on the matter—a sad commentary on society, really. At the same time, people don't commonly spit inside public buildings anymore. Again, there's no longer any need for a law on the matter—thankfully! At the very least, it's interesting to see how times have changed.

WATCH YOUR MOUTH

Foul!

A foul mouth could cost you $50 or get you locked away for 30 days in the town of Fahler, Alberta, in 1957. That year, the town council passed a bylaw "to promote peace and good behaviour" in their community.

Be Nice to the Lady

In 1898, you'd better have known what you're talking about when you suggested a lady in the North-West Territories was unfaithful to her husband, unchaste or guilty of reckless extravagance of any kind. If you were lying, you could face legal action, whether the young lady slandered could prove any personal damages or not.

The Name Says It All

Council members of the village of Nakusp, BC, have the sole right to determine the name of any new municipal parks. The 1988 bylaw highlights the fact that the village elite want to honour "persons or events in a tangible and lasting manner" and will use the naming of parks for that purpose.

MAINTAINING MORALITY

Public Morals

In 1893, maintaining public morals was a major concern for the town of Sudbury, Ontario, and to snuff out any potential problems, the council of the day enacted a bylaw addressing some of their concerns. Morality laws, as these laws came to be called, were common in communities across the country.

- ☛ Unless you were announcing the beginning of a religious service of some sort, the ringing of bells was strictly prohibited.
- ☛ Despite the lack of organized animal rights groups in the late 19th century, the town of Sudbury was serious about making sure animals under their jurisdiction didn't come to unnecessary harm. Residents were expressly forbidden from hosting, running, baiting or inciting in any way fights between any "bull, bear, dog, cock or other animal (whether of domestic or wild nature or kind)."

- Unless you were one of "her Majesty's soldiers," an on-duty militia member, a sheriff, a police officer or a member of a rifle club in the midst of target practice, you'd better not even think about firing "any cannon, gun, pistol or other fire alarm."

- You didn't want to let the town fathers catch you bathing or washing that naked body of yours in anything deemed "public water." You could be in deep trouble if you did—not to mention being embarrassed at being caught with your britches down.

- If you didn't like something town council was addressing, letting your representatives know was a little tricky. Disrupting the "order or solemnity of the meeting" was against the law.

- If you happened to own a wolf, bear or other wild animal, or were perhaps animal-sitting for a friend, you'd better not let your charge out of your sight. Should the animal happen to wander the streets of Sudbury, you could face a $50 fine.

- Down on your luck? You'd better make sure a member of the clergy or two justices of the peace signed a certificate stating that you were "a deserving object of charity" before you started strolling highways and public lanes or knocking on doors for a bit of bread or a piece of cheese. Without this document, begging for alms was prohibited.

- Wondering about your future? In 1893, you had to keep on wondering until it happened. Fortunetellers of any kind likely didn't stop by the town of Sudbury often, since they were prohibited from charging for their services.

Prim and Proper

In the interest of "peace, order and good government," the city of Moose Jaw, Saskatchewan, enacted a modern version of the old morality laws in 1999. People in that city can't

- ☞ deface a memorial plaque or sign,
- ☞ build a fence using barbed wire,
- ☞ leave a trail of nails, tacks or glass behind them while walking down city sidewalks,
- ☞ damage the bark of or uproot any trees and
- ☞ allow their doors swing out "over any part of any sidewalk or street within the city."

Behave yourself

Proper behaviour is something that's expected of a good citizen, but in the town of Jasper, Alberta, it's an expectation that's legislated. Inciting someone to fight, using profanity, defacing property or being generally annoying is enough to earn a fine— shouting obscenities alone will cost you a minimum of $150. Curiously enough, this isn't an old bylaw. It was just passed in August 2005.

ASK NICELY

Please, Sir?

Beggars in the town of Rat Portage (Kenora), Ontario, would go hungry if they didn't follow the rules. In 1901, it was made law that beggars going door to door or asking for food or money in the town streets had to have a certificate signed by "a priest, clergyman or minister of the gospel or two justices of the peace" allowing them to do so. It was also the responsibility of the beggar to have his certificate reviewed and renewed every six months if he wanted to continue to receive alms.

By the Book

Panhandling in Saskatoon, Saskatchewan, is perfectly legal. But panhandlers have to follow a few rules first. They can't coerce or pester people walking by, they can't bother someone sitting in a parked vehicle or one that's stopped at a red light and they can't beg for money on a Saskatoon transit bus. They also can't obstruct the doorway to a "bank, credit union, or trust company" or an automated teller machine, bus stop or bus shelter. If they do, they're going to find themselves in considerable trouble, since the fine for a first offense is $100. This bylaw was first enacted in 1999 but has been updated as recently as 2003.

ALL WET

No Swimming

Nude swimming was just fine at the turn of the 20th century in Summerside, PEI, as long as you took a dip between the hours of 8:30 PM and 7:00 AM. Any other time of the day, you'd better have been properly attired for the occasion.

A 1912 bylaw in the town of Edson, Alberta, similarly restricted bathing and swimming in town limits to between the hours of 9:00 PM and 6:00 AM. The interesting twist to this bylaw is it didn't only restrict swimming for those doing so in the nude.

DECENCY LAWS

Going Topless

In 1996, a young woman in Guelph, Ontario, decided to walk down city streets topless. It was, after all, really hot that day. While some folk didn't find her attire suitable, the Ontario Court of Appeal decided, on a unanimous vote, that the lady in question hadn't violated any "community standards" by going topless. Whether this was a good choice or not depends on who you talk to, but it's definitely still a matter of debate.

The Oldest Profession

Most communities with morality laws made some reference to the fact that it was against the law for folks to visit a house of ill repute or avail themselves of the services of a prostitute. A 1912 bylaw in Edson, Alberta, however, addressed citizens' concerns over "common prostitutes or night walkers." If a suspected prostitute was discovered wandering "in the fields, public streets or highways, lanes or places of public meeting or gathering of people," she was expected to "give satisfactory account of herself." I'm sure all will agree with Ann Dechambeau of the town of Edson when she said, "I'm not sure what a satisfactory account is!"

Keep It Covered!

Morality laws in the town of Rat Portage (Kenora), Ontario, were quite explicit when it came to public indecency. A bylaw passed in 1901 made exhibitionism illegal. You also couldn't make or display any "obscene picture, plate, print, drawing, statue or any other indecent exhibition" within the town, nor could you wash your naked body in any "public water."

AND MORE GOOD MANNERS...

Privy Business

It simply wasn't considered proper to move an outhouse in the town of Summerside, PEI, between the hours of 4:00 AM and 10:00 PM in 1897. After all, doing so would cause quite a stink!

Noise Pollution

Blowing horns, playing football, and using insulting language were all lumped together in the town of North Battleford, Saskatchewan, in 1906. All these activities, as well as ringing bells, playing cricket, baseball, lacrosse or any other game, swearing or using any kind of "loud, blasphemous" or abusive language, were against the law.

Bury Your Dead

Your neighbours are likely sad at the death of your loved one, but that doesn't mean you can exhibit the body in public and hope that sympathy turns into dollars and cents. A 1901 morality bylaw in the town of Rat Portage (Kenora), Ontario made it illegal for "deformed, malformed or deceased" persons to be displayed publicly for the purpose of gathering money from public sympathy.

Shhhhh…Don't Get Too Excited

Another 1901 morality bylaw in the town of Rat Portage placed a few restrictions on celebrations, including weddings. The party couldn't get too carried away, as any loud jubilation was considered a disturbance of the peace.

Private Parking

A bylaw passed by the town of Jasper, Alberta, in 2002 makes it illegal for tourists to camp out in the grocery store parking lot or on any other public land within town limits, no matter how many "no vacancy" signs they might have passed before nightfall. Close your eyes, even for just a few hours, and you could wake up to a fine.

Keeping Critters Happy

If you think rules for people are complex, the ins and outs of maintaining livestock, not to mention keeping a family pet, can prove to be just as complicated.

For some of the past and present bylaws listed below, you can easily imagine the rationale behind them, but others seem a tad extreme. Just take a look and you'll see what I mean.

HORSING AROUND

Oliphant's Amazing Law of Horses

In 1908, a barrister-at-law named George Henry Hewitt Oliphant authored a book, *The Law of Horses*, using British common law and applying it here in Canada. The following are just a few of the interesting dos and don'ts of that era:

☛ It was okay to hunt fox, otter or other "noxious animals," even if it took you through your neighbour's property. That's because these animals were considered "noisome vermin" and "injurious to the commonwealth."

☛ A horse injuring a person was a serious legal matter, even if that horse belonged to the local fire department. According to an 1872 case, a nosey voyeur was checking out a neighbourhood fire and was subsequently injured by an unattended horse. The judge found the Montréal fire department that owned the animal was liable for damages.

☛ Meandering bees killed two horses in one 1906 case. The court found the beekeeper liable for damages. After all, he should have known that his bees would wander and could pose a threat to his neighbours or passing traffic.

☛ Innkeepers in the 19th century were responsible for providing a safe place for horses belonging to their patrons. In one 1858 case, an innkeeper was held responsible for the actions of his staff, who were believed to have shorn a horse's mane and tail while the animal was in his care.

☛ Citing a law of King Athelstan, "merchandizing on the Lord's Day" was expressly forbidden. No "tradesman, artificer, workman, labourer or other person whatsoever, shall do or exercise any worldly labour, business or work of their ordinary callings upon the Lord's Day." However, anyone who wasn't a horse dealer could enter into a contract to sell a horse on a Sunday.

Road Travel Only

In 1967, the village of Airdrie, Alberta, first passed a bylaw restricting horses and riders from travelling on "sidewalks, boulevards and lawns." They were limited to street and alley travel only.

Secure Your Horse

If you plan to leave your horse unattended for any length of time, you'd better not plan on tying her to the nearest lamppost, water pump or hydrant. A 1901 bylaw in the town of Rat Portage (Kenora), Ontario, made it illegal to do so. Horses pulling a wagon, carriage or any other vehicle were also required to have two or more bells securely attached around their necks.

Registered Horses

Horse owners in city limits and within 1.6 kilometres of St. John's, Newfoundland, must pay a licence fee by July 2nd of every year. If you purchase a horse after July 1, you have to licence the horse before using it.

Chow-time Etiquette

Want to feed your horse after a long drive into town? In Yarmouth, Nova Scotia, a law was passed in 1918 making it illegal to feed your horse on the street "except by a nose bag."

It was also against the law to wash your vehicle while it was parked on the street.

Residents with horse-drawn vehicles such as carriages, wagons, sleighs and others, whether the conveyances are used only for personal use on private property or used for hire, must register these vehicles by July 2 of each year. These bylaws were still found in the 1990 version of the City of St. John's Act.

LIVELY LIVESTOCK

Control Your Critters

The municipal council of the town of Lloydminster, Alberta, read farmers the riot act in 1908. That was the year they made it law for animal owners "or any person having the custody or care of any horse, mule, jack, cattle, sheep, goat, swine, rabbit, goose, turkey, duck or poultry" to keep their critters off town streets at all times. Town fathers took great care to list every possible livestock of the day, and there were no exceptions to the rule. Those who broke the law faced a $20 fine or seven days in jail. Curiously, dogs and cats were absent from the list. And one can't help but wonder what might happen to any wild bunny bouncing through town.

By 1935, it was no longer legal for animals of any kind, "horse, mule, ass, cattle, sheep, pig, goat or goose," to run at large within the village limits of Falher, Alberta. Animals not on their owner's property were to be under "immediate, continuous and effective control" of a caregiver and "securely tethered."

In 1985, the city of Guelph, Ontario, passed a bylaw stipulating rules for keeping ducks, geese, poultry or pigeons in city limits. The approved pens couldn't be located closer than 50 feet (15 metres) from "any school, church or dwelling house not including the owner's dwelling house."

Keep Your Critters Penned

Allow your cattle to roam the streets of Port Coquitlam, BC, and you could be in for a pile of trouble. First, there's a fine of up to $2000, six months in jail or both. Then there are the initial pound keeper fees of $35, followed by an additional $20 a day for food and care. If the cow in question is a milking Holstein, the pound keeper must milk the animal twice daily, but you won't see a drop of it, since whatever is collected goes directly to the pound keeper to reward him for his efforts.

The same fees apply to other large animals, including stallions, horses, donkeys, bulls, goats, sheep, swine and mules. Geese, ducks, fowl, poultry and rabbits cost their owners a little less, with an impound fee of $10 and a daily care rate of $2.50. Curiously enough, this bylaw was first enacted in November 1970 and is still on the books.

Cow Census

In 1935, the city of Kelowna, BC, passed a bylaw requiring farmers to register all cows kept within city limits with the city clerk every 12 months. The registration included an inspection from the Medical Health Officer of not only the cow, but also the owner and all members of the family. This bylaw wasn't repealed until 1990.

Dairy Dos and Don'ts

The town of Cochrane, Ontario, was pretty specific when it came to regulations surrounding the production and sale of milk. In 1924, if a dog or cat happened to wander into the barn area or milk house, the farmer was effectively breaking the law. And it could cost as much as $50.

Animal Farm

Pound keepers in the city of Weyburn, Saskatchewan, had an entirely different set of responsibilities back in 1924 than they do today. According to a bylaw enacted that year, the pound keeper's job was to impound animals running loose. However, the term "animal" referred to everything except dogs and cats. Any animal—bull, stallion, horse, mule or the like—found wandering about with no owner in site could be captured by anyone noticing the vagrant and be brought to the city pound. Should the wandering animal trample through a farmer's field of ripened wheat or cause some other damage, the injured party had to submit a written complaint to the pound keeper in duplicate, together with a dollar amount for the cost of damages. The impounded animal was destined to remain behind bars until its owner paid his debt in full or until the court ordered the animal sold. The proceeds from the sale of such an animal was divided between the costs of the sale itself and any monies due to the original complainant.

To the individual initially delivering the wandering animal to the pound, a set fee would be paid as follows:

- ☞ Stallion or bull: $5.00
- ☞ Boar or ram: $2.00
- ☞ Horse, mule, jack, ox, or cow: $0.50
- ☞ Swine (other than a boar), calf or sheep: $0.25
- ☞ Domestic fowl: $0.10

The pound keeper added a receiving charge of anywhere from 10 to 50 cents for each animal, along with a daily maintenance charge of a similar amount. Add to that the notification fee of 50 cents, the delivery of a notice of sale for 50 cents and posting notices of the sale throughout town at $1.00, and pretty soon the owner was out of pocket a considerable portion of the animal's worth.

Whatever was left over from the proceeds of the sale would be returned to the original owner—once that ownership was proven.

A Pound of Many Species
According to a 1970 bylaw, the city of St. John's, Newfoundland council may, when required, establish facilities for the "impounding of horses, horned cattle, sheep and swine or other domestic animals which may be found straying, or at large, in streets or parks of the city."

Animal Access

Sidewalks in the city of Sault Ste. Marie are for pedestrians, period. Don't even think about taking your dog team and sled for a boot along the sidewalk. Sleds, toboggans and all other vehicles are banned from the walkways. The only exception to the rule is if you need to pass over a paved or plank sidewalk to enter a property.

Animals aren't welcome on the street either. So if you need to drive a herd of cattle, sheep or pigs, you can't use any of Sault Ste. Marie's city streets.

Special Permission
Since sheep roam about freely in some parts of the city of Fort Saskatchewan, Alberta, a herding dog is needed to keep them all in line. And to herd sheep, a dog needs to be able to roam about freely, and it isn't always under the direct control of a handler. So in 2002, the council reviewed its animal control bylaw to allow for the free movement of herding dogs.

Animal Control

Farmer Joe may have thought that by securing a cow bell around Ol' Bessie's neck, he'd have a clearer idea of her whereabouts, but town fathers in Orillia, Ontario, had a different idea. In 1883, they passed a bylaw making it illegal for cows to run "at large with bells attached to them" within town limits. Farmers had to be even more attentive to their livestock after another bylaw passed later that same year restricted the time of day cows could wander through town unattended.

In 1897, farmers faced another roadblock after a new bylaw prevented them from the "leading of, driving or pasturing of horses, cows or other horned cattle upon the sidewalks or boulevards in the town of Orillia."

Two years later, Orillia farmers had yet another area of their farming practices to pay a little more attention to—they had to be careful how they bred their horses. A bylaw passed that year made it illegal for farmers to breed their mares and studs "on or in any of the streets, hotels, yards or parks of the town." Basically, no more equine nookie in public view.

FINES FOR SWINE

The Problem with Pigs

In 1914, town council declared that swine pens in Ponoka, Alberta, should be built a minimum of 300 feet (91.5 metres) from any home or business, and "no more than two pigs of any one age shall be kept in any one pen." If your neighbours complained about any offensive odours wafting in from your direction, you could end up with town officials at your doorstep. Swine pens were to be kept "dry and free from offensive odours" at all times.

It wasn't until 1952 that the village of Airdrie, Alberta, took action when it came to dealing with livestock kept within their village limits. A bylaw enacted that year made it illegal to have any kind of livestock in the village. The only exceptions to the rule were dogs, cats, parrots and canaries "providing the council [did] not consider them objectionable." In unique circumstances, council could give special permission for an individual to contravene the law, but they'd have to reapply for this special permission every year, and council members could change their minds at any time, despite their initial approval. By 1968, "no horses, cattle or chickens" were allowed—under any circumstance—to be kept in any residential area of Airdrie.

THESE LAWS ARE FOR THE BIRDS

No Fowl Odours

Bird lovers in the city of Kingston, Ontario, have a list of rules to adhere to if they want to keep pigeons on their property. A 1957 bylaw stated that people with bird shelters must thoroughly wash the inside walls, ceilings, and floors at least once a year, clean droppings daily, turn the earth in the outside areas of the bird house regularly and dispose of collected bird droppings at least twice a week.

People with pigs weren't so lucky. In 1963, it was illegal to keep any kind of pig—even pets of the potbellied persuasion—if you lived within Kingston city limits.

While limitations were put on pig possession in the village of Lloydminster, Alberta, as early as 1918, the council didn't ban the beasts altogether. Instead, householders in that village were only allowed two pigs on their premises at any one time. The animals had to be kept in an appropriate pen located "not less than 100 feet from any dwelling." Just two years later, that bylaw was repealed, and pigs were no longer allowed in town under any circumstances.

The town of Cochrane, Ontario, passed an outright "no pigs allowed" bylaw in 1922. There was one difference, though. Swine could pass through the town, as long as they didn't stay more than five days.

Feathered Friends?
Birdhouses, birdbaths or bird feeding stations are okay in the city of Moose Jaw, Saskatchewan. But just try to raise any livestock, and you're barking up an entirely different tree.

According to a 1998 bylaw, you can't even have more than two hamsters or guinea pigs in your home without breaking the law.

Foul-feathered Frustrations

No, it's not the Wild West. But you might still hear a shotgun blast from time to time in the town of Carman, Manitoba. Because of an overabundance of nuisance birds, town council passed a law allowing animal control officers to shoot to kill… crows and grackles, that is. The law came into effect in 2001.

Fowl!

It was against the law for homeowners in the village of Quesnel, BC, to keep poultry or any other fowl in their home—and that included the basement! Business owners and shopkeepers had to follow the same rules, according to a 1950 bylaw.

Clip Those Feathers

If you lived in the town of Cochrane, Ontario, in 1913 and planned on keeping poultry, you couldn't let them wander—or fly—off your property. If your feathered friends got onto public property, you could face a $5.00 fine.

Don't Feed the Birds

Stroll along the shores of Lake Banook or Little Abro Lake in the city of Dartmouth, Nova Scotia, and chances are you'll meet a few feathered friends. But if you're inclined to share your sunflower seeds or toss a slice or two of bread in their direction, think again. It is illegal to feed the birds if you're within 50 feet (15 metres) of the lakeshore.

Not Good for the Goose

At an April 1853 town council meeting in Yarmouth, Nova Scotia, it was made law that geese were no longer allowed to waddle about freely in town limits. The penalty for ignoring the law? Five shillings.

Pigeon Police

Though a little more difficult to regulate, feathered fowl aren't exempt from a few rules of their own. A bylaw is still on the books making it illegal to feed the pigeons in Sault Ste. Marie, even on your own personal property. It's considered a public nuisance in that city for pigeons to land on private property, defecate when flying overhead or be too noisy.

DOMESTIC AND NOT-SO-DOMESTIC PETS

Dangerous Animals

If you want to own a pit bull in Grande Prairie, Alberta, you'd better check out the town's animal bylaws. Owning anything labelled a "Restricted and Dangerous Animal" means you'd better have a minimum of $500,000 in liability coverage just in case that pooch of yours bites the neighbour—or anyone else for that matter.

Not Allowed

In case there was any doubt, a 1988 bylaw in the city of Guelph, Ontario, outlined specifically the kinds of animals the ordinary Joe could keep as a pet. Kangaroos and opossums, gorillas and monkeys, wild cats and dogs, mongooses, civets and gents, skunks, weasels, otters and badgers, bears, raccoons, hyenas, seals and walruses, snakes of the pythonidae and boidae family, ostriches, rheas and cassowaries, eagles, hawks and owls, anteaters, sloths and armadillos, alligators and crocodiles, and all bats were among the banned species. Interestingly enough, while it is not a law, the town of Gladstone, Manitoba, encourages its residents to make bat houses to attract the flying mammals since bats eat mosquitoes, and mosquitoes carry the West Nile virus.

Here's One for the Birds

Cat owners in the town of Fort Saskatchewan, Alberta, had some rather unique rules to follow in 1938. Out of great concern for the preservation of the area's song birds, the town council of the day enacted a bylaw making it mandatory for every cat to wear a collar equipped with a bell at all times. Since cats were considered "an enemy to the songbirds," a wandering feline flittering through town without the legislated bell around his neck could find himself dodging bullets. The bylaw stated the feline offender could be "shot at large." Amazingly, Fort Saskatchewan had this bylaw on the books for 20 years before it was repealed.

Out of the same concern, the town of Stavely, Alberta, enacted a cat-belling bylaw the same year. In fact, they announced themselves the first community in the world to have such a law, responding to concerns at the time from the Audubon Society about deaths of songbirds because of domestic cats. Stavely's bylaw also allowed for the shooting of cats. Council even paid a man named Halvar "Red" Rostrum to shoot every cat or kitten he found wandering about without a bell—as long as they were shot before noon.

King of the North?

If you live in Yellowknife, Northwest Territories, and you are pondering the prospect of welcoming a furry friend of the lion persuasion into your family, think again. After a resident's pet lion attacked two people in that community in 1977, the city council enacted a bylaw making it illegal to keep a lion within city limits, and any such feline discovered could be destroyed. The owner of the pet lion responsible for initiating the bylaw was given 30 days to find a new home for his feline protégé. While one is hard-pressed to imagine another family setting up house with a lion in tow, the bylaw remains in effect to this day—just in case.

Speaking of Cats

In Taber, Alberta, all cats six months and older must be licenced—and if they aren't "altered," then the cost to the owner is considerably more than the $15 for a cat that's been spayed or neutered. All cats must wear a "harness and leash with a licence attached" whenever they are outside their homes, and any cats found wandering that aren't "altered" will be part of the town's trap-neuter-release program, where wandering unlicenced cats "will be spayed or neutered if appropriate." A cat might make be returned to its owner—if he or she coughs up the money to cover the costs. Otherwise, the cat will be adopted out.

Population Control, Animal Style
You might be a pet-loving family, but if you live in Inuvik, Northwest Territories, you'd better pick and choose your companions carefully. Unless you have a kennel or a registered dog team, you are forbidden from having "more than three animals exceeding the age of five months" in any one household or property, and that includes hamsters, parrots and guinea pigs. The bylaw, enacted in 1998, still requires residents with dog teams to register each and every animal by listing their name, type, colour, age and sex on a formal application form.

Rats!
You can own a pet rat in Port Coquitlam, BC, but there are limits. More than four pet rats or another combination of pet rodents in one household, and you're breaking the law. The penalty? A $2000 fine, six months in jail or both.

Keep It To Yourself!
Your pet might be lovable, but if it's a snake, tarantula or scorpion, chances are your neighbour or anyone else passing by won't be in too much of a hurry to see it. And in 1990, the city of Kingston, Ontario, made it illegal to carry this type of pet in any public place, considering it a public nuisance. The only exceptions to the rule were schools, zoos or veterinary offices. Anyone transporting a snake, tarantula or scorpion was required to place the creature in a cloth bag to be then "contained inside a durable box having a lid, which is securely fastened." Breaking the law could make a $2000 dent in your bank account.

Species Specifications
It is currently against the law to keep a pet poisonous snake in the city of Dartmouth, Nova Scotia. Nonpoisonous snakes are fine, unless they grow to an adult length of more than 2 feet

(61 centimetres). Pet scorpions, tarantulas and black widow spiders are also illegal. And it's against the law for any pet store in Dartmouth to sell these creatures.

The town of Bedford, Nova Scotia, takes these regulations a step further. Circuses or any other travelling shows passing through aren't even allowed to bring their pythons, scorpions or spiders while travelling through town.

The city of Guelph, Ontario, enacted a bylaw in 1978 making it illegal for anyone to have a pet snake that isn't indigenous to Canada. Zoos and research facilities are exempt.

The city of Halifax, Nova Scotia, has a similar bylaw that was enacted in 1992. While it appears residents can have pets outlawed in some of their neighbouring communities, they'd better keep their reptiles under lock and key. Should a pet snake end up wandering city streets, its owner could face a fine of up to $500—if anyone could find the snake's home, that is!

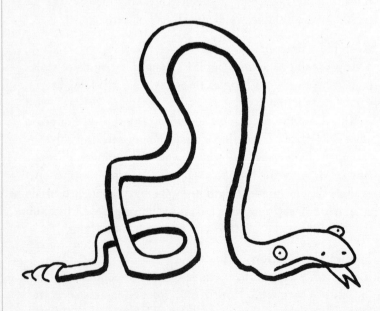

Pooper Scoopers

While it's in good taste to clean up after your pooch when he relieves himself on someone else's property while you're out for a walk, many dog owners choose to turn the other cheek, so to speak. Because of such inconsiderate behaviour, the county of Halifax, Nova Scotia, passed a bylaw in 1989 making it a fineable offence to ignore your duties. Now, if your neighbour catches you looking the other way, you could find yourself faced with a $100 fine or a 30-day jail sentence.

WILD KINGDOM

Gator Wrestling

It is a Criminal Code violation to fight or bait animals or birds, or encourage, aid or assist an individual fighting or baiting animals or birds. Strangely enough, a video depicting an alligator show at Winnipeg's Red River Exhibition might have disturbed one viewer, but despite visible contact between the "showman" and his alligator, the judge in the 1997 case did not find that there was sufficient contact to suggest any fighting or wrestling had occurred.

Bee Serious?

Urban dwellers may have few farming options open to them, but several communities in Canada allow beekeepers to run an apiary within city limits. In some places, a windowsill apiary can be operated, even in a high-rise apartment! Of course, there are laws for this type of operation. Vernon, BC, has a bylaw for the "keeping of bees." Beekeepers must ensure their hives don't pose a risk to their neighbours or anyone passing by on public property, and they must keep any damage to neighbouring private or public property "to a minimum." Vancouver, BC, has a similar bylaw for windowsill beehives.

Don't Touch a Hare

Circus performers and exhibitors had to check the bylaws in Digby, Nova Scotia, before they coaxed a lion to leap through a circle of fire or encouraged a bear troupe dressed in pink tutus to dance for the camera. In 1996, council enacted the Circus Performance Bylaw, making it illegal to encourage animals to perform "tricks, fight or participate in exhibitions or performances for the amusement or entertainment of an audience." There are exceptions. Magicians can still pull rabbits out of their hats, viewers can still bet on horse races and long live the rodeo!

Rules of
Employment

*Life is nothing if not complicated. And while running
a business obviously has its array of ups and downs, who
knew just hiring staff could lead to such a list of
interesting bylaws?*

EARNING AN HONEST DOLLAR

Child Labour

Young lads hoping to support their families in 1906 couldn't get a job in a coalmine in the province of Alberta, unless they were at least 12 years old and able to read, write and were "familiar with the rules of arithmetic." According to the same provincial bylaw, no girl of any age could be employed in a coalmine.

Child Labour Laws

Edmonton, Alberta, was pretty strict when it came to establishing child labour laws within the confines of that city in 1909. Young boys had to be at least 10 years old and young girls had to be 16 before they could sell newspapers, magazines or "small wares." They also couldn't operate as a "boot-black," or shoe shiner, without meeting the age qualifications.

Youngsters meeting the minimum age requirements still needed a valid licence from the city and had to wear an official badge at all times when they were working. To obtain these prerequisites, the child wanting employment had to obtain a written statement from their school principal outlining the status of their attendance, and the principal had to further explain that the youth in question was "of the normal development of a child of his age and physically fit for such employment, and that such principal or chief executive officer approves the granting of permit and badge to such child."

Further, no youth could work after 9:00 PM or before 6:00 AM. And any child working without the appropriate licence and badge or working outside of the specified time limits would be arrested and would face a trial in juvenile court.

Licences expired on January 1 of each year, and youth would have to reapply in order to keep working. The badges worn by these youngsters also listed their next-of-kin information along with their personal description.

Women's Work

In 1926, it would cost you more than just an hourly wage to employ a woman in the town of Wilkie, Saskatchewan. Following The Female Employment Act of the Revised Statues of Saskatchewan of that year, Wilkie council made it law that every business wanting to employ "female labour" had to apply for a licence from the town clerk and pay a $1.00 fee. The licence expired on December 31 of each year, so if you had a great employee and wanted to keep her for another year, you'd have to cough up another dollar.

Odds and Ends

A jaded individual might believe you can't breathe without breaking the law. Who'd have thought someone would come up with a law about fighting alligators, for example?

Or what about the guy who just can't keep himself from tempting fate by doing something most of us would find irrational?

If you can imagine something, chances are someone has tried it somewhere. And with each fate-testing adventurer, another law is likely born.

ELECTION TIME

No Excuses

The residents of Fort Saskatchewan, Alberta, have historically been encouraged to get out and vote on election day—so much so that the town council in 1969 passed a bylaw eliminating one more reason someone might be waylaid en route to the voting station. That bylaw prohibited the "sales of liquor within the municipality on voting or election day." Sheryl Exley, administrative assistant to the mayor and council in that city, noted that it appears this bylaw was only in effect for one year.

Advance Polls

Railway men were perhaps the first to get the chance to vote at an advance poll in the early days of the 20th century—after all, they were often away more than they were home. In 1919, the town of Cochrane, Alberta, passed a bylaw opening advance polls for three days prior to election day. The law was repealed several years later.

CANADIAN, BY THE RULES

The Value of Women

Believe it or not, it wasn't until 1929 that women were considered "persons" under Canadian law. While Canadian women made considerable accomplishments prior to that date, legally they were thought of as little more than property.

A Quiet Patriotism

Letting the Canadian flag flying in your front yard snap in the wind is against the law according to one judge in Collingwood, Ontario. Apparently, a 1999 incident resulted in a schoolteacher being summoned to court because of his wayward, noisy Canadian flag.

A LITTLE RESPECT

In His Honour

With few exceptions, retail shops, businesses and industries throughout the city of Edmonton, Alberta, were to keep their doors locked and businesses closed on Friday, February 15, 1952, according to a city bylaw passed just four days earlier. Sadly, it wasn't because of a festive occasion. Instead, the day was set aside as a day of mourning for King George VI.

Although it was obviously a one-time occurrence, the bylaw wasn't repealed until 1996.

Honouring Our Heroes

The War Memorial Monument in the city of Charlottetown, PEI, is a testament to the gift of freedom our veterans and war dead gave us through their service. It's meant for citizens to come and pay their respects and ponder the many sacrifices these brave people made. It is not meant to be used as a crash pad. According to a 2003 bylaw, anyone taking up "permanent or temporary abode" at the monument could be fined between $100 and $5000, spend up to 90 days in jail or both.

In Remembrance

Folks in Medicine Hat, Alberta, remember their veterans on November 11 in a unique way. All retail and wholesale businesses, with the exception of pharmacies and other essential services, are required to remain closed from 9:00 AM to noon under a 1985 bylaw.

NEAT AND TIDY

That's Not Junk

The 1957 Chevy frame you have sitting in your front yard might be your future dream car, but if it doesn't have a current licence plate, is spotted with rust and is in plain sight of other residents, then it's considered a junked vehicle in Regina, Saskatchewan. A bylaw in that city states owners of junked vehicles must "remove them, place them in a garage or licence them."

Hold Down Your Hay!

Loose hay, straw or other feed blowing about in the village of Lloydminster, Alberta, was considered a fire hazard and a nuisance, so the council took decisive action to prevent that from happening. In 1919, a bylaw was enacted that required farmers to keep hay and other feed enclosed in a building. Failure to do so could cost you $20 or 30 days in the nearest "common gaol."

Serious Business

Composting may be a great environmentally friendly option, but folks in the town of Legal, Alberta, better know how to do it correctly. A portion of their nuisance bylaw states it's an offence for property owners to place "cat feces, dog feces, animal parts or animal meat on a composting pile."

The same bylaw makes it an offence for residents to have an outside light that shines "directly into the living or sleeping area of an adjacent dwelling house."

Garage Sale No-nos

Whether you were planning on holding a garage sale in the town of Ponoka, Alberta, or just wanting to donate a few things to the local thrift store, it was once law that you had to have any items of clothing laundered first. A bylaw dating back to 1939 made it illegal to sell second-hand clothes, boots or accessories without cleaning them first. And if you thought tossing your used clothing in the washing machine should do it, you couldn't have been more wrong. All items had to be "disinfected by a method approved of by the local Board of Health." Dare to defy the bylaw, and you could be fined $50—likely more than what you could have made at the garage sale. Exactly how a bylaw officer would know if the items for sale were properly sanitized is unclear.

Leave it in the Dump

One man's trash is another man's treasure—unless you're in the town of Inuvik, Northwest Territories. A 1988 bylaw made it illegal for anyone to dig in and remove garbage from the town dump. The first time you're caught scavenging, you'll have to cough up $50. A second offence will cost you $100. And third and subsequent offences will cost you $300. In the end it's probably cheaper to buy it new! There is, of course, a loophole. The town does make provisions for people to obtain a Solid Waste Salvage Permit.

S'no Easy Job

If you're planning on clearing snow or ice from the sidewalk in front of your home and you live in Saskatoon, Saskatchewan, make sure you don't dump the contents of your shovel on the boulevard. A 1977 bylaw in that community says that's dumping waste contrary to the Anti-Dumping Bylaw, and the offence could cost you as much as $500 in fines.

No Loopholes Here

The anti-litter bylaw in Winnipeg, Manitoba, may have originated several years ago, but the city still takes the issue of litter seriously. In 2002, the council updated the city's anti-litter bylaw—and the definition of what constitutes litter is pretty all encompassing. As stated in the bylaw, litter "means animal and agricultural wastes, ashes, construction and demolition wastes, dead animals, garbage, industrial refuse, rubbish, solid wastes or refuse, abandoned or unattended shopping carts and special wastes, including but not limited to street cleanings, containers, packages, bottles, cans or parts thereof and any deserted or discarded article, product or goods of manufacture." And anyone carelessly disposing of any of these items, on public or even private property, will face the wrath of the bylaw officer.

Tragedy Strikes

The city of Windsor, Ontario, enacted a bylaw in 1953 stating that anyone discarding a refrigerator, freezer or other similar container must remove the doors. The need for this law emerged when two young children suffocated after they were unable to escape from the refrigerator they were playing in.

AN ORDERLY FASHION

Your Number Is Up

According to the most recent count, the town of Morden, Manitoba, is a community of about 6200 people. And yet it appears that prior to 2004, a considerable number of homes and buildings on "streets, roads or other thoroughfares" in town didn't have street numbers affixed to the front of the property. That's when Morden town council enacted a bylaw making it mandatory for property owners to do so. And they had to do it right, too. Numbers had to be a minimum of 4 inches (10 centimetres) in height and "clearly visible from the public street."

The town of Neepawa had a few additional requirements in a similar 2004 bylaw. A house number there has to be a minimum of 5 inches (12.5 centimetres) in height and has to be in a "contrasting colour to the building, house or structure to which it is affixed."

Publishing Practices

It is law in Newfoundland that book publishers provide three bound copies of newly published books to the government within one month of being printed. One copy goes to the Department of Municipal and Provincial Affairs, and the other two copies are placed in a library or other location as directed by the Lieutenant-Governor in Council.

Everywhere a Sign

Who knew regulating signs in your community could be so cumbersome? The district of Chetwynd, BC, takes the legalities around signs so seriously that in June 1996 they produced a 22-page bylaw documenting all the requirements to obtain a permit before a sign can be legally erected. Here are just a few of the highlights—the abridged version, of course:

☛ Aside from explaining what exactly constitutes a "sign," the bylaw goes on to define 21 different possible types of signs ranging from real estate signs and sandwich boards to illuminated, political, portable, fascia, directional, canopy and changeable copy signs, among others.

☛ When erecting your sign, you'd better have a clear understanding of the rules about its appearance, the allowable size, how far your sign can project from the outside wall of the building to which it may be attached and where you're permitted to place it, to name just a few restrictions. The bylaw provides minute details for every sign type.

☛ Disposing of redundant signs is also regulated.

☛ Oh, and one more thing. You may have a reprieve from following the rules after all. The bylaw doesn't apply to signs or "notices" issued by a provincial body, traffic control devices, vehicle signs or "signs located in the interior of buildings and not visible from a highway." Imagine that!

Of course, permits cost money. In Chetwynd, the permit fee for erecting a sign is complicated and depends on the "value of the sign and any supporting structure."

Just a few months after enacting the sign bylaw, the district of Chetwynd made one change to their initial rules by increasing the amount of liability insurance required to put up a sign from a minimum of $1000 to $2000.

While larger cities often have similar sign bylaws, for a small community like Chetwynd, this bylaw is unique indeed!

A Thundering World Wonder

A protected site it may be, but that hasn't stopped daredevils from around the world from tackling the thundering force of Niagara Falls. Common sense aside, the Niagara Parks Act is quite explicit about what visitors can and cannot do while visiting the park, especially when it comes to the falls itself.

Throughout history, a few adventurers have tried barrelling over the falls—quite literally—and lived to tell the tale. In fact, the attempts occurred often enough that officials decided to create a law forbidding any such stunts without written permission.

And if you're organizing a visit to this wonder of the world, you also shouldn't plan on playing an instrument of any kind, flying a flag, organizing a marching band or "performing any other act that congregates or is likely to congregate persons" without making arrangements first. You need written permission to do any of these activities as well.

For the Common Good

The city of Halifax, Nova Scotia, is mighty proud of its parklands. But one area, a park called the Commons, has special significance. In 1940, the city passed special bylaws to protect the area. Most are logical—no driving on the grass, no damaging the shrubs and trees. But when reading others, you can't help but wonder what may have happened to incite council to "spell it out," as it were. Apparently, it is illegal to dump a dead animal in the Commons, and don't even think about driving your herd of cattle through the area. Both offences could cost you $20 or 10 days in jail.

HOT BUTTON ISSUES

Squelch That Fire Pit!

Roasted weenies fresh from the fire are against the law in the city of Grande Prairie, Alberta. In 1989 the city enacted a bylaw to "prohibit open burning within the corporate limits of the city of Grande Prairie." Of course, a prohibition of any kind usually has its loopholes. In this situation, if you have an extreme case of the open-fire munchies, all you have to do is build a receptacle for the purpose, get permission from the landowner (if that's not you) and pay the city for a fire permit.

An Explosive Situation

Business owners in the municipality of Jasper, Alberta, cannot "possess, store, use, sell or offer for sale any explosive." Now, if you need to blast your way through a mountainside, you can apply to the town council for an explosives permit. But if you are granted your request, you'll still have to go elsewhere to buy the dangerous goods.

The Bell Tolls for All

While town fathers in Peace River, Alberta, didn't enact a bylaw on tolling the town bell, they did pass a motion in 1920 requiring the town constable to "toll the fire bell one stroke for every hour at 8:00 AM, 12:00 noon and 6:00 PM." While the practice is no longer followed to the letter, the motion is still on the books, and today, a bell still rings out every weekday at noon.

Banned, Banned, Banned!

That's all there is to say—in October 2005, the city of White Rock, BC, banned all sales, disposal, ignition and discharge of fireworks within city limits. People wanting to celebrate a special event can apply for a special permit, but they still have to travel to acquire the banned goods!

SHHH!

Censorship

The Censoring of Moving Pictures Act, passed in 1970, can still be found in the 1990 Revised Statues of Newfoundland. According to that law, "a quorum of the members of the board of censors present at an exhibition may, by oral or written notification to the proprietor of that exhibition or to the person operating the projection machine at the exhibition, summarily prohibit the exhibition of a moving or stationary picture, film or slide which they consider to be injurious to the morals of the public, or against the public welfare, or offensive to the public." Interestingly enough, adult videos are available from stores even in Newfoundland.

Music Mania

Perhaps it was a case of excessive musical gatherings popping up here and there without warning. Whatever the reason, in 1981, Grande Prairie made it illegal for any outdoor festival to strike its first chord without acquiring a permit. In fact, aspiring music festival organizers have to apply for the permit a minimum of 60 days in advance of a planned event.

Silence Please!

At the turn of the 20th century, Nova Scotia made it illegal for any on-duty policeman to utter a single word, phrase or sentence to the public. The only exception was if he was speaking in an official capacity.

Policemen had to be above reproach in their personal lives as well. In 1891, a policeman in Yarmouth, Nova Scotia, who was caught drunk, visiting a liquor store or gambling house (unless doing so in the execution of his duties) or using "ungentlemanly language" would be "immediately dismissed from the service." He could also face charges and fines.

EAT, DRINK, AND BE LEGISLATED

Real Butter

If you go by colour alone, there is no way you can mistake margarine for butter in Québec. That's because the vegetable-based spread can't contain more than "one and six-tenths degrees or less than 10 and five-tenths degrees of yellow or yellow and red combined on the Lovibond colorimeter scale." In layman's terms, that means the colour of margarine can't come anywhere close to that of butter.

What's the Buzz?

It is illegal for clear sodas to contain caffeine in Canada.

Information Mandate

The city council of White Rock, BC, enacted a bylaw in 1994 making it law for any business selling liquor to post signs in prominent locations warning women of the dangers of drinking during pregnancy. To send a consistent message throughout the community, all liquor outlets had to post the same warning.

THINK GLOBALLY, ACT LOCALLY

No Nukes!

Out of great concern for the safety of their citizens and the citizens of the world, the town of Fort Saskatchewan, Alberta, enacted a bylaw in 1983 stating a referendum on nuclear disarmament would be held in conjunction with municipal elections that year. While the referendum did indeed occur, the only record of any follow-up was a letter forwarded by the council of the day to the member of Parliament for that area "expressing council's concern regarding nuclear arms and asking the MP to bring to the federal government a referendum in the next federal election." Though council received a response to that request, there is no mention in the meeting minutes of what the reply was.

Check This Out!

The powers that be in Chilliwack, BC, recently enacted a bylaw that might be the first of its kind in Canada. On January 23, 2006, council members in that city passed the Hydroponics and Drug Paraphernalia Bylaw 2006. Simply put, anyone dealing in drug paraphernalia or in substances that in large batches could be used for narcotic production must be identified and potentially monitored under this act. Anyone selling drug paraphernalia has to register the following:

- the "name, residence, or street address and birth date of the buyer,"
- picture identification,
- a description of the item purchased,
- the price paid, and
- the date of purchase.

So, basically speaking, the RCMP will know of the sale of every item that could potentially have any association with drugs and drug production, along with the name and contact information of the purchaser. Yup, there's nowhere to hide in Chilliwack!

Don't Even Try It

Torture is against the law in the Yukon, no matter whether you are a public official or not. The 2002 Revised Statutes of the Yukon officially upheld the United Nations Convention Against Torture and Other Cruel, Inhuman or Degrading Treatment or Punishment. In the statute, torture means any kind of physical, mental or emotional pain inflicted on a person to elicit a statement or information.

CAUSE FOR A CELEBRATION

Happy Holidays

Most bylaws were established to provide restrictions of some sort, and if you broke those restrictions, you broke the law. But in 1959, in Williams Lake, BC, the village commission passed a happy law making January 2 an official holiday. The name of that holiday? Wrestling Day.

The origins of the holiday come from two pioneer merchants, Alistair Mackenzie and Syd Western. Legend has it the two shopkeepers were having coffee one January 2 some time in the 1930s. It was cold. The streets were empty. No one had come into their respective businesses all morning. And after talking to a few of other business owners on the town's main drag, they decided to close shop for the day. After all, the day after Christmas was a holiday. It seemed only reasonable that the day after New Year's would be a holiday as well. In 1943, the town declared January 2 a holiday, but it wasn't made law until 1959. The story goes that the holiday earned the name Wrestling Day because "half the town was wrestling with a hangover."

In 1976, all existing store-closing bylaws were abolished, including Wrestling Day. That put the town in an uproar, and after much public pressure, council reinstated the Wrestling Day bylaw the following year. It remains in effect to this day.

That's the Spirit!
While Boxing Day is a holiday we all take for granted, it evolved from community to community throughout the British Commonwealth at different times over the years. Here in Canada, the city of Windsor, Ontario, passed a law in 1937, making the day following Christmas a holiday. Council justified this law by stating it was "for the health, safety, morality and

welfare of the inhabitants of the municipality." But when the law was forwarded for approval to Ontario's Department of Municipal Affairs, it was returned unapproved. It was the opinion of the supervisor at the time that "the municipality has no power to fix such a public holiday." Two years later, the issue was raised again. Council proposed the day following Christmas would be a civic holiday called Boxing Day. The bylaw was passed and became law on December 19, 1939.

A Golden Celebration

Everyone loves a holiday, and councillors in Bowden, Alberta, decided that bestowing a day of rest on their residents was the best way to celebrate the province's Golden Jubilee. So for one day, August 17, 1955, a civic holiday was proclaimed to "augment the importance of the Alberta Golden Jubilee and the success of the Gigantic Community picnic."

Heritage Celebrations
Citizens of the Yukon are encouraged to "reflect on the history and heritage of their land and its peoples" on June 13 of every year after their Legislative Assembly passed the Yukon Day Act in 1998. The date was chosen because it was the anniversary of "the creation of Yukon as a territory within Canada" 100 years earlier.

Any Excuse for a Party

It doesn't take long to think up a reason for a holiday—or a festival. For folks in the town of Collingwood, Ontario, celebrating all things Elvis is reason enough. The annual four-day celebration is anticipated by residents and visitors alike. Although the town council hasn't deemed the King of Rock 'n' Roll worthy of a four-day vacation from work, they did pass a bylaw outlining rules and responsibilities for the Collingwood Elvis Festival Board in 2001.

ENVIRONMENT FRIENDLY

Tree Hugging at Its Finest

You can cut trees in the district of Hope, BC. Well, sometimes you can. That community's 1995 tree protection bylaw makes it clear that anyone who wants to cut down a tree must get a permit first. However, you'll only get a permit if your request follows some specific regulations. Among other things, you have to provide the city's municipal engineer with a letter explaining why you need to cut the tree, a tree survey and proof of liability insurance carried by the tree-removal company being used for the job.

Water Rations

In 1915, residents of the town of Cochrane, Alberta, were able to access drinking water from street taps—but not without paying for the privilege first. Using town water cost residents 75 cents every three months, and the fee had to be paid in advance. A midnight visit to the town's water source didn't mean you'd get off without paying. If you were caught, it could cost you $25—a whole lot more than the initial 75 cents.

I'm Even, You're Odd

The district of Hope, BC, deals with water conservation differently. In that community, water rationing isn't just a weather-related situation whereby residents are called to observe certain rules because of a drought. Since June 2005, homeowners there have been restricted to watering their lawns on even or odd days, depending on their particular street address, from May 1 to September 30 of every year. The penalty for getting your days mixed up is $100 a day and could increase to a maximum fine of $2000, depending on how long you continue the unlawful behaviour.

The municipality of Crowsnest Pass, BC, adds yet another twist to its watering rules. Council there passed a bylaw in 2004 restricting people with even house numbers to water their lawns on Tuesdays, Thursdays and Saturdays between 6:00 AM and 9:00 AM or 7:00 PM and 11:00 PM. Those with odd house numbers have Wednesdays, Fridays and Sundays to water their lawns. And "there shall be NO outside watering on Monday."

Water, Water, Nowhere...

In 1927, the watering of lawns and gardens in the town of Wilkie, Saskatchewan, was strictly regulated. A bylaw stipulated that watering with a hose could only occur between 6:00 PM and 10:00 PM from June to August. Break the law once and you could face a $50 fine or 30 days in jail. Break it twice in the same season, and the town could disconnect water services to your home for the remainder of that summer.

WILD TIMES

No Closed Doors Here

Using an escort service might seem a bit daring to most folk, but the city of Medicine Hat, Alberta, decided demystifying the situation was the best way to keep it on the up and up—and they did just that by enacting a bylaw to "regulate escorts and agencies." Before anyone can hang a shingle advertising escort services, he or she must obtain a licence from the city. Each licence issued includes the individual's full name, including all given names, their birthday and home address, telephone number, the agency they work for, any aliases and a current photograph. Get caught doing business without a licence, and the fine is anywhere between $500 and $1500 each time.

Age of Majority?

A 1958 bylaw that is still in effect today prohibits youth under age 18 years to "be or remain in a poolroom, or to play pool or any other game" inside a pool hall in White Rock, BC. Underage youth can't work there either—and anyone who does work there won't be clocking out any later than 11:30 PM. That's when all poolrooms must be closed for business.

LOCK 'EM UP

Jail Bait

It didn't matter how sorry you felt for your buddy who found himself locked up in the town clink. As of May 17, 1883, it was no longer legal in the town of Orillia, Ontario, for you to pass a flask of whiskey through the jail bars on your daily visit. Likely, inebriated prisoners were far more difficult to control than sober ones.

Twenty-five Stripes

From misdemeanours to felony charges or murder, criminals of all sorts in Newfoundland could face whipping and hard labour while serving time in jail in 1892. Each time a prisoner stepped out of line, the jail guard could privately or publicly issue three lashes "provided that not more than 25 stripes shall be given at any one time."

UNDERWATER

Out of Sight, Not Necessarily Out of Mind

Submarine telegraph cables in Newfoundland were protected like an endangered species. According to the Newfoundland Act of 1892, anyone breaking or damaging a submarine cable in any way could be subject to a prison term of three months or a fine of $500. Exactly how an ordinary Joe could manage the deep-sea vandalism is beyond imagining.

Pristine Waters

No one can cast stones—or ballast or anything else for that matter—into St. John's harbour in Newfoundland. Try it and you could face a $50 fine or 50 days in jail.

Fact or Fiction?

While I was researching this collection of unique laws
in this fine country of ours, a number of well-intentioned
individuals provided interesting tidbits they admitted
they were unable to confirm. Some were so wonderfully
bizarre that I simply couldn't help but include them in
this section.

Should you, dear reader, have any inside information
on one or more of these bylaws or know of a unique law
or two I didn't include, please don't hesitate call. Who
knows, maybe there's a volume two in the making?

BUT IS IT A LAW?

- Rumour has it that a bylaw in the town of Yarmouth, Nova Scotia, regulated the length of women's skirts until the 1960s.

- At least one curfew bylaw in Canada had a rather odd twist to it. Apparently, in the town of Yarmouth, Nova Scotia, African Canadians were not allowed in certain areas of town at night.

- It is illegal to drive your cows across Water Street in St. John's, Newfoundland, before 11:00 AM on Sundays—or is it?

- Exercise might be good for your health, but if your efforts at longevity frighten a horse in Quesnel, BC, then you could be in trouble—or so the story goes.

- It really is against the law to display advertisements in English in the province of Québec. On the other hand, it is rumoured that a Montréal bylaw states you cannot swear in French.

- Apparently, at one time in the province of Alberta, a newly released prisoner was provided with a handgun, bullets and a horse so he could safely ride out of town.

- Showing public affection on a Sunday in Wawa, Ontario, was supposedly against the law at one time.

- Maybe it's for the comfort of the cow, or the sensory well being of its caregivers, but according to one urban legend, it's against the law to keep a cow in your house in St. John's, Newfoundland. Rumour also has it that running cattle through city streets in St. John's has to happen before 8:00 AM, or you'll face a fine.

- Legend has it that the city of Toronto, Ontario, has had a few strange laws on the books at one time or another. Apparently, dragging a dead horse down Yonge Street on a Sunday was illegal. And riding a streetcar on a Sunday after eating garlic could also get you into trouble. A review of current bylaws seems to indicate these bylaws have been repealed—or were they ever in existence?

- In Canada, it is against the law to remove a bandage in public—or so some say.
- Allowing your dog to bark, especially during the night, is likely a no-no in many communities, but who ever heard of keeping your parrot quiet? One source suggests a $100 fine is laid against people in Oak Bay, BC, if they have noisy pet parrots.
- Apparently, it is (or was at one time) against the law to kill a sasquatch in British Columbia. Though the creature's existence has yet to be proven, should the sasquatch be anything more than a legend, it seems logical that killing one wouldn't be such a great idea.

- You can't depend on a roll of the dice while playing craps in Alberta.
- Rumour has it that cats older than six months had to be spayed or neutered in Port Coquitlam, BC, unless a special breeding permit was purchased from the city. It may have been a law in the past, but it's not currently on the books.

☛ Newly laundered clothes with that fresh-from-the-clothesline scent aren't possible in Kanata, Ontario. Apparently, it is illegal there to have a clothesline in one's backyard.

☛ At one time, a city bylaw restricted the colour of one's house and garage door in Kanata, Ontario. Beaconsfield, Ontario, apparently had a bylaw on books stating residents could not have more than two different colours of exterior paint on their homes. And in Outremont, Québec, exterior paint jobs weren't the only home improvement issue up for discussion. Apparently, in one case, the city of Outremont went to the Appeals Court over the type of division allowed inside a window frame.

☛ Youngsters have had their zest for adventure curbed slightly in Oshawa, Ontario. Supposedly, it is against the law for anyone to climb trees in that city.

☛ In Etobicoke, Ontario, bubble baths are likely a rarity since rumour has it that a bylaw states residents there can't have more than 3.5 inches (9 centimetres) of water in the bathtub.

☛ Theatre owners have to pay attention to the clock in Montréal, Québec. Apparently in that city it is illegal for a movie playing in the theatre to end later than 2:00 AM.

☛ If you like wandering about in your birthday suit and live in Winnipeg, Manitoba, you'd better make sure you have your blinds down and drapes drawn. If not, you could be breaking a city bylaw.

☛ Meeting the woman of your dreams wasn't possible for the men of Edmonton, Alberta, at least not if they were tossing a few back at their neighbourhood pub after work. One unconfirmed source suggests it was once illegal for a "man to drink with a woman in an Edmonton beer parlour."

☛ While the current existence of the British Columbia Grasshopper Control Committee has yet to be confirmed, it's said to be against the law to interrupt one of their meetings. Anyone doing so could be arrested.

☛ Wearing a bathing suit while "loitering, playing or indulging in a sun bath in any park or on the beach" was supposedly illegal in Victoria, BC.

☛ One source, apparently drawing their information from the provincial law books, stated it was once illegal to watch exotic dancers while drinking alcohol in Saskatchewan.

☛ A city ordinance in Churchill, Manitoba, states children there aren't allowed to wear furry costumes while trick or treating during Halloween. Apparently the concern is they could be mistaken for an animal, and in particular for a baby seal, and inadvertently attract polar bears to town.

☛ There's no excuse for sloppy dress in Fort Qu'Appelle, Saskatchewan. It's said to be against the law for teens to walk down Main Street with their shoes untied.

☛ It is—or was at one time—against the law in Ottawa, Ontario, for children to eat ice cream cones on city streets on Sunday.

☛ Public property must be treated with respect in Winnipeg, Manitoba. One source states a bylaw in that city makes it illegal for pedestrians to strike sidewalks with a metal object.

☛ Pigs weren't made for wandering. One source suggested pigs wandering the streets of Toronto, Ontario, in 1934 were in deep trouble.

☛ You'd think it would be considered fair play, but one uncon-firmed source states it's illegal to try and catch a fish with your hands in Saskatoon, Saskatchewan.

☛ It's been said that painting a ladder is against the law in Wawa, Ontario. The reasoning behind the law is simple—if the ladder is wet, it will be slippery, and someone could get hurt! Waiting until the paint dries to climb the rungs doesn't appear to have entered into the debate.

☛ The information highway has a predetermined speed limit in Uxbridge, Ontario. Apparently, residents there can't have an Internet connection faster than 56K.

☛ In Canada, you cannot pay for a 50-cent item with 50 pennies.

☛ If you find yourself bankrupt, and you have a predisposition to excessive alcohol consumption, one source points to BC as the best place in Canada to get locked up. That's because jailers there are supposedly required to "bring convicted debtors a pint of beer on demand."

☛ While you can purchase individual cans of beer in some Canadian provinces, it's apparently the law in Newfoundland and New Brunswick that the smallest unit of beer that can be sold in liquor stores is a six-pack.

Definitely Legend

*It's interesting how some sources cite chapter and verse,
and yet their claims are not easily verified.*

*While the following entry was said to be true, no date was
offered, and as of 2005, the citation was erroneous.*

THE LAW THAT WASN'T

Don't Ruffle My Feathers

An Internet site claims section 331 of the Canadian Criminal Code makes it "illegal to send a letter or telegram threatening a bird." The Criminal Code of any country is ever evolving, and today the section stated refers to "theft by person holding power of attorney." Whether the claimed law ever existed is doubtful.

No Such Law...Not Yet

On its way to legislation, a proposed law goes through a number of twists and turns and sometimes unorthodox processes.

Here are just a couple of hotly debated laws that can't help but evoke a response of some type.

SPICING THINGS UP... AT LEAST ONCE A YEAR

No Headaches Allowed

Leave it to the imagination of one of Canada's quirky authors to come up with an idea for a proclamation that could blow the roof off the fallacy that we Canadians are an uptight, sexually stunted lot. According to a 2004 article by *Toronto Sun* columnist Valerie Gibson, Chris Gudgeon, best-selling author of *The Naked Truth: The Untold Story of Sex in Canada*, suggested May 14 be declared National Sex Day. His chosen date was significant because it was the anniversary of the day Pierre Trudeau's government passed the Omnibus Bill, which addressed previously taboo topics including abortion and birth control.

Gudgeon wasn't alone in his quest. Sue McGarvie, therapist and *Sex with Sue* radio host, and Valerie Scott, spokesperson for Sex Professionals of Canada, added their voices to the cause. McGarvie was quoted as saying it would be a "fun" idea. "Sex is, after all, good for you!...Maybe everyone could spend the day in bed on National Sex Day?"

NO SUCH LAW...NOT YET

WATER, WATER, EVERYWHERE

Ancient Innovations

While it's not yet law in the town of Cochrane, Alberta, council members there has put their muscle behind a not-so-new idea they hope will take off. Running with the motto "You don't know the value of water until the well is running dry," residents in the western town are being encouraged to harvest rain in a rain barrel. After all, it takes no real effort, and it's such a shame to waste all that "free and pure rain water." They're even encouraging residents to consider attaching a hose to their barrel to make for "more practical, 'hands-free' watering." The hope is to reduce the amount of treated water used in lawn and garden care. Whether this actually becomes a bylaw is yet to be seen.

WHERE THERE'S SMOKE...

The Great Marijuana Debate

Marijuana was once clearly against the law, and those who flirted with Mary Jane were thought of by most Canadians as not the kind of people mother would like you to bring home for dinner. But legalizing pot has developed into one of Canada's judicial system's hottest topics of debate.

In 1923, marijuana was banned in Canada under the Opium and Drug Act. While the 1960s were a time of free love and experimentation of all sorts, it wasn't until the 21st century that Canada started seriously reviewing its stand on the matter. Was marijuana really a dangerous drug?

In a 2003 report, *Decriminalization of Marijuana in Canada*, then–Justice Minister Martin Cauchon was quoted as saying Canadian laws on the topic needed some updating.

The previous year, a special Senate committee on illegal drugs suggested marijuana be treated like tobacco or alcohol. The House of Commons was wading through intricate studies on whether marijuana was a gateway drug, how it affected users and if it was really prudent to saddle an otherwise-productive individual with a criminal record because he was found to have a joint or two in his possession. While those supporting decriminalization were hopeful that what they believed to be a strange and antiquated law would be modernized, others looked at Canada and wondered if our leaders had lost their minds. Interestingly enough, the proposed Act to Amend the Contraventions Act and the Controlled Drugs and Substances Act, originally tabled in May of 2003, died on the order paper once the 2004 election was called.

No matter what side of the fence you stand on, the situation is likely as weird, strange and odd as any other law in this collection. But regardless your view, possession of marijuana is still against the law in Canada.

THE PUBLIC EYE

Big Brother is Watching

Don't say that—someone might be listening! In November 2005, the House of Commons reviewed a proposed law that, if passed, would have allowed police and other officials to get personal information about people of interest to national security. If passed, telephone and Internet providers would have been required to "phase out technical barriers to police and security agencies seeking access to messages or conversations." The goal was to restrict communication between "terrorists and other criminals" and also prevent a child pornographer, for example, from "sending his disgusting images around this country and around the world," explained then–Public Safety Minister Anne McLellan in a statement to the Canadian Press.

Advocates for privacy rights argued it was against the Canadian Charter of Rights and Freedoms to do such a thing, and telephone and internet providers raised practical concerns about new equipment needed to preserve electronic data and the costs incurred by working with security agencies.

Although the law was introduced into the House, like the great marijuana debate, it too died on the order paper with the early January call of the 2006 election.

ABOUT THE AUTHOR

Lisa Wojna

Lisa Wojna, author of two other non-fiction books, has worked in the community newspaper industry as a writer and journalist and has travelled all over Canada, from the windy prairies of Manitoba to northern British Columbia, and even to the wilds of Africa. Although writing and photography have been a central part of her life for as long as she can remember, it's the people behind every story that are her motivation and give her the most fulfillment.

ABOUT THE ILLUSTRATOR

Roger Garcia

Roger Garcia immigrated to Canada from El Salvador at the age of seven. Because of the language barrier, he had to find a way to communicate with other kids. That's when he discovered the art of tracing. It wasn't long before he mastered this highly skilled technique, and by age 14, he was drawing weekly cartoons for the *Edmonton Examiner*. He taught himself to paint and sculpt, and then in high school and college, Roger skipped class to hide in the art room all day in order to further explore his talent. Currently, Roger's work can be seen in a local weekly newspaper and in places around Edmonton.

WEIRD CANADIAN PLACES

Humorous, Bizarre, Peculiar & Strange Locations & Attractions across the Nation

Dan de Figueiredo

BLUE
BIKE
BOOKS

The Publisher: Blue Bike Books

Library and Archives Canada Cataloguing in Publication

De Figueiredo, Dan, 1964–
  Weird Canadian places: humorous, bizarre, peculiar and
strange locations and attractions across the nation / Dan de
Figueiredo.

ISBN-13: 978-0-9739116-4-0
ISBN-10: 0-9739116-4-6

  1. Canada—Miscellanea. 2. Canada—Description and
travel—Miscellanea. I. Title.

FC60.D26 2006   971   C2006-901646-1

Project Director: Nicholle Carrière
Project Editor: Nicholle Carrière
Illustrations: Roger Garcia
Cover Image: Roger Garcia

PC: P1

CONTENTS

DEDICATION

This book is dedicated to the oh so many people who have let me be part of their lives and in some way nurtured any talent I might possess. To my mother, Sharon Lindsay, and my grandmother, Sarah Tilbury, for passing down the strength and ability to see beyond the hype that allowed me to take up the life of a writer and be "poor." Right, mum? To my Uncle Brian and Aunt Dawn for giving me a copy of Robinson Crusoe—I know that book started me on this path. To my mother-in-law, Gena Figueiredo, thank you for your openness, your *bacalhau* and all the laughter. To Max, for being my constant companion for more than 10 years. Sorry about the peeing, but I bet the boiled chicken is better than ever. To the three most important male influences in my life—Bob, Simon and Paulo—thank you for inspiring me to be better. And, I suppose, most of all, I must thank God for toying with my emotions, pulling the rug out from under me and never letting me get too full of myself. I've learned my lesson. I really don't think I'm the smartest person in the room. Not all the time, anyway. Thank God for those "gotcha moments" and for making my life a journey. You have some weird sense of humour!

ACKNOWLEDGEMENTS

This book could not have been written without the generous help of a great many "weird" Canadians. First, I have to thank my publisher who took a chance and let me write this book. I have had the best time researching, writing and putting this together. I also have to thank my editor, Nicholle Carrière. Having worked much of my professional career as an editor, I know that a good editor can make or break the final product.

I also have to thank a great many people from the various government tourist offices, town's, sights, festivals etc. If I've forgotten anyone, I do apologize. But here is a list of people whose help was invaluable. They include: Paul Figueiredo; Sharon Lindsay; John Fisher; Bill Lishman; Jane Sims; Gillian Marx, Market Development Officer, Media Relations, Newfoundland and Labrador Tourism; R. Randy Brooks, Manager, Media Relations, Nova Scotia

Department of Tourism, Culture and Heritage; John Marr, Waterfront Visitor Information Centre, Nova Scotia; Bernadette MacNeil, Destination Cape Breton Association; Carol Horne, Manager, Advertising and Publicity, Tourism PEI; Donna Rowley, Manager, Prince Edward Island Potato Museum; Diane Rioux, Media Relations-Tourism, Tourism and Parks, Tourism New Brunswick; Isabel Gil, Director Destination Québec/Tourisme Québec; Magalie Boutin, Destination Québec/Tourism Québec; Sophie Saint-Gelais, Agente de promotion touristique, Ville de Baie-Comeau; Ontario Tourism Marketing Partnership; Bev Carret, Manager, Government and Community Relations, Art Gallery of Ontario; Eunice Henning (the Big Adirondack Chairs); Daryl Demoskoff, Media Relations Coordinator, Tourism Saskatchewan; The Town of Wilkie, Saskatchewan; Harold Wasylenka of Wynyard, Saskatchewan (my Chicken Chariot race source); Rollie Bourassa, Regina, Saskatchewan (the Pemmican Pete insider); Marilyn at Danceland, Manitou Beach, Saskatchewan; Susan Fekete, Travel Media Relations Specialist, Americas, Travel Alberta International; Becky Fox, Coordinator, Information Services, Vulcan Tourism and Trek Station, Vulcan, Alberta; Carla Mont, Tourism BC; Brenda from HelloBC.com; Heidi Korven, Administrative Assistant, Kootenay Rockies Tourism; Miles Prodan, Director of Communications and Marketing, Thompson Okanagan Tourism Association; John Bass, Media Relations Coordinator, Northern British Columbia Tourism Association; Lana Kingston, Media Relations Manager, Tourism Vancouver Island; Kristine George, Manager, Travel Media Relations (Canada and Overseas), Tourism Victoria; Jeannie McLarnon, Travel Counsellor, Yukon Tourism and Culture; D'Arcy Butler, Marketing and Promotions Manager, Klondike Visitors Association; Samantha Cayen, Administrative Assistant, Klondike Visitors Association; Jennifer Horton, Northwest Territories Tourism; His Royal Highness SnowKing, www.snowking.ca; Brian Webb, Acting Director of Marketing, Nunavut Tourism.

I thank all of these people for their directions, clarifications, redirections, fact-checking and all-around assistance with this weird little book. I hope to run into some of you on my future travels.

INTRODUCTION

"Weird," to me, means odd, unique, interesting, out of the ordinary, not mundane and also fun! It can include the mystical, the paranormal and the unexplained. It includes things described as queer, incomprehensible and mysterious. It can be connected with fate, warning or just plain size. It's a word that can include a great many and varied things.

The question "why" is at the heart of "weird." Why does a headless brakeman roam the former CPR tracks in Vancouver? Why does Lumsden, Saskatchewan, hold an annual Duck Derby? Why does Father Goose live underground and build a replica of Stonehenge out of crushed cars? The answer to "why" defines the weirdness.

Weird does not, in my mind, have a bad connotation, though I do accept that many people got weirded out when I called them and said I was writing a book on weird Canadian places and wanted to include their place. I heard a lot of silence or the oft-repeated response: "This place isn't weird!" The protest response was all about not wanting to be ridiculed or made fun of. For some reason, the first place people go to when they hear the adjective "weird" is a bad place. Not me. I understand that no one wants to be laughed at, especially by a smarmy citified writer from Toronto. I hope I am not that. My intention is to highlight all the unique places that are everywhere in this country and do it in a lighthearted manner.

In my other life, I occasionally work in television. Please don't hold that against me, though I do not blame you if you do. Last year I had the opportunity to pitch a couple of show ideas to a room full of television executives at the Banff Television Festival. I pitched a paranormal idea that received a warm response. The second idea I pitched involved con games. The response I got from the executives (German TV,

FOX TV, Global TV) was "weird." They called it "weird"!
No one thought the paranormal idea was weird, but they all
said my con game idea was weird. I took this as a great compliment and a bit of a commentary about television executives—sheep dressed in Armani! I recount this story because
I really do think being called weird is a compliment, and I
hope that all the places that I've chosen for this book will
also accept the "weird" moniker as a great compliment.
Heck, why not include it on your town sign: "One of the
Weird Places included in the book *Weird Canadian Places*."

My angle of attack in writing the book was to use humour,
because other such books I've read like this are…a bit dry.
They are well researched, thorough and detailed, but they
are encyclopaedic in nature. You'll notice that my tongue is
firmly planted in my cheek as I write about each and every
one of my weird finds. My intention was to play with all the
weirdness that is Canada, not to offend, and I hope everyone
who reads this book will take my observations, questions,
extrapolations and wit with the intention with which I wrote
it. I really hope that you will be entertained. If you learn a
little something, that's okay, too.

I structured the book by subject as opposed to compiling a
straight province-by-province and location-by-location list.
I did this to again avoid the encyclopedic effect that I'm not
keen on, but also to show the interesting similarities and differences in weirdness across the country. We are all not as
different as we sometimes think.

One of the things that I've discovered about all of us from
sea to sea to sea is that we don't take ourselves too seriously.
Or if we do, we move to the United States, renounce our cit-
izenship and "are currently under investigation." My research
has afforded me the opportunity to learn a great deal about
some great places. I have to say that I think Alberta and
Saskatchewan "get it"! They, along with New Brunswick,

have embraced all that is weird in their parts of the world. They can laugh at it, have fun with it and bring tourists in and not just take their money, but also show them a great time!

There are so many places I now want to visit, though a few months ago I might not have thought so. I am fascinated by the paranormal, intrigued by the oddities that nature has to offer and celebrate all that is kitschy. I'd love to see a ghost train or a fire ship. I have actually seen a UFO, but I don't want to hold myself up for ridicule, so I won't go into that… Okay, I was nine years old, there were all these flashing lights; yes, it might have been an emergency vehicle, but I don't think so. Ambulances, fire trucks and police cars don't hover! Oh, and when I was five years old and living in Woodstock, Ontario, I thought the abandoned drum of an old cement mixer was actually a three-man splashdown capsule that NASA had left out behind my house. The eyes of a child! I turned a mundane old cement-mixing drum into a spaceship. Weird! That's the kind of weird that this book is about.

The choices I've made are, indeed, arbitrary. My interpretation of what is interesting, odd and weird is probably different from what many other people in the world would designate as weird. However, I'm the one who wrote the book, so enjoy it or go write your own… Seriously, there were so many weird places that I don't think I've even covered a quarter of them, and I suspect that the number will just continue to grow. Who knows, maybe there'll be a *Weird Canadian Places, Volume 2*.

There may be a great many weird Canadian "things" that I have omitted. However, the parameters of this book were specific to weird "places." Some weird things crossed over and could be directly pegged to place. A great many of the weirdest things do not lend themselves to this type of specificity, so they got tossed. I also tended to avoid places considered weird just because of their place names. There are enough of these in Newfoundland alone to fill a full volume. Those weird places that made it to final cut tend to be current, ongoing and recurring sites of weirdness. In general, I avoided one-offs, lone occurrences and, except in a very few instances, weird places that are only weird because of something that happened in the past.

Peppered throughout the book you will read all about the various "Big, Gargantuan & Ridiculously Oversized" things that have been foisted upon the Canadian landscape. There are a lot of "world's biggest" in this vast land of ours. Some might suggest it screams of a national inferiority complex. However, I choose to look at it differently and applaud all those ambitious little communities that have figured out how to get tourists to their "little piece of heaven." Whether that's to see the "World's Biggest Inukshuk" or "Mac the Moose," who cares! If you build it big in Canada, tourists will come a-runnin' with cameras in hand…

Embrace the weirdness!

Dan de Figueiredo

Underground
and Overhead

*In this chapter, we look at the weirdest places you'd never
be able to spot and those you can't possibly miss—the little
hidden gems literally beneath the ground and others that
are not only out in the open but scream "Look at me!"*

*It's monstrosities vs. little hidden wonders;
odd architecture vs. Cold War bunker; mysterious lost
mine vs. money pit; haunted tunnel vs. escape tunnel*

*You get the idea.
Here are Canada's underground wonders
and aboveground screamers.*

THE DIEFENBUNKER
CARP, ONTARIO

The promotional literature asks the question: "Looking for a different site for your tours to visit?" Well, you've definitely found it here. The Diefenbunker, as it is affectionately called, is one of those Cold War relics you'd think could only be found in the United States or Russia. But no, the Diefenbunker is real and is located just 35 kilometres east of Ottawa in the community of Carp…or more accurately, underneath the community of Carp.

The Diefenbunker was built between 1959 and 1961 and was intended to house essential government and military personnel in case of a nuclear attack. It's a four-storey facility built into a hill and is designed to survive a five-megaton blast a kilometre and a half away. Although the idea of such a Cold War relic serving as a Cold War museum is kitschy, to say the least, the Historic Sites and Monuments Board of Canada has called the Diefenbunker "the most important surviving Cold War site in Canada." And it almost didn't survive.

When Canadian Forces Station Carp (the official name of the Diefenbunker) was closed in 1994, the government gutted the facility. Some of its original artifacts were dispersed to the Canadian War Museum, the Canadian Museum of Civilization and the Military Communications and Electronics Museum in Kingston, but most of the contents disappeared for good. However, the museum's staff has done an amazing job of begging, borrowing and stealing (not literally) original artifacts and recreating others to fill the Diefenbunker and give it a real sense of its Cold War–era prime.

A 90-minute tour through the meandering facility takes visitors through a time warp into the 1960s. Visitors experience the blast tunnel, the air lock, the top-level hallway, the Federal Warning Centre, the machine room, the CBC Radio studio, the Bank of Canada vault, the War Cabinet room and the prime minister's suite and offices.

And I'll bet that in the cramped prime minister's quarters you can well imagine Prime Minister John Diefenbaker, with his jowls a-flappin', practising his bad French while commanding Canada's response to a nuclear attack (which I believe consisted of officially sitting and waiting to see what the Americans would do). For a weird and wacky blast from the past, the Diefenbunker is high on our list of special places.

THE TUNNELS OF MOOSE JAW
MOOSE JAW, SASKATCHEWAN

The town of Moose Jaw has one of Canada's weirdest tourist attractions—tunnels. That's right, tunnels! Apparently when Moose Jaw's downtown business district was originally constructed in the late 1800s and early 1900s, passageways were built that ran from the CPR station, under Manitoba Street and to the Maple Leaf Hotel (now called Brewster's) and from there under Main Street to the CER Restaurant (now called Capone's).

Although the locals don't know for sure why these passageways exist, it's thought they were built as utility tunnels. They allowed steam engineers easy access from building to building to maintain the town's boilers.

What's left of the tunnels includes basement rooms and interconnected utility corridors. Stories of bootleggers such as Al Capone using the tunnels for escape purposes and other illegal activities are rife in the town.

The "Tunnels of Moose Jaw" tour operator runs two interactive tunnel tours during which tourists become part of the experience while travelling beneath Moose Jaw. Visitors are apparently treated to "state of the art animatronic characters," a multimedia presentation and character tour guides.

The "Chicago Connection" tour explores Chicago's bootlegging connection to Moose Jaw and allows visitors to "lie low" with Al Capone himself. Participants get to be bootleggers who are in town to learn the ropes and buy booze from the Capone organization, all the while staying ahead of the Moose Jaw police. What fun!

The "Passage to Fortune" tour explores the early Chinese immigrant experience, which apparently involved hiding from authorities in the tunnels. This one includes visitors becoming "coolies," working at Burrows and Sons Laundry and ending up in Mr. Wong's Café. I guess with this one, you can experience turn-of-the-century prairie racism at its finest.

The tunnels of Moose Jaw are definitely an underground gem!

THE OAK ISLAND MONEY PIT
OAK ISLAND, NOVA SCOTIA

This may qualify as the weirdest place in Canada because of its strange, enduring, as-yet-unsolved mystery. Oak Island is a small island (57 hectares) in Mahone Bay, on Nova Scotia's eastern shore. Since 1795, people have been intrigued by, focused on and digging at a spot on this island where they think they're going to find some form of buried treasure.

Legend has it that Oak Island won't give up its treasure until its last oak tree has fallen. Which begs the obvious question, why not just cut down all the oak trees and then have at it? I can find no explanation for the wilful flouting of this obvious solution, but there must be some weird treasure hunters' code that forbids it…or in this day and age, provincial legislation against the wilful destruction of oak trees. Whatever.

As the story goes, in 1795, a teenager named Daniel McGinnis tripped over a "curious" circular depression in the ground that just happened to be underneath a tree with cut branches that looked like they'd been used as a pulley. Different place, different time, different type of teenager, I guess, because I have no idea what a branch used as a pulley would look like. Anyway, the enterprising young lad brought two friends on board, and they started digging, all the while with thoughts of Captain Kidd's treasure dancing in their collective heads.

Less than a metre below the surface, they hit flagstones. They became more excited, but found nothing immediately underneath. So they continued digging. At 3 metres down, they hit a layer of oak logs. Underneath that, more dirt… At depths of 6 metres and 9 metres, they hit logs again, but still no treasure. And 9 metres down was as far as they could go on their own. Eight years later, they came back to the money pit along with the Onslow Company and resumed their excavation. They found more and more logs and dirt at regular intervals.

At 27 metres below the surface, they found a stone inscribed with mysterious writing. They pulled that up, along with more oak logs and then the *agua* hit the pit. That's right, the designers of the pit had built an ingenious booby trap that flooded the pit with seawater. *Dios mío!*

Anyway, the boys never did find their treasure. And no one else has been able to get to it either. Attempt after attempt, failure after failure, and at least six deaths directly or indirectly attributed to the pit. And yet people don't give up. Modern technology has been no help either. Except in the area of spreading rumour, innuendo and far-fetched theories on who designed the pit and what the treasure might be. Theories on the pit's builders range from Egyptians, Mayans, Freemasons, Sir Francis Bacon, William Phips, the British, the Knights Templar, Captain Kidd, Blackbeard and the Vikings. Ideas about the treasure range from gold doubloons and pieces of eight to the Holy Grail.

So, if you're in the vicinity of Oak Island… I wouldn't advise digging your own hole, since the place is private property, and in 1985 when I was there, I was chased across the causeway (not really).

In 1995, the Woods Hole Oceanographic Institute (you may remember them from Titanic finding and Bob Ballard fame) was brought in to give their opinion on whether there is something valuable in the pit. Their report is confidential, but rumblings from people who have apparently seen the report say its conclusions are "not discouraging." I wonder if they used the mini sub to come to this underwhelmingly positive conclusion?

Oak Island is currently up for sale with a price tag of $7 million. The Oak Island Tourism Society is calling on various levels of government to purchase the island—pit unseen—and exploit its potential to the fullest. Now that's all we need, government involvement in a pit already known to be a money sucker!

THE LOST LEMON MINE
CROWSNEST PASS, ALBERTA

According to legend, "there's gold in them thar' hills" and murder, mystery, mayhem and a curse! Ewooooewww! In around 1870, as the story goes, a group of American prospectors came to Canada and started panning for gold along the North Saskatchewan River. Two of the prospectors, Frank Lemon and a second man named Blackjack (not to be confused with Yosemite Sam's cartoon character buddy, Black Jack Shellac—they're totally different fellas).

Anyway, Lemon and Blackjack struck out on their own and somehow stumbled across the motherlode of gold mines somewhere near the Crowsnest Pass. The evening of their big score turned from celebration to tragedy when Lemon ended up hacking Blackjack to death with an axe. Distraught, Lemon did the only thing he could and blamed it on Natives, who in turn may or may not have placed a curse on the whole sordid Lemon mining endeavour. Is this all sounding just a bit like that Bogart film, *Treasure of the Sierra Madre*?

Over the next bunch of years, Lemon tried to lead others back to the site of the mine, but whenever he got close, he seemed to go a bit nuts. Others too have tried, but with no luck. A man named McDougall, who was originally dispatched to bury Blackjack, drank himself to death. Another man, Lafayette French, may have found the mine, but he died when his cabin burned down around him. All this gave rise to the legend and curse surrounding the Lost Lemon Mine.

In the 1980s, a man named Ron Stewart claimed to have found the mine, but despite reports by the CBC, the mine turned out to be a pretty crappy gold strike—definitely not up to the calibre of the Lost Lemon's hype.

People continue to try and find the Lost Lemon Mine. Nobody has, but it's given Alberta a great little story about greed and gold and curses. Yeehaw!

~ Big, Gargantuan & Ridiculously Oversized ~

The "World's Largest Blueberry" is located at an Irving Gas Station in Oxford, Nova Scotia (northeast of Springhill). Oxford also claims to be the "Blueberry Capital of the World," so the giant blueberry does make sense. The blueberry is 2.4 metres tall and will take on all challengers!

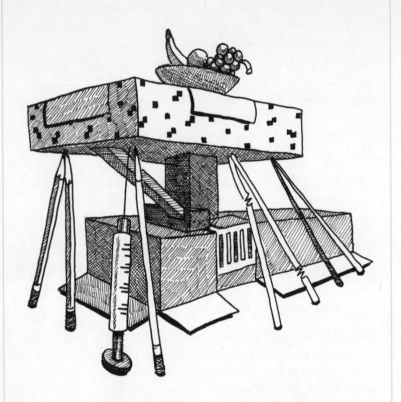

ONTARIO COLLEGE
OF ART AND DESIGN
TORONTO, ONTARIO

The "Tabletop" at the Ontario College of Art and Design is one of the strangest additions to any building in a city quickly becoming known for strange additions to buildings. The Sharp Centre for Design, as it is officially known, was designed by British architect Will Alsop and looks as though a child's black-and-white checkerboard pencil box has been precariously balanced atop 12 multicoloured pencils. And yet it's all just an illusion—a little magic mixed with some architectural wonder.

The black-and-white box is actually a conventional two-storey structure that provides classroom and studio space and is held up by the elevator's central core (if you care about engineering).

The Tabletop rests 26 metres in the air and allows great views of Toronto's downtown and the Grange Park, which it shares with the Art Gallery of Ontario. From dusk until midnight, 16 blue metal-halide lights illuminate the Tabletop, giving it a totally different look from its daytime configuration.

Unfortunately there are no public tours of the Sharp Centre. However, it is best viewed from the street where one can't help but be enthralled by its charm. Kitschy, bright, odd, unique and wonderful, the Sharp Centre is everything an addition to a college of art should be! This is one weird building that definitely screams, "Look at me!"

~ Big, Gargantuan & Ridiculously Oversized ~

The "World's Largest Permanent Historical Photo-Mosaic" (now that's a mouthful) covers the sides of a building in Port Carling in Ontario's Muskoka region. Thousands of historical postcards dating back to 1860 were arranged to create a scene 34 metres wide by 14 metres tall, showing a boat on a Muskoka Lake. If you look closely, you can actually see Kurt Russell and Goldie Hawn fighting off the paparazzi on the shore behind the boat. Not really.

THE ART GALLERY OF ONTARIO (AGO)
TORONTO, ONTARIO

Weird is something people have come to expect from world-renowned architect Frank Gehry... And his offer to the city in which he was born, while not quite as weird and wild as the undulating titanium structure in Bilbao, Spain, is nevertheless odd! It has all the hallmarks of becoming as inspirationally famous as Bilbao—it has garnered praise, been heavily criticized and caused both disdain and out and out glee!

The promotional material screams: "Transformation AGO is the vision of a new kind of art museum." One with eyelashes, a sneeze guard or a fallen eyebrow, we would suggest. What am I talking about? Well, the entire north façade rises 21 metres above street level and is 183 metres long. There are two cuts at the east and west extremities of the façade, which makes it look as if it has two eyelashes that are raised high and about to flutter shut. The PR person at the AGO compares them more to wings. Ohhhhhhhh!

Nevertheless, the centre portion of the front façade includes a 137-metre-long promenade on the second floor that allows visitors to look out onto traffic and streetcars on heavily congested Dundas Street, or affords those in their cars or on the streetcar to look inside the AGO while stuck in gridlock. This truly is an example of a museum "giving back." And when you look at the central structure of glass and Douglas fir, you can't help but think salad bar sneeze guard. And when you put the whole façade together and in context, it looks a lot like a Picasso-esque version of a fallen eyebrow...or so we think. We also think it is truly odd, wackily weird and positively wonderful.

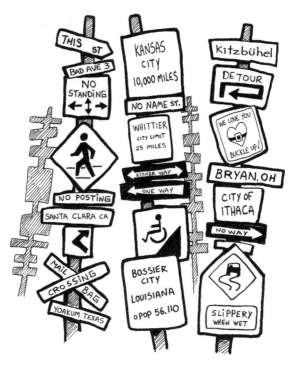

~ Big, Gargantuan & Ridiculously Oversized ~

The town of Watson Lake, Yukon, is located on the Alaska Highway in the southeastern corner of the territory. Watson Lake's best-known attraction is the "Signpost Forest." That's right—a forest made up of signposts. (Didn't they do this on *M*A*S*H*?) Located next to the Watson Lake Visitor Information Centre, the Signpost Forest was started in 1942 by a homesick U.S. Army G.I. who was working on the construction of the Alaska Highway. He erected a sign pointing the way to his hometown of Danville, Illinois, and giving the estimated mileage to get there. It wasn't long before sheep in the form of people without an original idea of their own followed suit and added their own signs. In fact, in July 1990, an American couple added the 10,000th sign to the forest—Bryan, Ohio. So, if you're heading to the Yukon, why not stop in at Watson Lake and add your hometown's sign. I'd call first, though. At 10,000 and counting, I'd hate to see you travel all that way and not be able to mount your sign.

ROYAL ONTARIO MUSEUM (ROM)
TORONTO, ONTARIO

Weird Toronto building number three is, we regret to say, our least favourite. It's definitely monumental, definitely costly and definitely big—it's also overhead and weird. But it looks way too much like it was ill conceived and hastily constructed by Homer Simpson, and when it didn't fit the rest of the building, he crammed it onto the Bloor Street side, where maybe people wouldn't notice. "D-oh!" Does that sound harsh?

Let me start again. Since 1914, the Royal Ontario Museum has been thrilling adults and school groups alike with its dinosaurs, exhibits of natural and cultural history and a really big totem pole (for those of us in Ontario, it's really big).

From the beginning, the ROM buildings themselves were an amalgamation of various architectural influences. So, when it was announced that Daniel Libeskind's crystal-inspired design was going to be added to the north side, it was no great surprise. However, Libeskind's original design involved a lot of glass and a lot of light. The revised design involves a lot less glass, a lot less light and a whole bunch of corrugated metal cladding that screams "suburban backyard." This is not a criticism of suburban backyards. A corrugated metal shed fits there perfectly. I can't imagine a better place for it. But as an addition to one of our country's important cultural institutions, it seems, at best, out of place.

I have, of course, short-changed the Libeskind shed design in one respect. It's not just a square box. In fact, it's a bunch of boxes piled on top of one another, so you couldn't get a right angle if you tried. And that makes it weird!

THE LISHMAN HOUSE
BLACKSTOCK, ONTARIO

How does a home that was featured in magazines such as *Harrowsmith* and *Canadian Architect* as well as on the CBC-TV show *Life and Times* qualify as underground and weird? Well, the "hole" thing has to do with its designer, builder and occupant, Bill Lishman. You could even say that this home transformed its designer from igloo enthusiast to mole man.

That's because Bill Lishman's home is a series of eight interconnected, igloo-like domes that were built with wire-mesh frames, covered with concrete and a bunch of waterproofing materials and then covered over with dirt. A 1970s igloo was Lishman's original inspiration for the structure.

The home features in-floor heating, overhead skylights and a roof that requires mowing. The whole unique structure reminds one of the dwelling in which Luke Skywalker grew up. You know, the one owned by Uncle Owen and Aunt Beru. There isn't a right angle in the entire structure. Arched doorways were hand-made, as was the furniture inside the home. Even the refrigerator is round. It pops out of the kitchen counter at the touch of a button, just like in the 1996 film *Fly Away Home*. Which is no great surprise since that film, about a man who taught geese to fly behind an ultralight plane, is based on the life of our home's designer, Bill Lishman.

KAY-NAH-CHI-WAH-NUNG (MANITOU MOUNDS)
STRATTON, ONTARIO

Kay-Nah-Chi-Wah-Nung ("Place of the Long Rapids") near Rainy River, Ontario, is the site of some of the most interesting underground archaeological digs in the country. As the press information says: "Kay-Nah-Chi-Wah-Nung and the surrounding lands hold the record of almost 8000 years. The Place of the Long Rapids contains the largest group of burial mounds and associated village sites in Canada."

And just what are these mounds and why are they so significant? The mounds are essentially a burial place. The Laurel Culture (300 BC–1100 AD) is thought to be the first group of First Nations people to have built mounds at this site. The Laurel mounds are up to 7 metres high and 18 to 24 metres in diameter. The mound builders would dig a shallow pit, place the deceased inside and cover the remains with earth. Over hundreds of years, more deceased were placed on top and covered with earth. The layering process created the mounds as they are seen today. Sometimes the deceased were buried with medicine bags, pipes, food, clay pots and tools they used in life and would need in death.

The Manitou Mounds site includes a visitor centre that explores the site as a ceremonial centre, its context within North America and the culture of the Ojibway peoples. It's a fascinating look back into the past of First Nations peoples and their burial rituals.

THE PHANTOM SUBWAY STATION
TORONTO, ONTARIO

Myth, folklore, urban legend or reality—that's what people have been asking for decades about the notorious phantom subway station known as Lower Bay. Well, I am happy to tell all that the phantom station does, in fact, exist. This will come as no surprise to older folks who were around when the station was actually used in 1966. So, how was it used, why isn't used anymore and how has the myth surrounding it grown? Hold your horses—I'm getting to it!

So as not to bore those who don't give a flip about Toronto's subway, I'll keep it short. Basically, when the Bloor–Danforth subway line opened in 1966, the Lower Bay Station was a transfer point between the University Line (Lower Bay) and the Bloor–Danforth Line (Upper Bay) in a similar way that the two lines cross at St. George.

The station was also designed and connected by a "phantom tunnel" to Museum Station, just like the one that connects Museum and St. George on the Spadina Line. The three stations formed a "Y" configuration with the purpose that every second train heading north on the University Line could take the right "Y" leg through Lower Bay, and would then connect to the Bloor–Danforth Line before it got to Bloor Station.

The system ran this way for six months, but the configuration was abandoned because it was confusing for passengers. Also, because the whole subway system was interconnected, a single problem anywhere on either subway line disabled the entire system instead of just one line, as it does now.

So Lower Bay was abandoned, and the myth of the phantom station grew. The station is still accessible from Upper Bay by those who have a key. Much of the time, it is used by film companies to shoot creepy subway scenes, which is probably where the myth about it being haunted arose. There are also stories of people who have travelled the "phantom tunnel" to get to Lower Bay, but it is ill advised since it is a dangerous route.

A second "phantom station," which is more like a roughed-in underground streetcar stop, exists at Lower Queen (Yonge and Queen). There are, however, no official documents about a third phantom station at Lower Osgoode.

THE SCREAMING TUNNEL
NIAGARA REGION, ONTARIO

This one falls under the heading of underground and creepily weird! The tunnel in question is not far from Queen Elizabeth Way on Warner Road near Garner Road. I've been there, and the tunnel is dark and smells of sulphur, not to mention that it's often full of water and empty beer bottles and used...oh, never mind.

It's either an abandoned or never-used railway tunnel that may have been built by the Grand Trunk Railway. The legend goes that if you light a match or lighter (any small flame will do) while you're standing in the centre of the tunnel, you'll hear a bone-chilling scream and your flame will blow out! Some variations on this legend say you have to light the match at midnight.

The explanation for the screaming and blowing out is something to do with an abused girl (now a ghost) who's afraid of fire. That's why she screams and blows out the flames.

Some stories claim the girl was set on fire by her father in a divorce dispute. Others claim she was raped in the tunnel (though that one doesn't link to the flame thing very well). Still others say she ran screaming and alight from a nearby burning farmhouse and died in the tunnel. The stories are as varied and creepy as you can imagine, matching this dark and stinky tunnel toe to toe for its creep factor.

~ Big, Gargantuan & Ridiculously Oversized ~

The "World's Largest Turtle" is located in Turtleford, Saskatchewan...
and in Boissevain, Manitoba. Say what? That's right, both towns
have a giant turtle statue that, measured from beak to tail, is 8.5
metres long...or tall. Besides variations in colour, the two turtles
are pretty much alike, except in Turtleford, "Ernie" is posed on all
fours, whereas in Boissevain, "Tommy" stands tall and proud on his
back legs. Tommy also holds Canadian and American flags in his
front hands/feet/turtlegrapplers? I guess the good people of
Turtleford were looking for realism with their giant turtle (turtles
have flippers and not hands, so can't really hold flags). And
Boissevain? I guess they were looking to bring together the people of two great turtle-loving nations.

Gruesome
and Ghoulish

Some of the weirdest places in this country have to do with the macabre, the gruesome and the ghoulish. If you are really up for some weird treats, you can tour the home of a murdered Irish family in Biddulph, Ontario, or you can make a jaunt to Kootenay Lake in BC to see the house built of embalming fluid bottles. No stink. No kidding?

But not to be outdone, there are a great many scary ghosts residing in this country in some very public spaces. You'll want to sneak up on them before they sneak up on you, or else you'll be the subject of a fright and suffer a big "boo" and maybe be pushed over the edge and find yourself crying "boo-hoo-hoo." Our motto here: "Scare the ghosts before they scare you." Read on, if you dare...

THE GRUESOME

THE DONNELLY HOMESTEAD
BIDDULPH TOWNSHIP, ONTARIO

Some people might call it the enterprising idea of a smart entrepreneur who saw a need and filled it. Others would call it macabre, gruesome, ghoulish, sick, scary and in bad taste. Either way, the publicity is likely welcome, and the business thrives.

We're talking about a business that highlights, celebrates and even exploits the massacre of five members of an Irish immigrant family. Now, if it was a recent massacre, I'm sure the ghoulish factor involved in all of it would be much more in question. However, because it happened in 1880, I guess the time factor allows the macabre exploitation to seem, well… less exploitative. And to be fair, Robert Salts, who owns the Donnelly Homestead and runs the tour, is not the first person to latch onto the Donnelly story and turn it into some form of economic gain.

Let's start at the beginning. In the early morning hours of February 4, 1880, five members of an Irish immigrant family are murdered in the mad melee of a blood-soaked massacre. Killed in the melee are patriarch James Donnelly, his wife Johannah, sons Tom and John and niece Bridget. Their house is burned to the ground in the massacre. The known murderers are neighbours and town rivals of the Donnellys. There's an eyewitness to the massacre, but no one is ever convicted. And so the myth surrounding the events grows and grows until there's a bit of a book industry surrounding it and a whole niche market involving more than just a few people.

And now there's a 90-minute tour of the former homestead of the murdered family. The tour apparently includes a look at artifacts and photographs and includes a tour of the Donnelly barn. Of course, the original barn burned down, and the one in the tour was built after the murders, but that doesn't stop it from being a tour highlight—no matter how irrelevant. You see, Salts thinks the barn is haunted.

I wonder if the tour contains moments like: "We think this is where Tom was pitch forked," or "This is thought to be where Johannah Donnelly swore vengeance on the murderers and took a last puff of her pipe."

Ghostly happenings surrounding the homestead have also been reported, including the murdered family materializing, horses being spooked and horses dying as a result of travelling the Roman Line (so named for the numerous Roman Catholic families who lived there) on the anniversary of the massacre. Talk about being tough on the animals!

The Donnelly Homestead site is located in Biddulph Township near Lucan—that's halfway between London and Exeter, Ontario.

~ Big, Gargantuan & Ridiculously Oversized ~

Well, it's not so weird finding totem poles in British Columbia, but they have got some unique ones. In fact, the province has cornered the market on big totems, and they'll soon be trading on the Vancouver Stock Exchange…kidding. The "World's Largest in Diameter Totem Pole" was carved by renowned West Coast artist Richard Hunt for the city of Duncan in 1988. The totem is 7.3 metres high and is 2.1 metres in diameter at its top. Duncan is also known as the "City of Totems." Before Duncan got its wide-body totem, Victoria already had the "World's Tallest Free-Standing Totem Pole." It was carved in 1956 from a single tree by a team that included Kwakwaka'wakw artist Mungo Martin. This very tall totem is located in Beacon Hill Park and stands a whopping 38.8 metres high. Victoria's tall totem title was usurped—albeit on a technicality—in 1972, when Alert Bay, BC, erected what is now known as the "World's Tallest Totem Pole." The technicality is that Alert Bay's 52.7-metre totem is made of two pieces, whereas Victoria's is just a one piece—sort of the sports model versus the bikini. The Alert Bay totem is unique in another respect. Most totems are specific to a particular family, but the 13 figures on the Alert Bay totem represent various tribes of the Kwakwaka'wakw Nation. It is located at the northern end of Cormorant Island (off the northeast coast of Vancouver Island), on the outskirts of the Nimpkish reserve.

THE GLASS HOUSE
BOSWELL, BRITISH COLUMBIA

So, just what does a retired mortician do with his newly found spare time? Well, he takes up house building, of course! But he can't remove himself from his former profession entirely, so he incorporates the former tools of his trade into a house—literally. So, what the heck am I talking about?

Well, the mortician can't use cadavers as building materials. I mean, that would be really gruesome. However, he does go on a campaign across western Canada to collect bottles from his friends in the profession. What kind of bottles? If he'd been a doctor, they'd probably be urine sample bottles. But no, David Brown collected half a million rectangular embalming fluid bottles.

In 1952, Brown began building his dream home overlooking Kootenay Lake using those same embalming fluid bottles. He used mortar to stick the bottles together to create a two-storey castle design, complete with watchtowers. The house was apparently a great success and a comfortable place to live until curious passersby started knocking on the door night and day to see the house. That's when Brown moved out of the Glass House and turned it into a tourist attraction. It remains such today.

I've been told the whole place has the stink of death surrounding it! Not really. Brown cleaned out all the bottles before reusing them. Or at least, one would assume he did…

The Glass House is located at 11341 Highway 3A, 40 kilometres north of Creston, BC.

AND NOW...
THE GHOULISH

Step into my lair and I'll tell you a tale of the evil that men do.
You'll hear about the scary, the ghouls without heads, the logs and
dogs and places where the undead spring out and say "Boo!" So,
come on in if you dare and learn where folklore and urban legend
meet and a terrifying mix of ghoulish fun begins.

DALTON HALL, UNIVERSITY OF PRINCE EDWARD ISLAND
CHARLOTTETOWN, PEI

Dalton Hall opened in 1919 and was only the second building to be constructed for Saint Dunstan's College at UPEI.
The five-level, red brick building sports a slate roof with
prominent dormers and bay windows with decorative stone
surrounds. It's a fusion of Victorian, Edwardian and Georgian
styles—pick a monarch, it's got them all! Oh, and it's creepy.
Just the type of place an urban legend could grow up around.
And it has.

The legend is folkloric and tragic and makes for a wonderfully gruesome story that may or may not be true! Such is
the stuff that legends are made of.

As the story goes, two roommates were out tying one on.
A blustery snowstorm blew in, and the guys started back to
their residence, Dalton Hall. For whatever reason, the two
friends were separated, and one arrived at the Hall ahead of
the other. When the second arrived, the priests (who were the
traditional gatekeepers of this residence at what was an institution originally founded for young men aspiring to the priest-
hood) had locked all the doors, intending to teach a curfew

lesson to the tardy student. He tried frantically to get inside, but to no avail.

Later that night, the first student heard a knock at his door and assumed it was his roomie. But when he answered the door, all that greeted him was a chilling draft of air that blew past him and a trail of water that led from his room to the staircase. The next morning, the second student was found outside the front door, frozen to death.

Ever since, a chilly breeze and a trail of water leading to the staircase often confront staff and students working late on blustery winter nights. Is this a reminder of the student who died an icy death? Or perhaps it's just a drafty old building with a mysterious incontinence problem.

ST. PAUL'S ANGLICAN CHURCH
HALIFAX, NOVA SCOTIA

St. Paul's is probably known to most as the oldest Protestant church in Canada. It's been serving Protestants since 1750. A pupil of Sir Christopher Wren designed the church, and its simple wooden design is essentially comprised of a box structure with a peaked roof and a steeple at one end. The building has seen a few additions over the years, including side wings and a chancel, but it's still a simple structure.

The church is located in the centre of Halifax. It's seen battles, been scarred and has survived a great many things that much of the rest of Halifax has not. It even survived the Halifax Explosion, which, as some may know, is still considered the world's largest non-nuclear explosion. In that 1917 disaster, two ships collided in the harbour, then exploded and flattened the city.

That's where the ghostly presence of one of those victims comes into play with St. Paul's. It seems ("seems" being the key word, meaning that it may or may not be true) that during the explosion a man (or clergyman) was blown clean through the glass on the Argyle Street side of the church. In the process, the man's silhouette was etched into the glass and continues to be visible. So, why not replace the creepy etching? Well, apparently it's been tried, but each time the glass is replaced, the silhouette of the exploding man appears yet again.

That's the story, though no one will confirm its veracity—which means the whole thing could really be true, or the apparition could be a shadow cast on the glass by one of the newer buildings on the block…or dirt…or nothing at all…or something strange and evil…or a marketing ploy…or…

~ Big, Gargantuan & Ridiculously Oversized ~

The "World's Largest Beaver" sits proudly on top of a log next to Highway 43 in (where else?) Beaverlodge, Alberta. The beaver is 4.6 metres high, 5.5 metres from nose to tail and 3 metres wide. The log he sits on is 6.1 metres long.

HALIBURTON HOUSE
WINDSOR, NOVA SCOTIA

Haliburton House in Windsor, Nova Scotia, is the former home of Judge Thomas Chandler Haliburton. It's a quiet little wooden manse all decked out in white with a slow-peaked roof and large windows. Built in 1836 and expanded upon after Chandler sold it in 1856 to move to England, the home overlooks Windsor and the Avon River. In terms of being creepy, well the house itself is charming and bright. But read on…

Thomas Chandler Haliburton was an immensely popular humorist who wrote the *Sam Slick* series of books. In the 1830s and 1840s, those books popularized phrases like "it's raining cats and dogs," "quick as a wink" and "facts are stranger than fiction"—which brings us to the house's scary ghost tale. Are facts indeed stranger than fiction?

The Judge was known for his humour, which might explain the fact that he left his face behind. What's that? Another face misplaced? Dump it in the lost and found!

On occasion, the Judge's smiling face can be seen coming through the wall in the reception hall of his beloved house. He may find it funny, but a disembodied face pushing through the period wallpaper is not a Benny Hill moment.

Other versions of this weird tale tell of the "Joking Judge" emerging from a secret panel in the reception hall and walking about the house. The "face" version of the story seems more the Judge's style, if you ask me. After all, no self-respecting ghost needs a secret panel to enter a room…unless he's about to be unmasked as a hoaxer by a bunch of med-dling kids and their Great Dane.

There's not much of an explanation as to why the Judge—or just his face—haunts this place. Could be that his first wife died while he owned the property or because he created Sam Slick here or just because it's a pretty place.

In any event, if you're in the Windsor area, go take a boo at the Judge's house or just see if you can catch some face time with the old joker. Come on, who doesn't respond to a smiling face?

VICTORIA GOLF CLUB
OAK BAY, BRITISH COLUMBIA

For more than a century, people have been hearing "Fore!" shouted near the Municipality of Oak Bay, BC. It's not a ghost or anything else gruesome, just middle-aged men in ill-fitting, plaid polyester pants playing golf. The Victoria Golf Club was founded here in 1893. It's the oldest golf club in Canada still on its original site, which just happens to be a rocky point overlooking the Strait of Juan de Fuca at the southern end of Vancouver Island. You can almost picture the craggy outcroppings, the fog and a dark and blustery night, can't you?

Since the 1930s, someone or something has been haunting the seventh green. Haunting the seventh green of the Victoria Golf Club in Oak Bay sounds kind of classy, doesn't it? It's probably a former lady golfer who was kept from the PGA tour—perhaps a story of sport and woe. But no.

There's not a lot to indicate that the ghost of Doris Gravlin is any sort of golf enthusiast…or that her former self was, for that matter. In fact, considering the circumstances of her death, old Doris probably has a bit of a golf tee on her shoulder.

It seems that Doris was strangled by her husband on the seventh green and buried in a sand trap. Talk about an ignominious end! But not actually an end. Doris is still there, in ghostly form that is, and she has often been seen right there on the seventh green. She's most frequently seen wearing a long, white wedding gown, but has also taken on the form of lights. Doris has been known to play chicken with passing motorists and even scare the heck out of some by entering their cars.

No word on exactly why her husband killed her, but the old girl sounds like a hoot, if you ask me! A ghoulish hoot!

FAIRMONT BANFF SPRINGS HOTEL
BANFF, ALBERTA

Located in Banff National Park, the Fairmont Banff Springs Hotel is nestled in the lush greenery of the Bow Valley among the majestic peaks of the Rockies and overlooks the Bow River. Styled after a Scottish baronial castle, the hotel is large and made from brown stone, with deeply peaked roofs and creepy-looking dormer windows.

The hotel was originally built by the CPR and only accessible by railway. It was the grandeur of the hotel that brought people to Banff, as well as the mineral spas. The original hotel opened in 1888, and the new, improved Banff Springs was rebuilt in the 1920s. And this leads to the hauntings... But first, a story.

So, I'm attending the Banff Television Festival at the Banff Springs Hotel in the spring of 2005. Scary, creepy and beyond gruesome! Anyway, this has got to be one the creepiest buildings you could ever visit. There are all these dark and gothic-like hallways. There are halls that go nowhere, rather dimly lit passages and nooks and crannies that you can stumble upon, but never find your way back to. And the whole place is rather dark.

Sitting on a bench collecting my thoughts, I'm trying to stay away from the kids who keep asking if I'm Trina McQueen or Fred Nicolaidis, and a rather odd woman approaches and sits down beside me. She doesn't say anything, but just sits there in a white wedding gown. I figured she was someone doing publicity for some "ripped from the headlines" CTV movie. That is, until she gets up, goes to the top of the stairs, turns around and starts down. The train of her gown then gets caught on a huge candelabra, and her dress catches on fire. She panics and rolls down the stairs. I figured out it wasn't a publicity stunt, so I rushed to her. But there was no her. There was no one there at all except for me. She was gone.

This is apparently the "Bride" who regularly re-enacts her Banff Springs wedding day horror for horrified onlookers. The story goes that she broke her neck in the fall, and she's been haunting the hotel ever since. This is not in the tourist brochure.

Okay, I never really saw this, but apparently if you're there at the right time, the Bride will do her show for you. There's also a ghostly bellman named Sam who'll help you with your luggage and then disappear. Which is all you really want from a ghostly bellman, isn't it?

All I got at Banff was treated badly and a crappy bag from Rogers! A Bride sighting would have been really nice—except things like that scare the heck out of me. So, treated badly was, I guess, okay after all.

~ Big, Gargantuan & Ridiculously Oversized ~

The "World's Largest Axe" is located in Nackawic, New Brunswick. It stands 15 metres tall and is made of stainless steel embedded in concrete. Nackiwac calls itself the "Forestry Capital of Canada," so what better way to symbolize the importance of the forestry industry than an axe? Well, what about a tree? Choices, choices!

PRINCESS THEATRE
EDMONTON, ALBERTA

In the Old Strathcona part of Edmonton, the Princess
Theatre has been doing business since 1914. The theatre has
hosted vaudeville shows, Hollywood movies and even some
blue ones. It's got a large marquee out front, and the inside
has been restored to its bygone glory—plush red seating, a
balcony and an arched roof that sports cherubs. There is also
a smaller theatre in the basement. With 90 years of history,
this place has seen it all...including a ghost or two.

As the story goes, a projectionist was doing his thing in the
projection booth. All of a sudden, he heard someone knocking at the projection booth window...the window that is two
storeys up, looks out onto the street and is not accessible by
anyone that is gravity-bound. When the projectionist looked
out, what he saw was someone, something, some "being"
floating two storeys up. The only explanation is a sprite with
a sense of humour and no vertigo...or wacky kids playing a
trick...or a barrage balloon that learned to knock at the
window...or...

MAHOGANY MANOR GUEST HOUSE
ST. JOHN, NEW BRUNSWICK

The Mahogany Manor Guest House is located on Germain
Street in St. John, New Brunswick. A local merchant named
William Cross built the manor in a hodgepodge of mixed
architectural styles at the turn of the 20th century. And as
we've seen with mixed architectural styles, that spells ghost-
story creepy!

Mr. Cross has long since passed on, but his good lady wife
refuses to vacate the premises. Perhaps she thinks she's one of

the fixtures that were sold with the house. She makes herself known on occasion when she materializes walking down the stairway, swinging a lantern as she descends. That's her whole shtick. Not very creative, but she'd freak the heck out of me. That's why I like to stick to the big chain hotels. More chance that the bedspread's never been laundered, but you're less likely to run into a ghost. Eeewww on both counts!

HOTEL VANCOUVER
VANCOUVER, BRITISH COLUMBIA

The present incarnation of the Hotel Vancouver is in the tradition of those grand Canadian hotels like the Château Laurier and the Royal York. Situated in downtown Vancouver, the hotel's distinctly green, copper-topped, peaked roofs dominate the skyline. The current Hotel Vancouver was completed in 1939 and built in the French Château style. It's a rather large, bunker-like structure, with ornate dormers and scary gargoyles. The opulent interior also contains some creepy spaces.

Like other grand railway hotels, there's also a bit of mystery here. Well, not that much mystery, just a whole lot of folk-lore. One of the hotel's elevators has often been known to stop on the 14th floor, even though the stop isn't requested. As the doors part and elevator patrons wonder "What gives?" a ghostly woman in red glides down the hallway…and then she's gone. It's always the Woman in Red, isn't it?

The legend, though interesting, appears to have no real explanation. But let's face it, when did truth or "real explana-tion" ever get in the way of a ghost story?

~ Big, Gargantuan & Ridiculously Oversized ~

In the town of Upsala, Ontario, northwest of Thunder Bay, there's a kitschy statue at the Can-Op service station of a giant mosquito carrying off a man. The mosquito also has a knife and fork in its hands…legs…feet…whatever those appendages are called.

Haunted Homes, Hostels and Theatres

I think every kid growing up knows of a building in the neighbourhood that is supposedly haunted. For me, growing up in Hamilton, Ontario, that building was a house that stood at the southwest corner of Manning and Hester on Hamilton's mountain. When I was a student at Ridgemount Public School, I passed that house just about every day. It was simply known to all as the "haunted house." It was two storeys high, I think—some kind of split-level place—and all the images I remember about that house involve it being devoid of colour, dark, mysterious and spooky. It had broken windows all around, and the front door was sometimes ajar and closed at other times, adding to the idea of ghosts coming and going. I'd heard stories of kids going into that house and having the wits scared out of them and even stories about kids entering but never leaving. These were talked about, but never with names or confirmation of the events. But that didn't matter—the house was evil! And as I later found out, with most ghost stories and haunted houses, confirmation is elusive. ☞

The house had become haunted, so our kid folklore said,
when the youngest son in the house murdered his parents.
Apparently the place still ran with blood, which of course
kept drying up and making the house darker and more
evil. One day, someone dared me to go into that house.
I actually tried, slowly making my way across the overgrown lawn. I even put a foot on the porch. But then I
heard the sounds of a creaking floorboard or a blood-
curdling scream—I'm not sure which. So, I turned tail
and ran. I never ever got that close to the "haunted house"
again. It was then, and still remains for me today, the
weirdest place in Canada.

Ghost stories have always scared the heck out of me. They
still do. While writing this book, I had terrible nightmares about the ghosts and ghost stories I was writing
about. And that is why today I turn to the ghost stories
I like. This chapter covers the fun ghosts. Fun ghosts, you
ask? That's right, and for some reason there are a great
many Canadian places haunted by benign, benevolent
and just plain mischievously fun ghosts. These ghosts
really just want to be noticed. They aren't out to scare
you or drive you away. They aren't headless, limbless or
screaming. And they don't remain, wherever they live, just
to claim exclusive squatters' rights. These are the ghosts
that rearrange the furniture, swing a light in the window,
puff a pipe, toss some popcorn your way, put the theatre ☞

seats up, sing, perhaps let their smelly presence be known or even clip-clap-clop along with their hooves on the top floor of a hotel.

These are my kinds of ghosts—those who want to have a little fun, don't want to be forgotten, and aren't out to scare.

Oh, and by the way, I was never so surprised as an adult as when I went back to Hamilton and discovered the "haunted house" was occupied…by humans. The whole place had been transformed into a brightly coloured suburban home where a family lived. A manicured lawn and a car in the driveway were its new assets. It was a shocker. I wanted to go up to the door and ask if they knew what evil was in that house before they moved in. But the place still scared the bejeezes out of me. Bright paint and a freshly cut lawn couldn't take the evil away. Anyway, forget that and read on about all our fun Canadian ghosts! No one's going to jump out and say "boo" in this chapter. Whew!

CASS SCIENCE HALL, UNIVERSITY OF PRINCE EDWARD ISLAND

CHARLOTTETOWN, PEI

Cass Science Hall opened in 1939 and was the original science building for St. Dunstan's College at UPEI. The four-level structure is made of concrete block and face brick. It got its current name in 1967, in memory of Father Frederick Cass, the first priest to teach chemistry at the school. His kind devotion to the campus, the building and his students created a lasting legacy that includes a ghost that just doesn't want to leave.

Apparently, a grateful Father Cass is so enthralled with the building and the fact it was renamed in his honour that he continues to hang about. But just as he was kindly, helpful and an all around boon to society in life, he continues to be that way in death.

Father Cass is a priest of the first order, continuing to help his students from beyond. He roams the halls of the building looking for any and all problems, safety concerns or untidiness. He's been known to shut off Bunsen burners, shut down the gas mains and put equipment into tidy piles. And he does all of this without ever being seen—like when my mother used to clean my room. I knew some entity had been there, but I couldn't prove it.

The good Father just looks for ways to help avoid disaster, and he does so in the most unobtrusive ways possible. He's not a scary priest, nor a hairy beast—he's just a top-notch ghostly guy with a penchant for safety. And no pension, I guess.

FAIRMONT HOTEL MACDONALD
EDMONTON, ALBERTA

This grand old lady of Edmonton has been host to politicians and pop stars, the restless and the royal, the living and the dead. No, really! Built in the Château style in 1915, the hotel Macdonald was named for Canada's first prime minister. Like many of the great railway hotels, it is copper topped and faced with Indiana limestone. The oh, so *trés* elegant hotel overlooks the North Saskatchewan River, and views from the newer turret suites in the former attic are quite spectacular. Being in a former attic, the rooms are probably also a little creepy. Solid, Victorian and a little creepy is what all of these grand, old palaces have in common. The "Mac" has seen some grand times and fallen on heaps of hard ones as well. It was nearly demolished in the 1980s, but it has found its way back, ghosts and all.

Well, the official word is that there are no ghosts. But as the folklore goes, during the hotel's construction in 1915, a bunch of horses worked and died in the basement. And now patrons and employees alike claim on a regular basis to hear the clip-clopping of hooves on the basement's concrete floor. Officially, no one's heard a darn thing.

Worse than the pitter-patter of hooves in the basement are the sounds of a horse and carriage racing the halls of the hotel's top floor. Talk about your show ponies!

~ Big, Gargantuan & Ridiculously Oversized ~

The "World's Largest Lobster" can be found in Shediac, New Brunswick. He's not a real lobster, thank goodness—I mean, he is 10.7 metres long and 4.6 metres tall. He's also quite climbable. *C'est un grand homard!*

EMPRESS THEATRE
FORT MACLEOD, ALBERTA

Fort Macleod's 1912 theatre, the Empress, is the oldest operating theatre in Alberta. Originally built by the Famous Players chain, the Empress has been a vaudeville theatre, lecture hall and movie house. Sandwiched between other buildings along Fort Macleod's historic Main Street, the distinctive red brick and elegant marquee can't help but stand out.

Inside, the theatre seats 372 people in plush red seats, including a little more than 100 in the balcony. Over the years, performers have left their mark on the theatre by autographing the walls of the basement dressing rooms. You can see the scribbles of Texas Tony and his Wonder Horse Bay Doll, the CPR Minstrels and Sammy Davis Sr. The theatre continues the tradition of using small Tiffany-style lamps for lighting, which gives the place an elegant glow and no doubt contributes to the legend that the place is haunted.

Yes, the ghost of the Empress Theatre is another unique sprite in Alberta's back pocket. "Ed" is apparently the former resident janitor, and he's either not too thrilled to be dead, not too thrilled with the place's state of cleanliness or perhaps just a bit of a curmudgeon whether dead or alive.

Ed's got a couple of issues. First off, he apparently has a rank aroma. Booze, cigarettes and cow dung are the three odours most often associated with him. But the odours may also be because Ed hangs out around the garbage. In fact, he rearranges the garbage—he's been known to flip popcorn containers out of the trash. Perhaps he's making a statement about garbage versus recyclables, but it's unlikely.

Ed also has a thing for flipping down already folded theatre seats, as if he's saying "So, is anyone sitting here? No…well, don't! Boo off!"

MACKENZIE HOUSE
TORONTO, ONTARIO

So, does the rabble-rousing newspaper editor, leader of the rebellions of 1837 and former first mayor of Toronto haunt this downtown Toronto house? Well, could be. There are, in fact, some people who think Mackenzie House is the most haunted place in Toronto. There are also people who think that the statue of Winston Churchill at Nathan Phillips Square talks. I certainly don't think the latter is true.

The house is situated in the heart of downtown Toronto. It's a gas-lit Greek revival, Victorian row house. Funny, how when you attach "Victorian" to something, it conjures up creepy nighttime images including fog, huh? Friends of W.L. Mackenzie took up a collection for him when he retired and bought the house. It changed hands several times after his death and was once even a boarding house. It's nearly been demolished a couple of times, but before the wreckers could start, something always saved it. Coincidence or ghostly happening? You be the judge.

The house has a fully functional 19th-century print shop like the one Mackenzie used to publish his rabble-rousing newspaper. It also apparently has a rabble-rousing ghost.

That's right! People claim to have seen the apparition of a short, bald man wearing a wig and a coat. Sounds like old William Lyon Mackenzie. Apparently old W.L.M. has a thing for indoor plumbing. It wasn't there when he was an official live resident, but in his ghostly form, he likes to run the taps and set the toilet a-flushing. He was a rebel, remember— ahead of his time and an agent for change. So the restroom fascination seems completely in line.

There are a couple of other ghosts hanging out in the house as well—one may be the last Mrs. Mackenzie. If you want a firsthand glimpse, head down to 82 Bond Street in Toronto and just ask the staff about the ghosts and the exorcism. They're quite happy to tell you about all of it. It's all an 1837-like rebellious hoot!

LAST CHANCE SALOON, ROSEDEER HOTEL
WAYNE, ALBERTA

Ten miles and 11 bridges south of Drumheller, Alberta, you'll come to the genuine, certified ghost town of Wayne. And within that former coal boomtown of the 1920s and 1930s, you'll come to the historic landmark, the Rosedeer Hotel. The hotel is a three-storey wooden slab of a structure that has changed little since 1913, except that over the years, a ghost has taken up residence inside its Last Chance Saloon.

Well, there's not a lot to say about the ghost at the Last Chance Saloon. He's thought to be the former owner. Seems to be taking a load off and sittin' a spell. His only eerie activity? He puffs a nice little pipe. And the aroma is cheery, not eerie. So head on over to Wayne and see if he'll offer you a puff. If he does, I'm sure you'll be quite chuffed… Take your camera.

CANMORE OPERA HOUSE, CALGARY HERITAGE PARK
CALGARY, ALBERTA

The Canmore Opera House is a log cabin located in Calgary's Heritage Park. The structure was actually used by Alberta Theatre Projects (ATP) for its first 13 years of operation.

Even though ATP has moved on, its productions must have inspired at least one of the Opera House's permanent residents. Apparently, on occasion, the voice of a beautiful songstress can be heard. She's wily and shy, though, because she never materializes in human form. But it's that voice that visitors swear they'll never forget.

~ Big, Gargantuan & Ridiculously Oversized ~

The "World's Largest Badminton Racket" can be found just north of Edmonton in the town of St. Albert, Alberta. In fact, you can't miss it—it's 4.3 metres tall, though it's skinny, like badminton rackets will be, so if you blink, I can't guarantee you'll see it. It stands tall and proud outside the Red Willow Badminton Club on Boudreau Road.

MASONIC TEMPLE
WINNIPEG, MANITOBA

Winnipeg's former Masonic Temple has housed many businesses over the years, including a Mother Tucker's restaurant. It is located at the intersection of Donald Street and Ellice Avenue in the 'Peg. It's a heavy, imposing structure (as Masonic Temples generally are) that dates back to 1895.

People have been talking about the building's mischievous sprite for years. He/she/it even once made an appearance in a CBC news report. Starring with Knowlton Nash didn't go to the sprite's head, because it continued its antics.

The lights have been known to flicker, and former restaurant workers claim on more than occasion to have come to work in the morning and discovered that some mystery rearrangements had taken place. Some suggested the ghost partied all night long, spending precious sprite time moving salt and pepper shakers and using all the napkins.

The ghost has also been known to do a bit of toe tapping in the attic. One former employee even said he'd seen the ghost decked out in 18th-century costume. The haunting is, of course, attributed to some evil done by the Masons in times gone by.

But who cares, really? Just go try the napkins...the ghost swears by them!

~ Big, Gargantuan & Ridiculously Oversized ~

At the junction of Highways 97 and 16 in British Columbia stands an 8.2-metre-tall mascot named Mr. PG. That's right, Mr. PG—"P" and "G" being the initials representing the community's name, Prince George. Mr. PG has a replica wooden log as a body, sports a yellow hard hat and waves a flag. The original Mr. PG was actually made of logs, but unfortunately, he eventually rotted away. The new, improved Mr. PG is made of metal painted to look like wood. Prince George is, of course, a logging community and the "Northern Capital of British Columbia." On special occasions, Mr. PG gets dressed up. He wears a tutu during the city's dance festival and sports a white cane and dark glasses for CNIB Week. It sounds like Mr. PG is quite the gad-about-town!

Nature's
So Nutty

Reversing falls, magnetic hills, white squirrels, black squirrels, sand dunes, pink lakes that are green, water, water everywhere, Hell's Gate and pingos. Take your pick. Whichever you choose, the naturally nutty nature of nature is, well…unnatural, naturally speaking.

Does that make any sense? Not really, but nothing outdoes the nutty nature of nature. It confounds, discombobulates and defies explanation—except by scientists, psychics and parapsychologists—provides tourist attractions and gives a bit of mystery to some places that might otherwise seem ordinary. Nature is so weird!

THE REVERSING FALLS
ST. JOHN, NEW BRUNSWICK

Although a bit of a misnomer, the "Reversing Falls" are indeed a phenomenon that happens nowhere else in the world… And no, it's not an optical illusion or something faked to get tourists to come see.

Some of the highest tides in the world are those of the Bay of Fundy. And twice a day, those enormous Bay of Fundy tides crash into the St. John River, forcing the river to flow backwards—in reverse, you might say!

Here are the details. Tidewater flows through the mouth of St. John Harbour and meets the downward-flowing St. John River. This is where the so-called "Reversing Falls" are created. The opposing flows of tidewater and the St. John River meet and create violent rapids as the water smashes into river-bottom ridges and is then forced through a bottleneck gorge.

The whole thing happens in reverse at high tide. (Ah, so that's where the moniker "Reversing Falls" comes from.) The falls, however, are not so much falls as they are turbulent rapids.

At high tide, the water in the harbour rises, then stops and pushes the St. John River backwards. Talk about nature's fury. The reverse flow is felt as far as 130 kilometres upstream at Fredericton.

Interestingly, the whole magical tidal action starts in the southern Indian Ocean, makes a right turn around the Cape of Good Hope and then makes a beeline for the Bay of Fundy. With that kind of run up, the St. John River doesn't stand a chance. That is some kick!

SKOOKUMCHUK RAPIDS
BRITISH COLUMBIA

Skookumchuk…Skookumchuk…Skookumchuk… That's just fun to say, isn't it? Skookumchuck is a word that comes from the Chinook language and means "turbulent water," which the "Skook" definitely is. The rapids actually appear to be boiling, as huge volumes of water are forced through the Skookumchuck Narrows.

In some ways, it's similar to the reversing falls in St. John, NB, since at the change of the tides, the flow of salt water switches and reverses the direction and power of the rapids. On a 3-metre tide, as much as 909 billion litres of water are squeezed through the narrows that connect Sechelt and Jervis Inlets. The most dramatic and visible motions occur when those billions of litres of water are sucked through cavernous whirlpools, creating standing waves.

The dramatic sight is easiest seen and experienced one hour after slack tide. Slack tide is, of course, when the narrows become flat and calm at either peak high tide or peak low tide. Of course! The whole thing can be rather dangerous, though the rapids attract surfers and kayakers from all over the world who want to experience the 10–14-knot currents. The effect is almost like a natural version of a wave pool at one of those water parks we all flock to in the summer.

The Skookumchuk Rapids are located in Skookumchuck Narrows Provincial Park, at the north end of the Sechelt Peninsula on the beautiful Sunshine Coast of British Columbia.

~ Big, Gargantuan & Ridiculously Oversized ~

It's an all-Prairie final in the "World's Largest Bee" category. And the winner is...Fahler, Alberta, with a bee measuring nearly 7 metres long. The "Honey Bee" in Tisdale, Saskatchewan, is only 5 metres long. Hang in there, Tisdale, you've got more weird things to offer!

HELL'S GATE
BRITISH COLUMBIA

The mighty water of the Fraser River being squeezed through a narrow gorge definitely creates a dramatic and turbulent sight to see. At Hell's Gate in the BC Interior, as much as 757 million litres of water are squeezed through a narrow 35-metre-wide gorge. All that water happens at spring runoff, and Hell's Gaters are quite proud to point out that it's twice the volume of water flowing over Niagara Falls.

This mighty whitewater area was named by Simon Fraser, who scaled the canyon's walls. There's an "air-tram," which is basically a cable car that travels over the river, giving visitors a great view. People have also been known to walk the suspension bridge just to freak themselves out.

It's a dangerous place, but there is a great story about a blind cow that found herself in the river and somehow managed to survive the violence of Hell's Gate. She was dubbed "Rosebank Rosie," and though cows don't swim, they apparently float pretty well. I'll bet it's their big, buoyant udders!

~ Big, Gargantuan & Ridiculously Oversized ~

Located on the western shore of Lake Winnipeg, Gimli, Manitoba, calls itself the "Capital of New Iceland" as a trubute to the Icelandic origins of many of its early immigrants. In ancient Norse mythology, Gimli was also known as the home of the gods. So what better centennial project to build than a 4.6-metre-tall fibreglass Viking? The Gimli Chamber of Commerce did just that way back in 1967. The structure was designed by a professor from the University of Manitoba and sculpted, horns and all, by the late George Barone. The Viking was unveiled in a grand ceremony in July 1967 by the then-president of Iceland, Ásgeir Ásgeirsson.

THE POCKET DESERT
OSOYOOS, BRITISH COLUMBIA

Dubbed the only "true" desert in Canada (because, I guess, the rest of the pretenders are lying), the Pocket Desert is located at the southernmost tip of the Okanagan Valley. It's also one of the most fragile and endangered ecosystems in North America and contains one of Canada's largest concentrations of at-risk species—more than 100 rare plants and more than 300 rare invertebrates. Some of those species include: the tiger salamander, sage thrasher, night snake and badger.

At the Osoyoos Desert Centre, visitors can walk along a boardwalk through a protected portion of the habitat. At the Desert Centre, the staff educates, does research and even validates parking—the first two, anyhow.

TUKTUYAKTUK PENINSULA
NORTHWEST TERRITORIES

The world's largest concentration of pingos is located on the Tuktuyaktuk Peninsula in the Northwest Territories. There may, in fact, be as many as 1450 pingos on the peninsula. So, just what the heck are pingos? Officially, it's an Inuit word meaning "conical hill." Which doesn't really clarify much, does it?

Pingos actually look like small volcanoes and range from 15 metres to almost half a kilometre across. They are, in fact, conical hills that often have a crater lake in the centre. Pingos have also been described as nothing more than nature's pimples. Their formation involves permafrost and standing water—all too complicated and uninteresting to read about, especially as compared to nature's magic!

Oh, and pingos aren't to be confused with that cartoon show about the penguin named Pingu. They are totally different. However, Pingu getting lost down a pingo sounds good to me! That little penguin drives me crazy.

GREAT SAND HILLS
LIEBENTHAL, SASKATCHEWAN

Sand dunes are not something you probably think of when you think about southwestern Saskatchewan. I mean, if you happen to think of southwestern Saskatchewan at all. But from now on, when you do think of southwestern Saskatchewan, think "Sand Hills!" In fact, think "Great Sand Hills"!

Twenty kilometres northeast of Liebenthal, Saskatchewan, you'll run into 1900 km² of active dunes, high, stable dunes and sand flats. These sand hills are what remain of a delta from an ancient glacier. Yet another thing I wouldn't have thought about when thinking about southwestern Saskatchewan.

The stable dunes make up most of what are the Great Sand Hills. They are covered with sagebrush, prairie grasses and other plants. The active dunes make up only a small part of the area (about 1%), but they also provide a crazy view. The place looks more like a little corner of the Sahara than it does like Saskatchewan. The active dunes change size and shape over time and are known to grow to 12 metres or more in height.

If you visit, sandals or desert boots are definitely the designated footwear of the day!

MAGNETIC HILL
MONCTON, NEW BRUNSWICK

For more than 70 years, savvy boosters from the New Brunswick berg of Moncton have been pushing their odd little tourist attraction known as Magnetic Hill. There are other magnetic hills, but none top the one near Moncton. They'll tell you: drive to the bottom of the hill, take your foot off the brake and put your car in neutral. You'll be absolutely amazed as your car coasts uphill! It works with trucks and vans and buses as well. Or so it would seem.

Here's a little secret about Magnetic Hill. There is absolutely nothing magnetic about it. Except, that is, for its ability to draw tourists. In fact, the whole thing is an optical illusion in which a slight downhill grade looks like an uphill grade. What looks like the bottom of the hill is actually the top of the hill. It's your eyes playing tricks on you, not the geography (in addition to a little sleight-of-hand marketing that's been done by some wily New Brunswickers).

There are many places around the world where a similar optical illusion can be experienced. It usually occurs on stretches of road where the level horizon is obscured and visual clues such as trees growing at an angle, not truly vertical.

This tedious, yet accurate description hasn't stopped the Moncton's Magnetic Mafia. They've been talking about Magnetic Hill since the 1800s, when, before there were cars, wagons rolled backwards up the hill…and I'll bet before that, Ezekiel's wheel rolled up the hill as well.

If you're looking to visit this most famous of Canada's growing number of magnetic hills, take exit 450 from the Trans-Canada Highway (#2) and follow the signs. Hopefully, they're right side up and not being dragged uphill by the perpetual motion of Moncton marketing gurus.

CÔTE MAGNÉTIQUE
CHARTIERVILLE, QUÉBEC

Not nearly as famous as Moncton's Magnetic Hill, nor as touristy nor as commercially marketed, the Côte Magnétique (Magnetic Hill) just outside Chartierville, Québec, is nonetheless just another optical illusion. And unlike the marketing minions of Moncton, here at Chartierville they admit the whole thing is quite natural. Although, that is perhaps why it's not as famous as the one at Moncton. I mean, a little magic, mystery and wonder goes a long way in drawing a crowd.

Chartierville is about 8 kilometres from the New Hampshire border. The instructions for experiencing this little bit of eye trickery are prominently displayed on a sign beside the road in both French and English. Those instructions read as follows: "Stop here. Put car in neutral. Look behind and experiment. Have a nice day!" Or, in French: *Arrêtez ici. Mettez le véhicule au point mort (N). Regardez en arrière et expérimentez. Bonne journée!* Bilingual, fun and polite! *Bonne route!*

MAGNETIC HILL
BURLINGTON, ONTARIO

Is it evil, I ask ya? Eeevvvilll? Ah…no!

The magnetic hill in Burlington, Ontario, is starting to rival the one in Moncton for fame. And that is mainly because a cheesy television show perpetuated mysterious folkloric tales involving the hill, many car accidents and the ghosts of children who died in a bus crash.

However, Burlington's Magnetic Hill is no more a mystery, magnetic or ghostly than any of the others. It is an optical illusion, pure and simple. I grew up in Hamilton, a stone's throw from Burlington's Magnetic Hill. I've been there many times and never felt anything creepy, dead-kid related or ghostly about it. And, as far as I can tell, there is no record of the purported bus crash. However, facts have never kept TV shows like *Creepy Canada* nor TV channels like CTV Travel from popularizing and publicizing the myth.

It has also been suggested that UFOs are somehow related to the phenomenon. Because, of course, aliens would take great pleasure in taking a jaunt over to Burlington and messing with the inhabitants' minds in the form of pulling their rather primitive vehicles backwards up a hill! I wonder what message they're trying to send to us? Perhaps it's "Boo!" or "You are such naïve fools!"

If you want to visit the Burlington Magnetic Hill, it's north of Highway 403 on a rural part of King Road. You'll want to stop your car at the Hydro right-of-way entrance to begin your ride. Make your way past the UFOs lined up on the right and ghost buses of dead kids on the left.

AND THE REST OF THE MAGNETIC HILLS...

Other magnetic hills starting to make their way into the tourist-marketing juggernaut include: Dacre, Ontario (near Pembroke); Neepawa, Manitoba; and Cantons-de-l'Est, Québec. There may also be one near Abbotsford, BC.

~ Big, Gargantuan & Ridiculously Oversized ~

In St. Thomas, Ontario, there is a life-sized statue of Jumbo, P.T. Barnum's famous giant elephant. The citizens of St. Thomas erected the statue in 1985 to commemorate the 100th anniversary of Jumbo's death. Jumbo never lived in St. Thomas, nor was he born there, and he didn't even perform there. He was unfortunately killed there when he had a run-in with a locomotive.

THE WHITE SQUIRRELS
EXETER, ONTARIO

So, do white squirrels actually exist or is this some twisted marketing campaign in which the tree rats with the furry tails are spray-painted as a come-on?

Well, actually they do exist—no paint, no come-on and no pink eyes. And that is one of the most unique things about Exeter's white squirrel population. Whereas other towns in North America promote their white albino squirrels—pink eyes and all—Exeter's white squirrels aren't albino. They are regular squirrels that just happen to be white.

And in Exeter, the townsfolk and visitors celebrate these unique tree-dwelling rodents with the annual White Squirrel Festival each September. There's a parade and white squirrel events with white squirrel mascots galore. The official mascot is named "White Wonder." Wonder why?

The origin of Exeter's white squirrels is unclear, though it's been suggested the following groups had something to do with it: Gypsies, tropical visitors and even Torontonians. If you visit Exeter other than at festival time, the white squirrels can be seen all over town and especially in MacNaughton Park. Exeter is located 50 kilometres north of London, Ontario.

THE BLACK SQUIRRELS
LONDON, ONTARIO

Not to be outdone by the Exeter mighty whites, London, Ontario, boasts a population of black squirrels in Victoria Park. No festival…yet…but these black devils were actually exported to the campus of Ohio's Kent State University in the early 1960s. I'm not exactly sure what else makes these black squirrels unique, odd or weird. I get the white squirrel oddity. Unusual, right? And a white squirrel definitely stands out in a crowd. The black ones, not so much! But what do I know?

PINK LAKE
GATINEAU PARK, QUÉBEC

For decades, people have been travelling to Gatineau Park to see the famous Pink Lake only to be disappointed when they find out the lake is actually green. The lake is actually named for a family of settlers, the Pinks, who originally settled the area in the early 1800s.

But Pink Lake isn't just an absurd colour mix-up. It does, in fact, fall under the category of "Nature's So Nutty." Why? Well, Pink Lake is actually a "meromictic" lake, which means that because of its depth, small surface and sheltered positioning, its waters do not mix. That is, the water in the lake is stratified into various layers. The bottom layer, for example, is deprived of oxygen, which means that organic matter accumulates there but does not decompose.

Not to be outdone by colour and water stratification, the lake is also home to some unique species, including the stickleback. Sticklebacks are an ancient type of fish with three spines and date back to the time when an arm of the Atlantic Ocean, called the Champlain Sea, covered the area. When the sea retreated 10,000 years ago, the stickleback got trapped. However, the crafty little devils learned to adapt to the lake environment. I guess when you have three spines, adaptation's a breeze!

MANITOULIN ISLAND
ONTARIO

So, what does being the largest freshwater lake in the world get you besides being a question on every quiz show ever broadcast on TV? Well, there are the tourists who tramp all over your beautiful wilderness and…well…the laurels. Let's not forget the laurels, because you are the "Largest Island in a Freshwater Lake" in the whole entire world. That's 2766 km^2 of island, don't ya know. Have I mentioned it's within a freshwater lake?

What is also interesting—or weird—is that there are also 110 inland lakes on Manitoulin Island. Within many of those lakes you've also got many islands. Say what? Well here goes: Treasure Island is within Mindemoya Lake; Mindemoya Lake is on Manitoulin Island; Manitoulin Island is in Georgian Bay; Georgian Bay is in Lake Huron; Lake Huron is in North America; North America is on Earth. That's pretty cool, eh?

Manitoulin Island…It's big and freshly watered and weird. No, really!

ROCHE PERCÉE SANDSTONE
SASKATCHEWAN

Roche Percée is a village located in the southeastern corner of Saskatchewan near Estevan. Just outside the village, there is a craggy sandstone outcrop that is both oddly shaped and "pierced." You see, Roche Percée is French for "pierced rock."

Over the centuries (maybe longer), Roche Percée has been worn down by wind and rain and marked mainly by human graffiti. We are such a creative species, aren't we? Names were carved on it by members of the North-West Mounted Police during their great trek west, Wild Bill Hickock may have left his mark somewhere on the rock, and ancient Natives also wrote their names on the rock with crude pictures. One of them translates to "Kilroy was here!" Not really.

Roche Percée was once also a sacred site to local Natives. Now, it's more or less just a weird curiosity near the American border. Progress!

SLEEPING GIANT ISLAND
LAKE SUPERIOR, ONTARIO

Looking out across Lake Superior from Thunder Bay, you can distinctly see the form of a giant in the water with his arms folded across his muscular chest… Or that's what they say, anyway. I've kind of seen it by squinting and unfocusing my eyes as if I was looking at a Magic Eye piece of "art." The phenomenon is not (surprise, surprise) a real sleeping giant. It's the formation of flora and fauna on an island.

However, First Nations lore says the Sleeping Giant is none other than the Great Spirit, Nanabijou. The rather long and somewhat complicated legend basically says that Nanabijou awarded a loyal Ojibway tribe with access to a great silver mine, with the stipulation that they keep the location a secret from the white men or else both the Ojibway and Nanabijou would suffer the consequences. Sioux rivals coveted the silver. A seasoned Sioux scout infiltrated the Ojibway tribe, learned the mine's location and then inadvertently told it to some white men after they got him drunk. The result was as warned: Nanabijou was turned to stone and became the Sleeping Giant in the water, and the Ojibway disappeared.

It's hard to say who's to blame here—Nanabijou for his poor judgement and showing off the wealth; the Ojibway for not doing enough to protect the secret mine; the covetous Sioux who couldn't hold their liquor; or the evil white men. In the end, life's too short, grudges are pointless and Sleeping Giant Island is rather picturesque.

THE BADLANDS
ALBERTA

They've been described as an alien landscape and are charac-terized by erosion formations, buttes, coulees, hoodoos, wind-ing canyons and gullies. These are Alberta's Badlands. Man, are they weird looking! And baaaad. Not street gang bad, just inhospitable, really. That's what early French settlers thought of the area. They discovered very quickly that the Badlands—*les terres mauvaises*—were not suitable for farming. Which may be one of the reasons Québec is in the east and not where Alberta is now. Location, location, location!

The heart of the Badlands is in and around the Drumheller area—about 140 kilometres north and east of Calgary. Drumheller and the Badlands are also known as "Dinosaur Country." As Canadians, we all know of the amazing dinosaur fossils discovered in the Badlands. Although the place is dry now, when dinos roamed the earth it was a thriving wetland. The Royal Tyrrell Museum is in Drumheller. It is Canada's only institution devoted entirely to paleontology. And though the museum's not exclusively about the dinosaurs, they do sit centre stage.

~ Big, Gargantuan & Ridiculously Oversized ~

A Viking ship (or at least the front half of one) greets visitors at the west end of Main Street in Erickson, Manitoba. Erickson was settled in the 1800s by Scandinavian immigrants and is known as the "Land of the Vikings." The ship is replete with red-and-white sails and two boatmen made of fibreglass. The boatmen were originally carved from wood like the boat, but were removed and later replaced after they were desecrated (their body parts were cut off and reattached in a sexually suggestive arrangement). No word on why the back half of the Viking ship was never built. Perhaps the idea wouldn't float with the town.

It's a Ghost What?
A Phantom Who?

The great outdoors seems to be a perfectly fine place to haunt, especially if all the homes, theatres, government buildings, trailers and outhouses are already taken.

The ghosts who favour the outdoors have a real creative spirit about them, too. Some disguise themselves as the sound of the whispering wind; others take a midnight ride on a horse, on the rails or on a fogbound ship.

There really are not a lot of restrictions to creeping out the great outdoors, so let's have at it...

PLACES WHERE THE GHOSTS TEND TO FLOAT

Aye's da bye dat builds da boat,
And aye's da bye dat sails her,
And aye's da ghost dat haunts near the shore,
And scares da bejeezes outta Liza.

MAHONE BAY
NOVA SCOTIA

Mahone Bay is a beautiful inlet of the Atlantic Ocean on the southeast coast of Nova Scotia. Fabled communities such as Lunenburg, Mahone Bay and Oak Island are located here. The bay is one of those almost mystical maritime places that casts a long shadow over quaint, mostly rural communities. The people are friendly, and the climate is mild year round. Although, because it's on the Atlantic Coast, Mahone Bay does not completely escape the battering winds and waves of the Atlantic Ocean. And sometimes, the fog rolls in like it's old London town. There are also more than 100 islands in the bay and just as many ghost stories.

Legend has it that on foggy nights, around the time of a full moon, the ghostly spectre of a fire ship has been observed there. The ghostly phenomenon is known as the Teaser Light and gets its name from an American privateer, the *Young Teazer,* that was chased into Mahone Bay in 1813 by a British warship. Trapped, with no way of escaping, *Young Teazer*'s crew set her ablaze to keep her from being captured.

The ship was carrying a substantial amount of ammunition. (It was the War of 1812, after all, and a ship without ammunition was like a peanut butter cup without its peanut butter—hollow and pointless!) Anyway, *Young Teazer* exploded in a spectacular fireball, and the shockwave was felt all along the shores of Mahone Bay and probably for kilometres inland. The entire crew of the ship perished in the explosion, which may explain why the ghostly ship reappears time and again. The crew is confused, I guess?

Today, landlubbers peering out into the bay are the most common spectators of the Teazer Light spectre. The ship appears through the fog, sails for a time on the bay and then disappears in a spectacular flameout. Sailors in the bay have also come a-runnin' and a-claimin' that the fiery spook ship tried to run them down. Which seems a bit far-fetched, since it's hard to come a-runnin' on water, unless you're "you know who," and he was really only ever seen walking.

As a way of commemorating the whole gruesome original death-inducing spectacle, as well as the recurring ghost ship sightings, the Mahone Bay Wooden Boat Festival sets ablaze a small replica of the *Teazer* each year.

~ Big, Gargantuan & Ridiculously Oversized ~

The "World's Largest Muskoka Chair" (or Adirondack chair, if you prefer that name) is located in Varney, Ontario. This largest wooden cottage chair is 6.7 metres high. There was some controversy over who had the biggest Muskoka chair, because the town of Gravenhurst, Ontario, also claimed the title. But at just under 4 metres high, clearly Gravenhurst's chair has come up short.

NORTHUMBERLAND STRAIT
PRINCE EDWARD ISLAND AND NOVA SCOTIA

Northumberland Strait is an arm of the Gulf of St. Lawrence
that separates Prince Edward Island from Nova Scotia and
New Brunswick. The strait is 290 kilometres long and
between 19 and 48 kilometres wide. It's big enough to get
lost in, but not so big as to be inaccessible…except in the
winter months, when it freezes over. The strait doesn't get as
cold or as wild and woolly storms as other maritime locales,
but it has its own mystery.

On cold, warm, dark, foggy, clear and windy nights, a fiery
phantom ship has often been seen on the Northumberland
Strait. Since 1876, people have been reporting sightings of
this glowing or fiery three-masted ship in the channel
between the north coast of Nova Scotia and the south coast
of PEI. But in sharp contrast to Mahone Bay's Teazer Light,
the strait's phantom ship doesn't just appear in foggy weather.
The only common weather phenomenon related to sightings
of the phantom ship seems to be that it often appears with
the advance of a northeast wind and storm. So, it's kind of
like a spectral version of that Channel 7 Accuweather warning: "There's a blowhard of a nor'easter a-comin'!"

The phantom ship sometimes starts out as a fireball and
magically transforms into a glowing ship. There are reports
of people being seen on the fire ship's deck, as well as unsuc-
cessful attempts to rescue the fiery sailors by "real" ships.
Theories as to why the phantom fire ship keeps appearing
have included pacts with the devil, pirates and a little bit of
Disney Imagineering. My theory—young kids and olde-tyme
shenanigans!

BAIE DE CHALEURS
NEW BRUNSWICK

Baie de Chaleurs is an arm of the Gulf of St. Lawrence. It separates Québec's Gaspé Peninsula from New Brunswick's north shore and extends 137 kilometres from one end to the other. That's a pretty big area. In fact, it's the largest bay in the Gulf of St. Lawrence. The name Baie de Chaleurs translates to English as "bay of warmth." However, that's just another one of those geographic jokes, since the water in the Baie can stay cold even in summer. Sandy beaches can be found all over the Baie, as well as a huge natural sandbar.

This body of water, like many others on the East Coast, is associated with remarkable tales of sightings of a fire ship. The fire ship in the Baie is not much different from that seen in Northumberland Strait. It has the requisite glowing presence, the three masts, the year-round appearances and a penchant for foretelling a storm. For 200 years, people have been reporting sightings of what the Acadians called *le feu du mauvais temps*, which of course means "bad weather fire."

There are various theories explaining this ship's appearance. They range from the ghostly reappearance of various shipwrecks to ships destroyed in battle to devilish death warnings for people on shore! More scientific reasons include rotting vegetation, natural gas being released under the ocean and St. Elmo's Fire. Translation: digestion, sea fart or a bad 1980s "Brat Pack" movie. No matter how you slice it, it's pretty silly!

THE GRAVEYARD OF THE PACIFIC
BRITISH COLUMBIA

The West Coast of Vancouver Island is known as the "Graveyard of the Pacific." More than 200 ships have foundered there since the early 19th century. Rocky shores, powerful ocean currents and stormy weather have all contributed to its well-earned moniker. Wind and rain and fog, oh my!

Once of the most famous wrecks and ongoing mysteries of the "graveyard" is that of the passenger ship *Valencia*. The ship left San Francisco for Seattle in January 1906, but crashed on the rocks off Vancouver Island near Panchena Point. Attempts at evacuation and rescue were more than muddled and went on for two days. Other ships tried to help in the rescue, but the *Valencia* broke apart and took at least 117 souls with her to the bottom.

Since then, a phantom ship resembling the *Valencia* has been seen steaming the Pacific near the wreck sight. Sailors have even reported seeing ghostly forms clinging to the ghost ship. Of course! What other kind of form would cling to a ghost ship? One of the most interesting aspects of the whole story is that one of the *Valencia*'s lifeboats washed up on shore in perfect shape—27 years after the ship sank. And the East Coast thought they had great ghost ship stories!

~ Big, Gargantuan & Ridiculously Oversized ~

Travelling east along Highway 14 from Saskatoon, motorists are greeted by a unique sign at the entrance to the town of Biggar, Saskatchewan. The colourful sign reads: "New York is Big, but this is Biggar." The slogan originated in 1909, courtesy of a survey crew who had too much to drink one night and decided to play a joke on the town. However, the joke was on them. The town loved the slogan and has been promoting it ever since. Oh, and by the way, the town is named after the former general counsel for the Grand Trunk Pacific Railroad, W.H. Biggar. It's not just a spelling mistake.

PLACES WHERE THE GHOSTS RIDE

SCUGOG ISLAND
ONTARIO

An hour's drive northeast of Toronto, near Port Perry, lies Scugog Island in Lake Scugog. Lake Scugog and the island were created when a dam was built at Purdy's Mills (now called Lindsay) in 1827. The lake covers 100 km², and the island is mostly rural, though it's large enough to have farms and villages. With that rural area comes the story of a lonely and desolate road island where a legend of woe has grown up.

In fact, the road is where a motorcyclist is supposed to have died and whose phantom continues to ride and haunt with vim, vigour and speed. Oh, and not much skill, since the accident that killed him in the first place in the 1950s or 1960s keeps stopping him in his tracks.

The legend says that the young man in question was trying out a motorcycle on a straight road, misjudged his speed, lost control, flew off the bike and hit his head on a rock. Oh, and he died. Judging from the type of crash, his riding skills were questionable. In any event, he apparently won't leave and making fun of him is probably not going to help.

This modern "haunting" phenomenon takes the form of a round, white light (which looks like a motorcycle headlight) that travels down the road and becomes a small red light when it passes you. So, headlight one way, brake light in the other direction. Got it? Some people have even suggested that they've heard the sounds of a motorcycle with the lights. They later had their hearing checked, but nothing was found. So they had their heads examined—still nothing!

Psychics, paranormal researchers and even reporters have examined the phenomenon. Explanations range from the reflection of car headlights, lights caused by a nearby geological fault and a complete and utter hoax. Still, people who have been there swear there is something to the ghostly lights of the poor and unskilled ghostly motorcycle-riding kid! Vroom, vroom!

~ Big, Gargantuan & Ridiculously Oversized ~

The "World's Largest Oil Can" sits on the edge of town in Rocanville, Saskatchewan. It was built in 1973 to commemorate the Symons Oil Can Factory and its 50 years of continuous operation. The oil can stands 7 metres tall and is bright red, so if you're driving by, there's no way you can miss it. It doesn't really contain oil, though.

ROUTE 230 BETWEEN PORT REXTON AND PORT UNION
NEWFOUNDLAND

Something freaky this way comes on the Bonavista! Route 230 between Port Rexton and Port Union, Newfoundland, is a quiet place. It's a lonely stretch of road where nary a person, nor other cars, nor beasts are encountered. So why does a phantom train or phantom hitchhiker or a combination thereof keep popping up? Who knows, but that is apparently what happens. Along this spooky route, people have reported encountering moving lights and even a phantom train running beside the road. There's no track, but there are spectres of people travelling on a ghostly train.

Also along this route, startled travellers have reported people picking up hitchhikers, only to have them disappear from the backseats of their cars when they get to their destinations. The one question I have to ask about this scenario is: If I picked up a hitchhiker, why would I let this stranger sit behind me in the backseat of my car? I mean, I'm just asking to be mugged, murdered or carjacked, aren't I? Or perhaps the drivers of these cars didn't realize it, but they are actually taxi drivers and the passengers who disappear have done a runner. You know—the old "drive and dash." Could there be an alcoholic beverage involved in these incidents? Maybe there's a little freaky "screech" action going on?

WATERFRONT SEA BUS AND SKY TRAIN STATION
VANCOUVER, BRITISH COLUMBIA

The Waterfront Sky Train Station and Sea Bus Terminal on Cordova Street between Granville and Seymour is a rather lonely and remote part of downtown Vancouver. This is the sight of the old CPR terminal, and in fact, the station can be entered through the old railway station on Cordova Street.

This is also the place said to be haunted by the "Headless Brakeman." The questions raised by this moniker are many and varied. If he's headless, does he bump into things? If he's headless, how does he know when to brake (no eyes, no ears)? And my mother would have my head if I didn't ask this one— is he headless because he forgot his head because it wasn't attached? The answers to those questions are no, no and no.

Way back in 1928, a railway brakeman slipped off one train and was run over by another. Now, that's some bad luck! Worse, his head was severed in the accident, giving him his illustrative name. Since then he's been seen, especially on stormy nights, hopping on and off railcars (and now the Sky Train, I guess), apparently feeling around for his head. He feels for it because he can't look for it because his eyes…well, they're in that other part that he's looking for.

~ Big, Gargantuan & Ridiculously Oversized ~

Both the cities of Burwash Landing, Yukon, and Quesnel, BC, claim to have the "World's Largest Gold Pan." The Gold Rush was big in these here parts! The pan at Burwash Landing is 6.4 metres in diameter and the pan at Quesnel, sadly, is only 5.5 metres across. The Yukon wins out on this one! The Burwash Landing gold pan also sports a scenic painting of Kluane Lake and is located beside the Burwash Museum of Natural History at historic Mile 1093 (Kilometre 1759) on the Alaska Highway.

RAILWAY BRIDGE
WELLINGTON, PRINCE EDWARD ISLAND

A railway bridge west of Summerside, PEI, is the setting for an odd little East Coast mystery. On December evenings since 1885, a phantom train has often been seen crossing the bridge near Wellington. It's a train, so the bridge thing makes sense. I mean, a train in a lake would be really odd. People have reported seeing the chug-chug-chugging phantom engine with multiple railroad cars and even passengers at times when no trains were scheduled, none were running late and nothing named Via was in the area.

PLACES WHERE GHOSTS FROLIC IN THE GREAT OUTDOORS

CROWSNEST PASS

ALBERTA

The Crowsnest Pass is where the CPR crosses the Continental Divide from Alberta to BC. It's located in the Canadian Rockies at an elevation of 1357 metres. Weather can be, at times, extreme, and neighbours are few and far between in what can be a quiet and lonely area. It's a place of legend and lore.

They say that when the wind blows in "The Pass," Montie Lewis, the haunting hooker of Turtle Mountain, is out looking for her jewels…and perhaps still attempting to practise the world's oldest profession. A well-known turn of the century "lady-of-the-evening," Montie was also known for her great love of gems. Apparently she was always seen wearing jewels, whether she was dressed in clothing or frolicking about in the altogether!

Montie's bejewelled life took a tragic turn when she was found murdered. (That's got to be a drag!) She clearly learned the hard way that "you can't take it with you." However, evidence suggests that one of Montie's gentleman callers had just that in mind. He had a thing for Montie's precious gems—which does not refer to any particular part of her body. The lout offed poor Montie in the bed where she lay and then up and disappeared with her diamonds that day. Ya don't say.

So now, whenever the wind blows around Turtle Mountain, it's said that Montie's a-moanin'! I don't know. It seems a bit rude to suggest that a wind blowing across the pass is actually a hooker moaning over a trick gone bad!

~ Big, Gargantuan & Ridiculously Oversized ~

St. Claude, Manitoba, is a dairy community located an hour southwest of Winnipeg. The town has a rich French heritage, which is why "La Pipe" is located there. And just what is "La Pipe"? It's the "World's Largest Smokable Pipe." That's right, a very large pipe just like your grandfather used to smoke…not the water kind that your cousin Dave uses. And it was, indeed, built for smoking. If you've got enough tobacco and gigantic-sized lungs, I guess you could sit back with a newspaper and enjoy a puff. The pipe is 6 metres long and was built to commemorate early settlers who came from Jura, France, where the main industry was making pipes.

CANOE LAKE
ALGONQUIN PROVINCIAL PARK, ONTARIO

Algonquin Provincial Park is the second oldest provincial park in Canada. Established in 1893, the park covers 7723 km² —an area larger than Prince Edward Island. The vast park includes woodlands, lakes and rivers and is situated on the south edge of the Canadian Shield between Georgian Bay and the Ottawa River. Algonquin is remote, easy to get lost in and full of stories that include ghosts, murder and mystery.

And that's how we come to Tom Thompson. His death and what followed have become one of the best examples of Algonquin's mysterious lore.

The ghost of Tom Thomson haunts Canoe Lake in Algonquin Park. That's right! The late and venerated painter of the Canadian wilderness and affiliate of the Group of Seven—but not a member, because he, like Groucho Marx, would never join any group that would have him as a member…or something like that…

We all remember the story forced on us in history or art class where they talked about how old T.T. was an accomplished outdoorsman and talented painter, but somehow in 1917, turned up dead under his canoe with a gash on his head and fishing line wrapped around his ankle. I don't know about you, but I am clearly seeing an ironic Mister Bean–like moment that, if it weren't tragic, would actually be sitcom funny.

Anyway, since 1917, people claim to have seen a lone and ghostly figure paddling a canoe through the mist on Canoe Lake. So, he's kind of a benign haunter, because he doesn't say anything to anyone or scare them or even do a quick sketch that they could sell to the National Gallery for a fin or a million.

Explanations for his mysterious death include a love triangle gone wrong—oh, you know those artists! There's also some controversy surrounding the fact his family had him moved from his original burial site beside Canoe Lake to Heath, Ontario, with some other body showing up in his Canoe Lake grave in the 1950s.

CAMPOBELLO ISLAND
NEW BRUNSWICK

Campobello Island lies at the mouth of the Bay of Fundy, off the southeast coast of New Brunswick and the northeast tip of Maine. It is 16 kilometres long and only a couple of kilometres wide. Not the largest island you'll ever visit, but F.D.R. sure did like it. That's right—the island served as a retreat for U.S. President Franklin Delano Roosevelt. It also spouts a weird tale of haunting.

The haunter in question is known as "Bingo Man." On Monday nights, the ghost of this elderly man rises from his grave and treks down to the local bingo barn! No word on who he might be, whether he's ever yelled "Bingo!" or if he pursues time-honoured bingo rituals involving chachkas, coloured dabbers or green-haired gnome dolls

LITTLE LEPREAU BEACH
LEPREAU, NEW BRUNSWICK

Leapreau, New Brunswick, is a friendly little village south of Saint John. It's a place where you can get groceries, gas or a quick lunch. Nearby, there's a provincial park with a picnic area and the pride of the area, Lepreau Falls, where the Lepreau River meanders ever lower over flat rocks until it finally roars over a rocky ledge.

Nearby is Little Lepreau Beach. It may be picturesque during the day, but visiting the beach in the depths of darkness can be a scary experience. It starts with the sounds of chains rattling in the distance, but nothing can be seen. And if you hang around until morning, you may be lucky enough to see markings in the sand that look disturbingly like those of dragging chains and huge metal balls.

What does all this mean? What's the explanation? Well, this little stretch of Atlantic beach is said to be where people suffering from cholera during an epidemic were chained together and left to die, en masse, on the beach. And apparently, they still aren't happy about it and refuse to move out. They rattle their chains…from the grave! And smoosh the beach sand from there, as well.

~ Big, Gargantuan & Ridiculously Oversized ~

If you visit Duncan, BC, just north of Victoria on Vancouver Island, you will find yourself in the locale that possesses the "World's Largest Hockey Stick and Puck." The hockey stick is 62.5 metres long and is attached to the community centre. The Government of Canada commissioned this classic kitsch of Canadiana for Vancouver's Expo 86. After the Expo ended, the stick was floated by barge from Vancouver to Duncan. No word on how the puck got there, but my hope is that it was a slapshot from the DEW Line.

~ Big, Gargantuan & Ridiculously Oversized ~

The town of Porcupine Plain, Saskatchewan, east of Saskatoon, is home to (what else?) the "World's Largest Porcupine." The town's mascot stands in a roadside park atop a wooden platform with his name on it. He's called Quilly Willy, and according to the town's web site, Quilly Willy "represents the genuine welcome all residents of Porcupine Plain extend to its visitors." Quilly Willy is nearly 4 metres tall, so let's hope his genuine welcome doesn't involve a prickly hug.

BASTION SQUARE
VICTORIA, BRITISH COLUMBIA

Bastion Square is the site of the original Fort Victoria. It's located in the heart of British Columbia's capital city. Many small shops, arts and crafts stands and restaurants frame the square. It also has several benches for catching the great view of the inner harbour, or if you're lucky, a ghost. That's right, ice cream and postcards and sprites, oh my!

Bastion Square is often called the most haunted spot in Canada's most haunted city. In Victoria's not-so-distant past, a jail was situated in the square, where executions actually took place, And, I guess, some of the executed are a little peeved at their fate, so they won't leave and like to play a little "scare the living" game.

People claim to have heard the sounds of rattling chains and are then confronted by the ghostly apparition of a man dressed in a prison uniform—black and white stripes and all. He may have been killed on his way to being executed by a prison guard who thought he wasn't moving quickly enough. And so he wanders Bastion Square today looking for justice...or the gallows, so he can be executed all proper-like.

So, if you're in the vicinity, visit Bastion Square, where you can eat, drink and be merry because you aren't a ghost!

~ Big, Gargantuan & Ridiculously Oversized ~

The "World's Largest Tin Soldier" is located at New Westminster Quay in the Vancouver-area city of New Westminster, BC. It stands almost 10 metres high and weighs in at a portly 5 tonnes—though I understand most of that is water weight. Weight Watchers has been contacted and the steel Gomer Pyle is being put on strict diet. The soldier was modelled on the Royal Engineers who founded the city of New Westminster back in 1859. He's got a bright red coat, yellow belt and black pants, and was unveiled at the Royal Westminster Regiment Armoury in July 2000. Workers and management of the BC Sheet Metal Industry built the soldier in support of the Simon Fraser Society for Community Living and their programs for children with special needs. When the big guy was moved to his permanent home at Westminster Quay, a time capsule was added, which will be opened in 2025. Gosh, I wonder if there are tin soldier accessories in it? Maybe a tin horse or a tin riding crop or maybe a big metal key they can use to wind the soldier up so he can dance a jaunty Royal Engineers jig?

Lakes and Bays and their Soggy Inhabitants

People who go to sea in ships and out on lakes in boats and generally swim and splash and float on Canadian waters…should look out!

There are mysterious creatures great and small that will scare you, rub up against you in a suggestive manner and generally make you look foolish talking about them on TV. They may even eat you or part of your dinghy. Who knew Canada had such a rich quantity of unknown, mysterious and slightly shy aquatic life that may have resided here even longer than our First Nations peoples.

British Columbia captures the title of "Sea Serpent Capital" with the creepiest waters and the most famous of these large, but shy, overgrown denizens of the deep.

OKANAGAN LAKE
BRITISH COLUMBIA

Okanagan Lake is found in one of the most beautiful regions of what is arguably the most beautiful part of Canada. Located in south-central British Columbia, Okanagan Lake is deep, long (155 kilometres) and relatively narrow. It's also the largest of the five main and interconnected lakes in the region. The area is known for its numerous sunny days, beautiful beaches and agriculture, and is one of the most abundant fruit- and wine-growing regions of the country. Hiking, biking, sailing, golf and skiing are enjoyed by residents and the tourists who flock to the area's many resorts. Sounds like the perfect place, doesn't it? But in truth, not so perfect, for a monster resides in Okanagan Lake, and he's a publicity hound.

> *The legend lives on from the Salish on down*
> *Of the deep lake they call Okanagan*
> *The monster was the pride of the demonic side*
> *And Squally Point was the place where they'd feed him...*

Now, just how famous would Okanagan Lake's monster be if Gordon Lightfoot had penned these lyrics instead of the ones about that sinking ship? I would guess probably not a lot more famous than he is today. That's because, since the 1920s, the people of this fine region have promoted the heck out of Ogopogo.

Before modern day promotion however, local Natives knew the "snake in the lake" as N'ha-A-Itk. Representations of the many-humped creature go back to pre-contact petroglyphs. The Natives also identified the creature's home specifically as the caves beneath Squally Point, and when they were out canoeing in the area, they would drop sacrifices to him in the form of chickens or pigs. Somehow the drowning of a small animal proved to them the existence of the beast.

Fast forward to 1926, when sharp local promoters latched on to an old dancehall song about the lake's serpent and rechristened the creature "Ogopogo." The BC government even got in on the Ogopogo ride that year, announcing that the new ferry being constructed for the lake would have monster-repelling devices. Later, they even put up a sign officially naming Squally Point Ogopogo's home.

Ogopogo is generally reported to be green, but he has also appeared as dark blue, black or brown. With those muted tones, he's either a fashion-conscious enigma or a true water chameleon. He's somewhere between 4.5 and 25 metres long, has numerous humps and reportedly moves at an astounding speed in an undulating motion. His head is shaped either like that of a horse or a reptile. These descriptions led a British zoologist to speculate that Ogopogo is a primitive serpentine whale of the genus *Zeuglodon*.

Ogopogo sightings are numerous, officially dating back to 1872, and continue right up to today. One of the most intriguing of those sightings involves a man swimming the length of the lake

to raise money for cancer. He claims that two Ogopogos swam underneath him for two hours. He was frightened and got out of the water. He continued his swim some time later, and the Ogopogos were apparently waiting for him like a loyal set of dogs. I guess the benign creatures like to support a good cause.

Over the years there have been sightings by "reputable" individuals as well as small and large groups of people. Ogopogo has been seen "frolicking," "chasing his tail" and "sunning himself on the beach." These are, coincidentally, the major recreational activities associated with the lake. Ogopogo has also been mistaken for a log, a sturgeon and even a beaver…or perhaps with enough alcohol, it's the other way around.

Most recently, a group of local businessmen offered a $2 million prize for proof of Ogopogo's existence. Disappointingly, no definitive proof was found, and the prize went unclaimed. There are, however, many blurred photos, inconclusive videos, and let's not forget the investigations by TV's *Unsolved Mysteries*, *Inside Edition* and the Japanese media.

CADBORO BAY
VICTORIA, BRITISH COLUMBIA

Cadboro Bay, British Columbia, is located within the Municipality of Saanich, which is part of the Greater Victoria area. The area has a Mediterranean-like climate, with warm, sunny summers and moderately wet winters. It's scenic, residential and adjacent to the University of Victoria. The bay is also known for its soggy and mysterious resident.

That's right, sleepy little Cadboro Bay is where you'll find the home of "Caddy," the saltwater counterpart to Okanagan Lake's Ogopogo. In 1933, *Victoria Times* newspaper editor, Archie Willis, latched on to the sea serpent as a local mascot and dubbed him "Cadborosaurus." The creature quickly became known by the shorter and much more adorable name "Caddy."

Caddy's emergence as mascot and "terror" came a scant seven years after Ogopogo's star took off. Mysterious coincidence or copycat marketing scheme? You be the judge.

Caddy has two large flippers and either a mane or a jagged crest. His head is either horse-shaped or camel-like, and like all sea serpents, he is long (up to 30 metres) and thin and moves at incredible speeds in an undulating motion. He has either a scary or a dopey face, depending on the sighting report…or is that the sighting reporter?

Caddy has a couple of legs up (though no actual legs) on Ogopogo in that he has a much smaller mate who goes by the equally adorable name "Amy." He's also been seriously studied by at least two scientists: Paul LeBlond from the University of British Columbia and E.L. Bousfield from the Royal British Columbia Museum. The pair gave Caddy his scientific name, *Cadborosaurus willsi*. Bousfield went so far as to notify the American Society of Zoologists that Caddy actually existed. Bet that was an interesting conversation: "A what? Who is this?"

Although Cadboro Bay is the designated home of Caddy, he has been seen up and down the coast of Vancouver Island. The similarities between Ogopogo and Caddy are so numerous that my personal theory is that they are one and the same. I will even go so far as to suggest that Ogopogo, like many other retirees, has chosen to spend his golden years in Victoria under an assumed name.

~ Big, Gargantuan & Ridiculously Oversized ~

The municipality of Moonbeam, Ontario, has built (what else?) a flying saucer as a town landmark. Get it? Moonbeam…flying saucer? Located in Moonbeam's major town of New Liskeard, the flying saucer doesn't actually fly—it's anchored to the ground. The saucer is 5.5 metres in diameter, 2.7 metres tall and has rotating flashing lights on its saucer edges, just like the real ones.

LAKE CHAMPLAIN
QUÉBEC

Often called "America's Loch Ness," Lake Champlain lies partly in Québec, partly in New York State and partly in Vermont. The lake is 200 kilometres long and quite deep, just like Loch Ness. Lake Champlain also has a monster. This one is lovably (and not terribly creatively) called "Champ."

Champ has been sighted more than 240 times. He's dark in colour, has a long neck, a couple of humps and may be as much as 8 metres long. He's probably a plesiosaur... Notice any similarities here?

As with all of our aliens of the waters, there are many photographs that prove very little. However, in 1977, a Connecticut woman named Sandra Mansi caught Champ sunning himself and snapped a very good photo with her Kodak Instamatic (remember those cameras?). Scientists studied the picture and declared it hadn't been retouched. The photo drew a lot of attention and even appeared in *Time* magazine on July 13, 1981.

There are have also been at least two scientific soundings done on the lake that showed something was there. No word on what that "something" was nor whether that which lies below the surface of Lake Champlain is considered intelligent...

~ Big, Gargantuan & Ridiculously Oversized ~

The "World's Largest Moose" stands next to the Trans-Canada Highway at the Moose Jaw Visitors Centre in Saskatchewan. He's named Mac after the late Moose Jaw alderman, Les McKenzie. Mac, the moose, not the alderman, stands nearly 10 metres tall and weighs in at a gargantuan 9000 kilograms. At that size, you must be able to see him as far away as Winnipeg.

LAC MEMPHRÉMAGOG
QUÉBEC

Lake Memphrémagog is 100 kilometres east of Montréal near Sherbrooke, Québec, and crosses the border into Vermont. The lake is 40 kilometres long, finger-like and nestled between mountains. It's a deep, cold, freshwater lake that contains another of Québec's weird lake creatures, "Memphré."

Memphré resembles Ogopogo in most respects. Memphré's got the long neck, the humps and the horse face, as well as the undulating motion and the shyness about having his picture taken.

The first European settlers encountered local First Nations people, who reportedly wouldn't swim in the lake because they were afraid of the monster. Since then, there have been well over 200 sightings, dating back to the 1800s. The local expert on the subject is a man named Jacques Boisvert. He founded an organization to study Memphré called the International Dracontology Society. He's collected much anecdotal evidence, but nothing conclusive. Darn, I thought maybe this time we had one!

If you're in the area and looking to waste some time looking for Memphré, he's said to make his home in a cave at the base of Owl's Head Mountain. Good luck!

LAKE POHÉNÉGAMOOK
QUÉBEC

Lake Pohénégamook is 60 kilometres south of Rivière-du-Loup and 250 kilometres from Québec City. It lies just north of the Québec–Maine border. The lake is 11 kilometres long and takes its name from a First Nations word meaning "mocking"…Now, we're talking!

LAKES AND BAYS AND THEIR SOGGY INHABITANTS

La bête du lac (the beast of the lake) goes by the name "Ponik." Unlike the other two Québec lake monsters, Champ and Memphré, Ponik is 100% Québecois. No cross-border Yankee serpent trash here!

Ponik, though, has seen better days. The heyday for sighting reports really peaked back in 1957 and 1958. In 1957, Ponik startled a local abbé, Leopold Plante, while he was fishing, and the abbé began promoting the existence of the creature. He said Ponik looked like "a long overturned canoe crossing the lake, leaving a wake behind."

Ponik has also been variously described as being black or brown, hairless and having some sort of "crenellation" in the middle of his back. The standard serpentine body, two to three humps, flippers and horse head have also been mentioned previously. He's also said to be about 10 metres long.

A number of studies of have been carried out, but no official study has produced evidence of a creature living in the lake. This hasn't, however, stopped the speculation about Ponik's existence or that he might actually be some form of sturgeon, plesiosaur or a giant and ancient snake.

TURTLE LAKE
SASKATCHEWAN

Turtle Lake is located in west-central Saskatchewan, 120 kilometres northwest of North Battleford and about a two-and-a-half-hour drive from Saskatoon. It's not a densely populated area, at least by human standards. The area is known for its recreational activities such as boating, fishing and golfing. The lake got its quaint name because someone thought it looked like a turtle. There are no turtles in Turtle Lake, but there are fish. Which is a good thing, because lake monsters need something to eat. And, as the theme of this chapter implies—you guessed it— there is a monster in Turtle Lake.

Tales of the monster go back to First Nations people. Their legends speak of a terror in Turtle Lake and say that people who entered his territory were never seen again.

There have been numerous sightings of the lake creature over the last 40 or more years. He's described as smooth…or scaly…with a dorsal fin…or without a dorsal fin…and his head resembles a dog…or a seahorse…or a pig. So, with this pinpoint accuracy, he could be either a plesiosaur or one of my half-cousins twice removed. He also has the requisite earth-tone coloration.

Sadly, this poor lake serpent does not have a kitschy name like Ogopogo or Champ! Perhaps a catchy name contest will eventually be had and the "Terror of Turtle Lake" will get what's coming to him, and more t-shirts can be mass-produced and sold!

~ Big, Gargantuan & Ridiculously Oversized ~

The "World's Largest Grasshopper" is located in the farming town of Wilkie, Saskatchewan, 160 kilometres west of Saskatoon. It's made of cedar, painted brown and green, and is 5.5 metres long and 1.8 metres wide. The Wilkie grasshopper was designed by local artist Byron Hansen and is based on smaller versions of grasshoppers that he is well known for making.

LAKE MANITOBA
MANITOBA

Lake Manitoba is a 200-kilometre-long, irregularly shaped lake that lies northwest of Winnipeg. It has marshy shores and is fed from Lake Winnipegosis, eventually draining into Lake Winnipeg. Winnipeg, Winnipegosis? Looks like someone was coasting when they were naming Manitoba's lakes.

Lake Manitoba is home to "Manipogo," another lake serpent very similar in size, shape and blah, blah, blah to Ogopogo (still king!). In fact, there have been reports of "animals of unclassified type" not only in Lake Manitoba, but also in Lakes Winnipeg, Winnipegosis, Dauphin, Cedar and Dirty. Speculation has been that Manipogo travels throughout the Manitoba lake system. And why not, if you've got flippers and frequent serpent miles to spare!

The most intriguing story of the elusive Manipogo involves a hoax perpetrated in 1997. The media were informed that Manipogo had been captured, killed and put up for auction by a Manitoba farmer who wanted $200,000 for it. The story quickly unravelled when the local RCMP denied that they had seen or heard anything about it. However, that did not stop various news organizations from running the story as though it was gospel.

~ Big, Gargantuan & Ridiculously Oversized ~

As you enter the town of Watson, Saskatchewan, you'll be greeted by a 7.6-metre-tall statue of Santa Claus, his right arm outstretched as if waving to you. Be polite and wave back! Watson claims to be the home of the original "Santa Claus Day," which continues to be commemorated in Watson and other copycat communities to this day. Thus, the statue is clearly apropos!

LAKE SIMCOE
ONTARIO

Lake Simcoe is an hour's drive north of Toronto. It's an oval-shaped lake with a couple of irregular fingers that jut out north, south and west. The major city on Lake Simcoe is Barrie. The lake is known for offering much recreational activity and has a scary little secret—there's a lake monster there that, depending on where he's seen, goes either by the name "Igopogo" or "Kempenfelt Kelly." Doesn't it just figure that Ontario needs two names for a creature, whereas other provinces can make do with just one?

Igopogo is, of course, a direct ripoff of Ogopogo. Kempenfelt Kelly gets his name from Kempenfelt Bay, a place on the north-west side of the lake, where the creature has often been spotted. The creature resembles Ogopogo in every respect except one— he's actually quite tiny. Igopogo Kelly has been described as being no more than 3.5 metres long.

Igopogofelt seems to move at a much more leisurely pace than other lake monsters. He's got a sense of humour, though, since many sightings involve him startling picnickers or sneaking up on unsuspecting boaters. And alcohol, I'm sure, had nothing to do with any of the encounters.

There's been speculation that Igofeltpogo Kelly is more mammalian than serpent-like. Infrequent sightings have also raised the possibility that IgoKelly-PogoFelt has passed on.

~ Big, Gargantuan & Ridiculously Oversized ~

The town of Baie-Comeau, Québec, has a life-sized statue of a man paddling a canoe. The statue doesn't represent Cartier or Champlain or even one of those *coureurs de bois*. It actually represents the town's founder, Colonel Robert McCormick, who was also the owner of the *Chicago Tribune* newspaper. The statue was erected in 1956, a year after the colonel passed away. Other "big" sites in the area are Manic-5, the world's largest multiple-arch and buttress dam, and Manic-2, the world's largest hollow-joint gravity dam. Baie-Comeau is also famous for being the hometown of Canada's former larger-than-life prime minister—Brian Mulroney.

LAKE UTOPIA
NEW BRUNSWICK

Lake Utopia is in southwestern New Brunswick, not far from the Bay of Fundy and northeast of St. George. The lake is 8 kilometres long and 3 kilometres wide and drains into the Magaguadavic River. The river was named by local First Nations tribes and may mean "River of Eels." Ominous, no? *Mais oui!* (Nice to be able to use my high-school French!)

According to one researcher, naming the river Magaguadavic apparently helps prove the existence of Lake Utopia's monster, since eels spawn at sea but return to their native lakes to live. That's what's been suggested to explain the existence of Lake Utopia's monster.

Just like Saskatchewan's Turtle Lake monster, there's been no catchy moniker attached to this one in Lake Utopia…no Utopia Tom or Uta of Utopia or even Kyle. That may be because sightings have been less frequent than some of the other serpentine lake denizens—on average only every three to five years.

There's a strange Native legend about the Lake Utopia monster chasing a canoe with its huge jaws snapping and another about it breaking through the surface ice of the frozen lake. However, like many of the other lake monsters, Utopia's is most often reported as being rather playful and docile and is most often seen sunning himself. Yep, another lazy-ass monster that likes to suntan!

For the sceptics among you, you'll be glad to hear that sceptical *Enquirer Magazine* investigated the lake. The results—they're sceptical! Actually, they're sure there's nothing there. Which I guess isn't much of a surprise coming from sceptics. As for the believers, they still believe. Good for you!

CAPE BRETON ISLAND
NOVA SCOTIA

Cape Breton is a beautiful island linked to the rest of Nova Scotia by a causeway. It's known for its friendly people, windswept coastline and majestic mountain ranges. As with many maritime communities across the globe, strange stories of the sea are ingrained.

Stories of sea serpents and lake monsters in this area have been reported for hundreds of years. There may be some eel-type monster in Lake Ainslie, for instance, but no name has been attached to it nor any marketing budget allotted to promote it.

Fishermen have been reporting encounters with strange creatures for centuries. The most recent seems to have occurred in 2003, in the cove off Point Aconi. A lobster fisherman claims to have had an encounter with a creature he thought at first was a big log. Oh, that old ruse! But it turned out to have a snake-like body, a turtle's head, smooth skin, brown coloration and was about 8 metres long. Although wary of the creature at first, the fisherman followed it for some time. The creature allegedly raised its head out of the water several times during the soggy surveillance.

The Nova Scotia Museum of Natural History couldn't say for sure what the creature was, but suggested it could be an oarfish. Oarfish have ribbon-like bodies and usually grow to 8 metres in length. Cryptozoologists debunked the explanation calling it, well…bunk. The Nova Scotia Museum of Natural History recanted, and everyone agreed they didn't know what it was. Talk about getting along. Those people on the East Coast really are friendly!

AND THE REST OF THE WEIRD AND SOGGY PLACES…

There have also been sightings of various "unexplained creatures" off the Grand Banks in Newfoundland, in Lake Erie at Kingston, Ontario (where they call him "Kingstie"), at Harrison Lake in BC, and even perhaps in Saddle Lake, Alberta. What a mosaic of a country this is!

~ Big, Gargantuan & Ridiculously Oversized ~

You'll see dinosaurs overlooking a group of small islands at the entrance to the Manicouagan Peninsula in the municipality of Ragueneau, Québec. There's a "mama" dinosaur and a "baby" dinosaur but no "papa" dinosaur. So, what gives? Is this scene a harmless bit of roadside fun or a commentary on the modern fractured family? *Mon dieu! Ce n'est pas possible!*

Interplanetary Kraft, Neither Orange Nor Individually Wrapped

One of the most fascinating subjects for me has always been anything and everything to do with UFOs, abductions and aliens. As I already mentioned in my introduction, I did, in fact, see a UFO when I was a kid. I admit it is much more a fuzzy, kid-remembered image than a solid, discernible and provable fact, but such is the stuff that the UFO phenomenon is based on.

I have studied so much UFO literature—from books to the wackiest of Internet web sites. I even once had an e-mail correspondence with an American woman who claimed to be in contact with 12 different alien races— we're talking interplanetary aliens, not the illegal types that Americans normally talk about.

Over the years, the hype, the hardcore believers and converted masses have all pushed me more towards scepticism than to belief. This is why I have, oh so cleverly, titled this chapter "Interplanetary Kraft, Neither Orange Nor ☞

Individually Wrapped." For those individually wrapped pieces of glow-in-the-dark cheese could as easily be UFOs or sites of alien abduction as most of the thousands of sighting/abduction reports filed in Canada each year.

Weird Canadian places that are related to UFOs are elusive. UFO sightings happen all over the place, in every region of the country and rarely in the same place twice. This makes my task difficult. If you want to see UFOs, apparently they most often hang out at nuclear power facilities or military installations. With the number of military bases dwindling, it becomes far more difficult to see them there year after year. However, with power consumption increasing and nuclear power production growing, it seems to me that's where to look.

I have included a couple of places in this section that count as weird UFO sighting places: Shirley's Bay, Shag Harbour and Falcon Lake. However, head for the nukes and you'll be in weird country. As well, some conveniently provided UFO sighting areas have been designated and funded by various levels of government, including St. Paul, Alberta, with its UFO Landing Pad, and Vulcan, Alberta, where a replica Starship Enterprise will welcome alien visitors of the extra-Alberta kind and the extraterrestrial kind alike.

Let's face it, the UFO thing used to be a dirty little secret, barely talked about in serious conversation and relegated to off-colour ☞

jokes and snickers behind the whackos' backs. But that is no more. The whole thing has developed from a niche market into a huge industry. And give the province of Alberta credit here, when the rest of us were still laughing, they were embracing the phenomenon full on.

Oh, and there's one more likelihood for seeing those elusive UFOs. If you live in the middle of nowhere, are out tipping cows and your name is Bob, you're bound to see one. Perhaps you'll even get to appear on Canada AM. Good luck, Bob!

PLACES TO HAVE FUN WITH UFOS

UFO LANDING PAD

ST. PAUL, ALBERTA

This, in fact, is no joke. No, really. In 1967, as one of Canada's centennial projects, the town of St. Paul, Alberta, built a landing pad for extraterrestrial and UFO visitors to our planet. I repeat: this is no joke!

In the mid-1960s, the Government of Canada encouraged all Canadian communities to undertake centennial projects to commemorate Canada's first 100 years. St. Paul put many projects in the works, but the one that garnered the most attention, and still does, is the UFO Landing Pad.

The idea for the pad actually came from W.R. Treleaven of Hamilton, Ontario, and Ken Reed of Calgary. And they actually convinced Alberta's lieutenant-governor, the Honourable Grant MacEwan, to turn the sod at the inauguration ceremony.

The round, 118-tonne pad is made out of concrete and steel and includes six 76-centimetre pylons that form the main column. It is raised above the ground and stands out...well, as a landing pad. A map of Canada, made of stones donated by each Canadian province, is embossed on the landing pad's backstop, and provincial flags are flown atop the backstop.

When the project was originally built, a time capsule was sealed into the backstop with letters addressed to Canadians from the likes of Ernest Manning. The time capsule will remain sealed until 2067, Canada's bicentennial. That will surely be an interesting "opening" ceremony.

The whole pad was completed and unveiled on June 3, 1967. Canada's Minister of Defence, Paul Hellyer, flew in by helicopter to officially open the pad. It was a joyful and wacky time, no doubt.

A sign beside the pad reads as follows: "Republic of St. Paul (Stargate Alpha). The area under the World's First UFO Landing Pad was designated international by the Town of St. Paul as a symbol of our faith that mankind will maintain the outer universe free from national wars and strife. That future travel in space will be safe for all intergalactic beings, all visitors from earth or otherwise are welcome to this territory and to the Town of St. Paul."

But St. Paul hasn't rested on its 1967 laurels. In 1993, they built a saucer-shaped structure beside the pad to serve as a tourist information booth. Then in 1996, they built an addition to the booth to house a UFO Interpretive display. The display shows actual (?) photographs of UFOs, crop circles and cattle mutilations, among other things. It also explains the various degrees of sighting reports (Close Encounter of the First Kind, Second Kind, Third Kind, etc.).

Along with the interpretive centre, the town also created and mans a toll-free UFO sighting hotline. The number is 1-888-SEE-UFOS (733-8367), for anyone who has something to report. The hotline has received reports on UFO sightings, cattle mutilations, crop circles, abductions and encounters of all kinds.

And we're not quite finished yet. St. Paul's UFO Landing Pad has attracted attention from all over the world. In fact, two of the most famous visitors to the pad were Queen Elizabeth II and the late Mother Theresa. However, there still haven't been any intergalactic visitors, though the town's collective fingers are crossed.

St. Paul is located in Alberta's Lakeland region, approximately 200 kilometres northeast of Edmonton.

~ Big, Gargantuan & Ridiculously Oversized ~

The "World's Largest Pair of Cross-Country Skis" (with poles) is located in the BC Interior town of 100 Mile House. The skis are 12 metres long and the poles are 9 metres long. They were commissioned by the ski manufacturer Karhu and dedicated by the Man-in-Motion himself, Rick Hansen, way back in 1987. The skis are located in front of the Visitor Infocentre on the west side of Highway 97. The town is also known for successfully fighting the federal government to keep their town's name from being metrically converted to 160.9344 Kilometre House. I mean, really!

VULCAN TOURISM AND TREK STATION

VULCAN, ALBERTA

Vulcan is, of course, the birth planet of *Star Trek*'s Mr. Spock. Vulcan, Alberta, is of course, yet another Alberta town that knows how to have fun and capitalize on its name in connection with a defunct, but highly popular TV show! And I say: Way to go! Or live long and prosper. And from the look of things, Vulcan will.

Vulcan has long been a farming community. The area was actually surveyed in 1910, so the town had its name long before *Star Trek* ever existed. However, it wasn't until 1998 that the Vulcan Tourism and Trek Station opened, so the question is, who is capitalizing on what's fame?

The Tourism and Trek Centre consists of a main building, which was designed to look like a landing spaceship, and the replica *Star Trek*-like starship. They've put some nifty fibre optic lighting on the centre's soffits to enhance the idea of the landing spaceship. Inside the tourism centre, the captain and the ever-friendly crew greet each and every visitor.

The tourism centre boasts *Star Trek*-related displays and a replica *Starship Enterprise* main bridge, where people can dress up in *Star Trek* costumes and have their photos taken with cardboard cutouts of *Star Trek* cast members. You can also obtain tourism information and maps of Vulcan and Vulcan County. How odd!

Clearly one of the highlights of the Tourism and Trek Centre is the replica *Starship Enterprise*. The starship is 9.4 metres long and sports the insignia "FX6 -1995-A." "FX6" is the identifier of Vulcan's airports, 1995 is the year the ship was unveiled and "A" designates the first project launched under the Science and Trek theme.

Each June, the town hosts the annual Galaxyfest and Spockdays Festival. The two events used to be separate, but I guess Starfleet can only sponsor so many events in a single green-blooded town. Last year, the actors from the *Star Trek: The Next Generation* TV show, the Klingons Gowron and Martock (Robert O'Reilly and J.G. Hertzler), were the festival's guest speakers. Apparently they killed the crowd with their version of a Klingon hip-hop song. They also answered questions from the hundreds of fans dressed as Romulans, Borg, Klingons and Ferengi. Must have been a sight for sore Betazoid eyes to see. Galaxyfest events also include fireworks (phaser fireworks, I'm guessing), bed races, an art walk and a parade.

If you want to visit the Vulcan Tourism and Trek Centre, beam yourself over to Vulcan. Better yet, drive the hour or so from either Calgary or Lethbridge. Starfleet awaits you!

PLACES FOR THE SERIOUS UFO NUT

THE WORLD'S FIRST FLYING SAUCER SIGHTING STATION
SHIRLEY'S BAY, ONTARIO

In the 1950s, the Canadian government was apparently not afraid to say that it was looking for UFOs. In fact, the government, under the guidance of the eminently respected Wilbert Smith and the Department of Transport, was not even afraid to say they'd set up the world's first officially sponsored Saucer Sighting Station, just 16 kilometres outside Ottawa in the community of Shirley's Bay. The program started in 1952 and ran for more than three and half years.

The Saucer Sighting Station was housed in a 3.6-metre square shack. It wasn't manned, but it was linked by some form of alarm system to a fully manned ionospheric station nearby. Inside the sighting station was expensive and complex equipment able to detect radio noise, magnetic fluctuations and gamma rays.

At one point in 1954, station personnel detected what they thought was a flying saucer. The bells and alarms apparently went off, and Smith and others ran outside to see what they could see. Nothing, as it turned out, because the whole area was fogged in. But this didn't stop Smith from announcing to the press that he thought he'd caught one. He was quickly reprimanded, and the project was officially shut down within the month. It was an ignominious end, to say the least. However, Shirley's Bay will always have the distinction of being the site of the world's first flying saucer sighting station.

~ Big, Gargantuan & Ridiculously Oversized ~

Pemmican Pete has been the ubiquitous mascot of Regina's summer exhibition, "Buffalo Days," since the mid-1960s. Pete is a buffalo
hunter clad in buckskins. He sports a beard and carries a rifle and
is most often seen sitting astride a giant buffalo. What else would
a buffalo hunter be doing? The Buffalo Days people had four replica
mascots built and positioned around Regina's exhibition grounds.
The 2.4-metre-tall Pemmican Pete rides his 2.1-metre-tall buffalo
buddy who's stuck on a really tall pole. When one of the original
mascots was damaged, Pete was removed and brought down from
his high post over the grounds, and people began dressing up as
Pemmican Pete and sitting astride the buffalo to have their pictures
taken. That's how the "real life" Pemmican Pete was discovered back
in the 1970s. Rollie Bourassa, one of Buffalo Days' founders, discovered a buckskin-clad fellow named Tom Doucette. Doucette was
apparently the spitting image of the mascot and went on to play
the real-life Pemmican Pete throughout the '70s, '80s and '90s.

CANADA'S ROSWELL

SHAG HARBOUR, NOVA SCOTIA

In UFO circles, the Shag Harbour incident is about as close as Canada gets to a Roswell-like incident. It involves the apparent crash of a UFO, many witnesses, government and military investigation, surveillance and strange and odd smells, sights and sounds.

The whole thing began on the night of October 4, 1967, above the waters of Shag Harbour, Nova Scotia. Shag Harbour was, and still is, a tiny fishing village at the southern tip of Nova Scotia. Just after 11:00 PM, witnesses claim to have noticed strange orange lights above the water that may or may not have numbered four and flashed in sequence. Sounds a bit like a Spielberg movie, if you ask me.

At some point, the lights turned at a 45-degree angle and dove towards the water. There may have then been a bright flash and an explosion. But whatever happened at that point, many people called the RCMP detachment at Barrington Passage to report the incident. The incident report refers only to the crash of a large aircraft into the harbour. The subject of UFOs apparently never came up.

Three officers were dispatched to the area. When the officers arrived at the shore near the crash site, they could still see the UFO with its bright yellow lights floating on the surface of the water. Apparently it was 18.3 metres in diameter and trailed some sort of yellow foam behind it on the surface of the water. It also gave off the distinctive odour of sulphur.

When government agencies and the military were asked if one of their aircraft was missing, the answer was no. Boats tried to reach the crash site, but by the time they did, the UFO had submerged and the lights had gone out. Some foam remained, however.

The next day the Canadian military sent the HMCS *Granby* to investigate. Divers spent four days in search of "something," but found nothing. And this is where the myth and folklore explode.

The whole incident was basically forgotten until the 1990s, when it took on mythic proportions and additions to the story emerged. Those additions involve underwater surveillance of the UFO over a 40-kilometre trek, a second UFO and the eventual escape of the otherworldly craft from the ocean depths. They also involve cover-up, trailing of witnesses and more murky yellow foam. Well, not more, but the whole thing might as well be covered in it.

So, if you're on Nova Scotia's south shore, have a look out over Shag Harbour. Lots of other people have.

FALCON LAKE

MANITOBA

The year 1967 seems to be a big one for weird Canadian UFO-related places. Clusters happen, I guess. Despite my scepticism and love of a laugh, there's something about the Falcon Lake incident that is both intriguing and has the ring of truth to it. Or at least it does to me.

Falcon Lake is east of Winnipeg, almost at the border of northern Ontario. On May 20, 1967, an amateur prospector from Winnipeg named Stephen Michalak found himself prospecting in Whiteshell Provincial Park. A flock of geese alerted him to the skies, where he spied two UFOs. One of the UFOs landed, while the other hovered for a time before departing the scene.

Michalak was both intrigued and a bit scared, so he stayed back for a time, sketching what he was seeing. He eventually approached the UFO and even heard voices from an open doorway, so he looked inside. However, his actions must have spooked the UFO's inhabitants, because the next thing he knew, the UFO turned, moved and sped off. But in its haste to depart, the UFO let blast go a blast of exhaust, which hit Michalak in the chest, setting his clothing on fire and leaving him with a large mark. He was forced to remove his burning clothes and suffered painful burns and illness.

Eventually, Michalak made his way back to the town of Falcon Lake and back to his home in Winnipeg, where he was treated for his burns and sickness. The RCMP got involved, interviewing Michalak several times. Tests on soil samples and Michalak's clothing came back with the result that the soil and clothes were radioactive. Well, that's weird.

And when Michalak finally took the RCMP to the landing site, they noted a semicircular barren spot, 14.6-metres in diameter, from which the naturally growing moss had some-how been removed.

The Department of National Defence marked the case "unsolved." So, this makes Falcon Lake a true government-certified weird place.

~ Big, Gargantuan & Ridiculously Oversized ~

The "World's Largest Fire Hydrant" is located in the town of Elm Creek, Manitoba, next to the fire hall. At 9 metres tall, it's more than just a kitschy photo-op for the practical people of Elm Creek—the hydrant is actually the town's water tank. For years, there have been plans to build a giant dog beside the fire hydrant, but nothing has appeared so far. I'm keeping my fingers crossed for them, though!

Odd, Mysterious
or on the Verge
of Being Offensive

*Oddities, mysteries and offensive finds, lions and tigers
and bears, oh my! No animals, actually. But these utterly
odd Canadian splunks are the things that dreams—or
nightmares—are made of. Splunks, by the way, are places
where you'll find odd, mysterious and possibly offensive
stuff. The word is new and was created by me, but
I predict it will soon be listed in Canadian dictionaries...*

*Anyway, Sam Spade may have had the mystery of the
Maltese Falcon, but he never got to consider the oddities
of root cellars, gopher holes or a horsehair-padded dance
floor. Sam missed out on the secrets of the Hammer of
Thor and mystery rocks in Saskatchewan. And the
"Spademan" never got to consider Saskatchewan's
"Land of Rape and Honey" or outhouse racing—that's
not racing to an outhouse, we're talking the actual
racing of an outhouse.* ☞

It's all here—the oddest of the odd, the most mysterious of mysteries and that thing that might offend.

And how offensive might it be to learn that secret midnight flights by the CIA are passing through a Canadian airport? We're talking terrorism suspects, no warrants and covert ops.

Who said Canadians are cold and staid and conservative? This little chapter should prove that statement wrong once and for all!

THE ODD

THE GOPHER HOLE MUSEUM
TORRINGTON, ALBERTA

In 1996, odd little Alberta (I mean that in the best possible way), opened yet another odd little attraction—the Gopher Hole Museum. The Gopher Hole Museum isn't so much a museum celebrating gopher holes, as it is a reason for someone to dress up dead gophers in costumes and pose them in a bunch of quaint little scenes. Each scene is considered a "hole." Thus, it's the Gopher Hole Museum. Get it?

Another redirection is in order here. The gophers are actually Richardson's ground squirrels, but I'm from the city, so you could tell me they are goldfish, and I'd believe you. The gopher hole scenes include: the Royal Canadian Mounted Gopher, a Gophersmith, the Reverend Gopher, a Gopher Hairdresser, Olympic Gophers and oh, so many more.

Torrington's Gopher Hole Museum has generated a great deal of controversy. Some people are apparently offended by the fact that the museum uses real, non-living gophers in their displays. Since before the museum opened, the People for the Ethical Treatment of Animals (PETA) have been urging the Gopher Hole Museum to use fake gophers instead.

The town and the museum have seen no reason to honour PETA's request. The town has huge problems with the beasts and has to off them anyhow. So, why not use what's leftover and put it on display? Or even create a silly tourist attraction. You could say it's a case of turning vinegar into wine, a negative into a positive (or road kill into a furry priest?). Anyway, the controversy probably won't soon die down, and the museum is thriving. Thanks to PETA, the museum has attracted international media attention and visitors from all over the world. You have to admit it's a pretty successful little endeavour for a minor amount of government grant money. Every little community should be so fortunate to garner such publicity and tourists.

When you visit Torrrington—and you will—you'll also see various gopher statues around the town. The largest statue is 3.7 metres tall and features an overall-clad gopher named Clem T. GoFur. You'll also notice that all the fire hydrants in town are painted to look like Clem's relatives. Go phigure!

Torrington is an hour northeast of Calgary. The Gopher Hole Museum is open daily from 10:00 AM to 5:00 PM from June 1 to September 30.

~ Big, Gargantuan & Ridiculously Oversized ~

The "World's Largest Snowman" (obviously not made of real snow) is located in Beardmore, Ontario, near Lake Nipigon. At 10.7 metres tall, it easily beats the one in Kenaston, Saskatchewan (south of Saskatoon), which also claims the title. The Beardmore snowman also comes with removable seasonal accessories: in summer, he sports sunglasses and a fishing pole; in winter, he's got a curling broom and a scarf. Snowmen are stylish to a fault!

THE ROOT CELLAR CAPITAL
OF THE WORLD
ELLISTON, NEWFOUNDLAND

I didn't even know there was such a thing as the "Root Cellar Capital of the World," let alone that it would be in Newfoundland and that they'd actually tell people about it. But, in fact, in the year 2000, Elliston declared itself the "Root Cellar Capital of the World." And no one seems to be disputing that. I'm making a bit of fun here, but this little piece of weird is taken very seriously in Elliston, which in my books makes it that much weirder.

There are apparently 135 documented root cellars in Elliston, which makes it some sort of nexus of the root cellar universe. The oldest root cellar still in use today dates back to 1839.

So, just what is a root cellar? Root cellars originated before the time of electricity—in the dark times, I guess you could say. People built these structures to keep their vegetables from freezing over the winter or to keep them cool in summer. The cellars have also been known to house homemade alcoholic beverages.

The cellars were often dug into the sides of hills or built from the ground up using rocks and sod. The newer root cellars are, however, made of concrete. If you're ever in Newfoundland, the good folks of Elliston want you to come and see their proudest attractions, the root cellars! It's a world capital, remember?

You'll find Elliston on the Atlantic Ocean, not far from Bonavista.

THE SINGING SANDS
BASIN HEAD BEACH, PRINCE EDWARD ISLAND

Generally speaking, I prefer my sand to be silent…oh yeah, and inanimate. So, that's probably why I wouldn't visit Basin Head Beach near Souris on the eastern tip of PEI. The beach is beautiful—a golden sand paradise. But as you walk along that beach, you'll think someone's following you. That's because the sand sings—more accurately, it kind of squeaks.

Scientists aren't actually sure why the sand on some beaches whistles and sings, but the squeaking phenomenon is found where quartz sand is extremely well rounded and spherical. Other squeaking, whistling, singing and even barking sand beaches have been found in the north of Wales on the Scottish island of Eigg, at a few other places along the Atlantic Coast and on the island of Kauai in Hawaii.

So if you're looking for a quiet little paradise-like beach, you'll want to avoid those and the Singing Sands of PEI. The fiddle music in the area is pretty good, but rarely does it keep time with the squeaking beach. Different unions, I guess.

~ Big, Gargantuan & Ridiculously Oversized ~

Now, what kind of gift does one get for a Manitoba town? Giant fly swatter? Big can of polar bear repellent? Maybe a town-sized parka… All good ideas, but none of them would fly for the officers and men of the soon-to-be-closed Canadian Forces Base Gimli. In true flyboy fashion, they gave the town of Gimli one of their T-33 Silver Star jets. Apparently in the move, they ended up with a spare. The base closed in 1971, and the "T-Bird" was stuck on top of a concrete pillar at the south end of First Avenue. Colonel Jim Dunlop formally presented the T-33 to the town of Gimli on July 17, 1971. I wonder how he wrapped it?

THE IGLOO CHURCH
INUVIK, NORTHWEST TERRITORIES

Officially, it's called Our Lady of Victory Roman Catholic Church, but throughout the Arctic, it's simply known as the Igloo Church. And why is it called the Igloo Church? Well, it's a church that's shaped like an igloo. Duh!

Brother Maurice Larocque and Father Joseph Adam designed the Igloo Church in 1958. Using largely volunteer labour, it took two years to build the structure, which opened in 1960. The church is nearly 23 metres in diameter, circular and 21 metres tall. It's also topped by a dome with a cupola and cross.

And the big question—why is it shaped like an igloo? Largely to keep from melting the permafrost, which if it did melt would cause the building to shift. The Igloo Church was designed and built with a double shell and sits on a bowl of gravel that's set into the ground, which apparently overcomes the permafrost issue.

It's innovative, functional, worshipful and one of the most photographed structures in the Arctic! It's no inukshuk, but it's outstanding nonetheless.

Inuvik is 3298 kilometres north of Edmonton, Alberta. If you're heading that way, I'd suggest you go by plane.

DANCELAND
MANITOU BEACH, SASKATCHEWAN

A place called Danceland that's located at the edge of a Saskatchewan lake doesn't sound so strange. In fact, I went back and forth on whether to include this one or not. However, when I started talking to people about it, their expressions were full of puzzlement, and that's when I knew the place was definitely weird.

Danceland is known as the "Home of the World Famous Dance Floor Built on Horsehair." Horsehair, you say? I do.

When the place was built way back in 1928, the maple hardwood floor was laid atop two subfloors with 15-centimetre rolls of horsetail (horsehair) wrapped in burlap sandwiched in between. The 15-centimetre layer of horsehair allows the floor to give up to 4 centimetres and dancers to almost glide across the 465 m² dance floor. Danceland also has other advantages such as its arched roof, which gives it great acoustics.

When Danceland was built, there were three similar halls in North America. They've all since been demolished. Danceland, with its horsehair-cushioned floor, remains unique. And nothing, apparently, compares to it for dancing on!

Danceland is open year round and is located 113 kilometres southeast of Saskatoon in Watrous, Saskatchewan.

COCHIN LIGHTHOUSE
COCHIN, SASKATCHEWAN

The only lighthouse in Saskatchewan is located in Cochin. And, as one might likely predict of a land-locked province, the Cochin Lighthouse serves no real seafaring purpose. It overlooks both Cochin and Jackfish Lakes from a narrow isthmus between the two. It provides great views for tourists as well.

The Cochin Lighthouse sits atop Pirot Hill. More than 150 steps lead up the hill to the base of the lighthouse. The structure is almost 12 metres tall, painted white and octagonal in shape. The lighthouse also has the requisite rotating beacon that can be seen for miles around.

You'll find Cochin nestled amongst rolling hills and scenic lakes, just 30 kilometres north of North Battleford in, where else, north-central Saskatchewan.

HÔTEL DE GLACE
LAKE ST. JOSEPH, QUÉBEC

Each January, just 30 minutes west of Québec City, you can slip and slide into North America's only ice hotel. Open from January to April, the Hôtel de Glace is made entirely of ice (360 tonnes) and snow (11,000 tonnes) There are 34 rooms than can accommodate a total of 84 people each frigid night. If you do the math, that's a little more than two people per room. Clearly some icy Québecois fun is going on in the *chambres*.

The architecture of the hotel changes each year, as does the unique and original ice artwork and ice furniture found inside. The hotel's walls are over a metre thick, and the ceilings are 5.5 metres high, keeping the inside temperature hovering somewhere between a balmy –2 to –5°C. There's a bar, a dance club and a chapel included in the icy *pension* for those wishing to consume an icy cold beverage, boogie or get married.

Just in case you're wondering, the ice hotel does, in fact, also include bathroom facilities… Apparently they are heated, and we say thank gawd to that! I mean, can you imagine a midnight pee where you go "whee" because it's so icy?

~ Big, Gargantuan & Ridiculously Oversized ~

The "World's Largest Fiddle" used to be 7.3 metres tall in Cavendish, Prince Edward Island. The fiddle is still in Cavendish, but its "world's largest" status has been usurped by the 16.8-metre-tall fiddle in Sydney, Nova Scotia. "Big Ceilidh Fiddle," as it is officially known, is owned by the Sydney Ports Corporation and was built to capture the attention of visitors. As well, a 4-metre-high fiddle commemorates the great Don Messer in his home-town of Harvey, New Brunswick. Clearly the Maritimes aren't fiddling around with their big fiddles!

THE MYSTERIOUS

MYSTERY ROCKS
SASKATCHEWAN

About a 45-minute hike from Fort Walsh in Cypress Hills Interprovincial Park, there is an odd formation of rocks that has mystified folks and defied explanation. Giant rocks appear to be fitted together to form a kind of road or wall. But no one seems to be able to explain how the rocks got there. They may even have been there for thousands of years, which just adds to the mystery.

People, including scientists, have been debating the origin of the rocks, and theories range from a geological anomaly to an ancient civilization and even to alien or UFO construction. So far, no solid explanations have been found.

Some people think the rock formations have similarities to the mysterious underwater formation called the Bimini Road in the Bahamas or look somewhat like the giant interconnected rocks found at Machu Picchu in Peru. But again, how did the rocks get there? The mystery continues and is not likely to be solved anytime soon.

The rocks are actually located on private property, so if you want to see them you'll have to ask permission at Fort Walsh.

Cypress Hills Interprovincial Park is located in southwestern Saskatchewan, near the Montana border. The visitor centre is located in Val Marie, about 120 kilometres south of Swift Current.

THE HAMMER OF THOR
PAYNE RIVER, UNGAVA, QUÉBEC

In far northeastern Québec, just north of Payne Bay, there stands a 3.3-metre-tall obelisk that looks like a crude hammer. It was discovered in the 1960s, but has actually been there for longer than anyone in the area can remember.

The Inuit don't claim it as theirs. In fact, they say it predates them. Although there is no proof, the "Hammer of Thor," as it's been called, has been attributed to Europeans—the Norse, to be more specific. It's been held up as evidence of Viking occupation of the Ungava region 1000 years ago.

Others claim the Hammer of Thor could be Inuit in origin or possibly Scottish. The debate rages, but conclusive evidence is elusive. The Inuit continue doing their thing on the Ungava, and life goes on whether Thor's Hammer has a maker or not.

DEFINITELY ON THE VERGE OF BEING OFFENSIVE

THE LAND OF RAPE AND HONEY
TISDALE SASKATCHEWAN

Tisdale, Saskatchewan, is known as "The Land of Rape and Honey." No, it's not a slogan that celebrates a heinous act—though it sure sounds like it does! The town's slogan is actually in reference to the fact that the community produces large quantities of both rapeseed or "rape" (now known as canola) and about 10% of Canada's honey. And that's how they got the slogan "The Land of Rape and Honey."

I understand that the people of northeastern Saskatchewan are practical, straightforward and shoot from the hip, but what that slogan lacks in subtlety, it more than makes up for in its fresh-faced, naïve offensiveness!

~ Big, Gargantuan & Ridiculously Oversized ~

The town of Kimberley, BC, is the home of North America's largest free-standing cuckoo clock. The Rocky Mountain town was already known for its Bavarian theme when the clock was originally built back in 1972. Instead of a cuckoo bird popping out on the hour, Happy Hans, a strange and demonic (just kidding!) bearded figure yodels each hour. If you can't wait for the top of the hour, you can drop a quarter in the clock and Happy Hans will emerge a-yodelling. The clock and Happy Hans are located at the Platzl Mall downtown.

COVERT CIA FLIGHTS
ST. JOHN'S INTERNATIONAL AIRPORT, NEWFOUNDLAND

With growing concern in European countries about covert CIA flights spiriting unnamed and perhaps illegally kidnapped persons to covert internment camps and information retrieval sites, Canadians woke up in November 2005 to discover that our airports may be being used in similar ways.

Canadian press reports identified a 40-seat turboprop landing in St. John's, Newfoundland. It was a private plane registered to Devon Holding and Leasing Inc. of Lexington, North Carolina—a company that has been linked to the CIA. The turboprop flew in from Iceland, made a stop in St. John's, travelled to Manchester, New Hampshire, and then to its final destination, Johnston County Airport in Smithfield, North Carolina—an airport that is thought to be a centre for covert American air operations.

Clearly, there's definite proof about the flights and their alleged covert nature. There's also a lot of circumstantial evidence mounting. Only time will tell how offended Canadians will be at the idea that their airports are being used as a weird stopover for mysterious CIA flights. This is especially true in the light of the Maher Arar case and inquiry.

If I Can Celebrate There,
I Can Celebrate Anywhere

It's official!

*All the ballots are in, and the first annual winner of the
Provincial or Territorial Award of Distinction with
Regard to Short-Term Weirdness—aka Crazy Canadian
Festivals—is New Brunswick. That's right, that quiet
little Maritime gem; that beguiler of bilingualism; that
place sandwiched between Maine, Québec, PEI
and Nova Scotia.*

It's a winner!

*Why? Well, New Brunswick is home to festivals cele-
brating molluscs, Brussels sprouts, fiddleheads, giant
pumpkins, chocolate, dory boats and peat moss.
That is one eclectic mix!*

*Ontario may have albino woodchucks and squirrels of
both the white and black variety; Saskatchewan may* ☞

have the Duck Derby and Chicken Chariot Races. Hey, Newfoundland even has the "Root Cellar Capital of Canada." But New Brunswick's mix of food, fun and frolic puts it way ahead of the rest of us.

So, let's hoist one on high for New Brunswick and proclaim: Spem reduxit ("Hope was restored")—that's the provincial motto, don't ya know!

FESTIVAL PROVINCIAL DE LA TOURBE
LAMÈQUE, NEW BRUNSWICK

Lamèque lies on the tip of New Brunswick's Acadian Peninsula. It's a small community of about 1600 people. The area has an eco-park nearby, some pretty good campgrounds and great scenery. None of this makes Lamèque particularly weird. What does make Lamèque, at least in the short term, particularly weird is the Festival provincial de la tourbe.

And I say, where better to have the Festival provincial de la tourbe than Lamèque, New Brunswick. Since Lamèque is the province's capital de la tourbe. So, just what is the Festival provincial de la tourbe? It's a peat moss festival, of course. *Mon dieu!*

Lamèque lies at the very northeastern tip of New Brunswick, and its moist climate and flat terrain make it perfect for growing peat moss. In fact, New Brunswick is the second largest world exporter of the moss known as peat. During the festival, you can visit the peatlands, wave to the peat, act like peat and even pet the peat. I wonder how many locals are named Peat? Or Pete?

Apparently the locals take their harvest celebrations seriously. A highlight of the festival is the way people decorate their homes, offices and harvesting areas with bales of peat. I'm imagining giant doilies made of peat moss, or perhaps a peat moss dragon, or even a peat-like mollusc named Peat! But let's hope the Lamèque decorators don't do what my cousin Bill does with his Christmas lights. I mean, they're up all year round. I bet if you do that with peat, it starts to get a bit musty…for peat's sake!

The festival takes place each July.

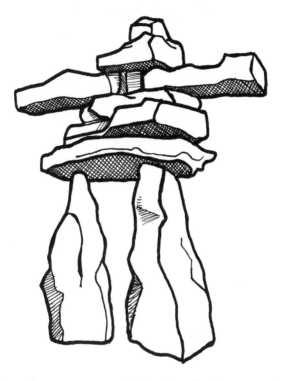

~ Big, Gargantuan & Ridiculously Oversized ~

Inukshuks are quickly becoming the most ubiquitous symbol of Canada. They may soon rival long-heralded symbols such as the moose, beaver and maple leaf. Perhaps there should be a contest, or even a cartoon reality show in which Inukshuk, Moose, Beaver and Maple Leaf duke it out in goofy, pointless contests with the winner becoming Canada's official symbol, sign and mascot…or maybe not. However, inukshuks are everywhere. Two—a male and a female, if there is such a thing—in Newmarket, Ontario; a squat-looking one in Marmora, Ontario; an extremely fat one in Collingwood, Ontario; a very large one in Vancouver, BC; a tall, sinewy one in Hay River in the Northwest Territories; and the grand-daddy of them all, a very tall one at Rankin Inlet, Nunavut. The Rankin Inlet one is large enough, in fact, for an average-height man to stand comfortably between its legs. That photo-op alone has got to be worth the trek to Rankin Inlet!

FESTIVAL DES CHOUX DE BRUXELLES
ROGERSVILLE, NEW BRUNSWICK

Rogersville is a community of about 1300 people located 100 kilometres north of Moncton and 35 kilometres south of Miramichi. According to the region's tourism materials, it offers guests "a panoply of events, historical sites to visit, plus great places to stay and eat." A panoply, huh? Read on... You can relax at Parc Mille Pas (Park of 1000 Footsteps), visit the Trappist Fathers 5 kilometres north of the town or head to the town in the summer for its big and weird festival celebrating the Brussels sprout.

Yuck!

What in gawd's name would make anyone, anywhere, anytime celebrate Brussels sprouts? I apologize to the good people of Rogersville, but this is one vegetable-like substance that I just cannot abide! I know they're supposed to be full of cancer-fighting vitamins, but the only thing I can think of doing with them is packing them into a blunderbuss and firing them at the enemy coming over the hill. This, apparently, is not one of the activities at the Festival des choux de Bruxelles.

Festival activities include breakfasts and barbecues. It just gets better and better! Sprouts on the barbecue and for breakfast! I'll bet there's some form of sprout shake involved. Perhaps they could contact the good folks of Lamèque (see previous weird place) and top it all off by adding a fashion show in which all the dresses include a sprout motif with a peat fringe!

Other activities at the sprout festival include a mini-sprout pageant (I'm seeing a portly version of the Jolly Green Giant), a treasure hunt (oh, I can't wait to line up to find the golden sprout), sprout dances, sprout bingo, sprout bike and car rallies, a sprout strongman competition and the always popular sprout parade.

What about a good tossing event? You know what I mean, like in the village of Buñol in Spain, where they pelt each other with ripe tomatoes. Think about it! The festival would build up to the great sprout rout, where teams grab handfuls of the tiny cabbage-like chokers and whip them at each other until everyone is black and blue from the green… And then I never have to taste another one of them in my life.

It's starting to sound a little more fun, don't ya think?

The Festival des choux de Bruxelles takes place annually during the last week of July.

~ Big, Gargantuan & Ridiculously Oversized ~

Sundial Folly is located at the foot of York Street in Harbour Square Park West in Toronto and is oft used as a meeting place or point of reference. People call it "that cracked egg thing," the "concrete ball" or "that round thing over there." It's made up of a ramp leading into a 6.7-metre-diameter hollow concrete sphere with a 1-metre piece removed from bottom to top on the harbour side. This harbour-side cut allows sunlight into the sphere and frames a view of the inner harbour and the Toronto Islands. There is also a cascading wall of water beside the orb and a circulating pool beside and inside it. The whole thing kind of looks like Mork from Ork just landed and his egg ship is sinking into the harbour because he forgot to shut the door. No, really. Picture it. Sundial Folly was unveiled in 1995 and was the first project of two talented and enterprising architecture grads fresh out of the University of Waterloo. Their winning design beat out 144 other proposals, some of them from well-known and established artists. That's got to hurt! The unique sculpture has been used for many things, including a homeless shelter, peeing hut, teenage drinking place and, my absolute favourite, the stage for a 1999 performance piece featuring a dancer, a mezzo-soprano and musicians playing clarinet and hurdy-gurdy. Folly, indeed!

FESTIVAL DES MOLLUSQUES
BOUCTOUCHE, NEW BRUNSWICK

The Mi'kmaq originally called the New Brunswick town of
Bouctouche "Chebooktoosk," which meant "big little harbour." The town dates back to 1785, when François and
Charlitte LeBlanc carved a cross in a tall pine tree, setting the
symbolic stage for making the banks of the Chebooktoosk
their home. It's large for a small port, but too small to be a
large one—the Mi'kmaq clearly knew what they were talking
about. The town is located where the Bouctouche River
empties into the Northumberland Strait. It's noted for its
silken shores, as the birthplace of that giant of East Coast
business, K.C. Irving, and for the Festival des mollusques.

That's right, a festival of molluscs. A festival celebrating all
that is mollusc, mollusc-like and mollusc to be.

And for the $250 prize: What is a mollusc? Anyone?

Answer: According to the Oxford dictionary, molluscs are
any invertebrate of the phylum Mollusca, having a soft body
and usually a hard shell… So, does that help? What we're
talking about here is slugs, snails, oysters, mussels, clams,
scallops, squid and octopi.

Every July, the tiny village of Bouctouche sees an influx of
visitors, who are basically there to sample and devour the great
bounty of molluscs that New Brunswick has to offer. In 2006,
the 31st anniversary of the festival will include lobster boils,
beer gardens, races, fireworks, a really big parade and, of
course, the festival's highlight, the Pageant des guidounes.
Guidounes is, of course, a slang word in French for "tramps,"
so I suspect the "Pageant of Tramps" is some weird and wild
thing to see! Other highlights include a strongman competition, bluegrass music and country fiddlers.

You can get a sampling of true Acadian cuisine with the infamous *poutine râpée*, which is, of course, grated, raw and mashed potatoes wrapped around fresh pork. Not terribly mollusc-related, but how many molluscs can one devour? No really, how many? Anyone have an estimate?

The Festival des mollusques takes place in mid-July. Bouctouche is halfway between Shediac and Miramichi along Route 11 on New Brunswick's beautiful and scenic East Coast.

~ Big, Gargantuan & Ridiculously Oversized ~

As if a town having the name Goobies, Newfoundland, isn't enough of a tourist draw, in front of a local Irving Big Stop Gas station stands a giant moose named Morris. Presiding over the number 210 intersection, Morris stands 3.5 metres tall and is 3 metres long. He was built as a tourist attraction and to remind people to be mindful of moose while driving. Fatalities from moose-car-people encounters are more than a little common in these parts.

THE FIDDLEHEAD FESTIVAL
FREDERICTON, NEW BRUNSWICK

Let's face it, capital cities in every province are a bit off-kilter. They have their own way of doing things. They dance to their own drummer, to put a clichéd, yet positive spin on it. Or at least that's the take if you're someone not living in a capital city. So why should New Brunswick's capital, Fredericton, be any different? Well…it's not.

Fredericton has been home to notorious American traitor Benedict Arnold, sports a "little nude dude" atop its City Hall Fountain and was the place where the "railway flanger" was invented. That's a sort of a snowplow-clearing device for tracks.

But in my mind, the weirdest aspect of Fredericton is its middle of May festival celebrating the unassuming little fiddlehead…That's right! Each year, the St. Mary's First Nation celebrates the fiddlehead. Fiddleheads, you know, are those highly perishable young fronds of the ostrich fern. This is all new to me! I've never had one! Didn't even know what they looked like before I did my research. But apparently the tightly curled green shoots are picked before their leaves unfurl. I'm from the city, so I have no idea what all of this means.

Anyway, the fiddlehead is a symbol of the Wolastoqiyik along the St. John River. The Fiddlehead Festival includes a whole lot of fiddlehead eating, a fiddlehead dance, great moments in fiddlehead history and fiddlehead stories. Like the one about the two fiddleheads who go into a bar and pick a fight with a Brussels sprout, a mollusc and some peat…

THE WIARTON WILLIE FESTIVAL
WIARTON, ONTARIO

Wiarton is a small and more than pleasant town located on an inlet of Georgian Bay at the southern end of Ontario's Bruce Peninsula. The town has a population of about 2300 and was incorporated as a village in 1880. The community originally thrived on the success of its lumber industry, but is now known for great area beaches and tourism.

And in this quaint little slice of Canadiana, a strange little annual event takes place. In the dead of winter, a guy dressed to the nines and standing next to another guy in a white groundhog costume reaches into the town-sponsored den of the famous White Woodchuck, Wiarton Willie, pulls Willie from his snug-as-a-bug-in-a-rug den, hoists him high into the air and hopes the pink-eyed little albino can give some indication as to whether he sees his shadow or not. I don't know—I think this annual ritual definitely falls under the "weird" heading…way weird!

Wiarton may be the location of the granddaddy of all weird Canadian festivals—the Wiarton Willie Festival—or as it is known to most of us in North America, Groundhog Day (February 2). Wiarton is 240 kilometres northwest of Toronto, which puts it in a good position for people from southern Ontario to flock there for the annual event. Ka-ching!

They've been celebrating Groundhog Day in Wiarton since 1956. Early groundhog prognosticators were named Grundoon, Sandoon and Muldoon, but were rather ordinary as groundhogs go.

Upon the arrival of the first Wiarton Willy in the 1980s, things really heated up for this weird festival. The first Wiarton Willie, as well as his successors, have all been albino groundhogs. That's right—they have white fur and pink eyes and can't see too well, which is interesting considering that W.W.'s main job is to look for his shadow once a year. Oh, the stress of it all! Sounds like a government job.

It may actually be a bit strenuous, considering that the first Wiarton Willie died tragically just before the festival in 1999. W.W. number one was replaced that year by a stuffed, reasonable facsimile of himself. Since then, they've kept two Wiarton Willies on hand just in case a tragedy befalls one of them.

The Wiarton Willie Festival actually runs for two weeks and includes hockey tournaments, dances, parades, snooker tournaments, Monte Carlo night, a fish fry and a circus.

The big question? How accurate is Wiarton Willie in his predictions of a truncated winter? Well, about the same as all the groundhog psychics. In general, groundhogs are correct less than 40% of the time. Neither America's Punxsutawney

Phil, Manitoba's Brandon Bob, Alberta's Balzac Billy or Nova Scotia's Shubenacadie Sam do any better. In 2006, Wiarton celebrated the 50th anniversary of its white-woodchuck-centred festival. I'll bet a good time was had by all!

~ Big, Gargantuan & Ridiculously Oversized ~

The self-proclaimed "Sunflower Capital of Canada," Altona, Manitoba, is also the home of the "World's Largest Painting on an Easel." Not surprisingly, the painting is a replica of one of Vincent Van Gogh's sunflower paintings. The easel is 25 metres tall, and the reproduction painting is 7 metres wide by 10 metres tall. This was the first completed giant easel erected as part of the Van Gogh Project. The intent of the project is to erect similar giant replicas all over the world. The second was erected in Emerald, Australia. A third is being constructed in Goodland, Kansas, and others are being discussed for South Africa and Japan.

CHICKEN CHARIOT RACES
WYNYARD, SASKATCHEWAN

Wynyard is the self-proclaimed "Chicken Capital of Western Canada." I guess *Harrowsmith* magazine doesn't have a category for this, so the town had to proclaim it for itself. It's also because the town's processing plant is known for raising and doing other things to a whole heck of a lot of chickens. The town proper has a population of fewer than 2000 people and is located 150 kilometres west of Yorkton, Saskatchewan. Wynyard was first settled by Icelanders and is named for the English family of the wife of a railroad official. She must have been something to have her family's name on the town and not his. It's a quiet town full of typically hard-working Saskatchewanites who once a year blow the lid off, get a little funky and do some odd, odd things to chickens…other than sell them to Colonel Sanders.

Each June, the Wynyard Carnival plays host to the annual Chicken Chariot Race. I have to say, I think this one has to be seen to be believed.

I chatted with a former Kinsmen (the Wynyard Kinsmen run the event) named Harold Wasylenka. He described the whole chicken-lickin' good proceedings for me. There are four lanes per heat, all separated by Plexiglas runners. A single chicken pulls each chariot. I asked if chickens need training to pull chariots. Harold told me that some people think the chickens need training. However, he says, if you attach something to the back of a chicken, it wants to run! Practical advice from a Saskatchewan native! Chickens, so I've been told, aren't that bright. And they are easily frightened. The record for the fastest race is somewhere in the vicinity of 20 seconds. And with a course length of about 15 metres, the poultry is flying like s*** through a goose.

DUCK DERBY
LUMSDEN, SASKATCHEWAN

Lumsden is a town of about 1600 people situated just 30 kilometres northwest of Regina, Saskatchewan. The town has a lot to offer, including an arena, a petting zoo and the nearby Last Mountain Provincial Park, which recreates a former 19th-century fur-trading post. In 2002, *Harrowsmith Country Life* magazine named Lumsden one of Canada's top 10 prettiest towns. In 2003, the same magazine named Lumsden Saskatchewan's prettiest town. Seems this pretty little town is getting a little greedy with the *Harrowsmith* accolades, don't ya think? But that may just be my jealousy talking, since I'm originally from Hamilton.

But with all this prettiness, there must be something else going on—something, odd, unusual or perhaps even a bit weird? Yeah, I'd call the annual Duck Derby weird!

And just what the heck is a Duck Derby? Well, unlike Saskatchewan's equally famous Wynyard Chicken Chariot Races, the Lumsden Duck Derby does not involve actual animals. Well, not living, breathing animals, anyhow. Basically it involves thousands of rubber duckies drifting down a kilometre-long course on the Qu'Appelle River. Say what?

Okay, each year, veteran "Duckettes" (people dressed up as duck mascots) sell $5 tickets. Each ticket buys a rubber ducky for the race. On race day, a parade assembles that each year resembles less and less a race to the post—like with the Kentucky Derby.

Following the parade, everyone gathers at the river's edge. A large metal cage is hoisted into the air, and then the cage is opened and thousands of ducks spill out. The ducks race, or more accurately, float really slowly, to the finish line. The first 10 ducks to cross the line are the winners, and each corresponding sponsor wins a prize. Races have ended in less than 50 minutes. However, they've also taken as along as five hours.

The whole fun and ridiculous derby was started to help pay for the town's arena $1.5 million arena. That's been paid off since 1998, so now the funds go to other fun projects. A duck derby wins the day. Charity casinos indeed!

The Duck Derby takes place each year on Labour Day.

YUKON RIVER BATHTUB RACE
YUKON RIVER, WHITEHORSE TO DAWSON, YUKON

So what can one say about the Yukon River? It's definitely long—2300 miles and tied with the Mississippi/Missouri as the second-longest river in North America. Only the Mackenzie is longer. Most of the river lies in Alaska and is navigable by ships from Whitehorse to the Bering Sea, though the Dawson to Whitehorse part is only navigable by smaller ships. The river is frozen over for more than six months of the year, leaving little time for wet and wild fun and frolic. Which brings us to the weird part.

The annual Yukon River Bathtub Race has been dubbed the longest and toughest bathtub race in the world. At 782 kilometres, the race traverses the Yukon River from Whitehorse to Dawson City in mid-May. The race celebrates its 15th anniversary in 2006.

Competitors are called tubbers. Some of the craft less resemble bathtubs than small speedboats, though according to the official rules, each craft must conform to the general shape and design of an old-style edge bathtub.

The promotional material for the 12th annual race explains the race's history this way: "Once upon a time, a very bored northern man looked upon his equally bored northern wife and said, 'Let's say we get all the boys together and race bathtubs down the Yukon River!?!?…' She replied, 'Whatever…'"

The race starts in Whitehorse, apparently "at the crack of 9(ish) and sends a dozen or so of the world's most adventurous souls down the Yukon River in 5-foot x 3-foot bathtubs!" Or so says the web site for the race. On the first day, tubbers traverse the Five Finger Rapids, and their day ends in McCabe Creek with a mandatory shower and barbecue. No word on whether the shower and barbeque come as a combo unit.

The second day of the competition sees the tubbers completing their trek and crossing the soggy finish line in Dawson City. In Dawson, tubbers are cheered on by crowds, copious drinks are served and thousands of dollars in prizes are awarded. The first-ever race took 33 hours to complete. Now it's a bit shorter, but no less fun!

THE GREAT KLONDIKE INTERNATIONAL OUTHOUSE RACE
DAWSON, YUKON

Dawson lies on the bank of the Yukon River near where it meets the Klondike. Formerly known as Dawson City, the community grew out of a marshy swamp after the discovery of gold in Bonanza Creek in 1896. It became the largest city in Canada west of Winnipeg in a scant two years, with 40,000 inhabitants. The town was founded by a former prospector named Joe Ladue, who figured out that merchants prospered more in gold camps than did prospectors. The town was the capital of Yukon from 1898 to 1952, when Whitehorse got the nod. Since then the population has declined, but the settlement still retains a hardcore citizenry of about 2000 people. And these hardcore citizens are known for their sense of fun, their love of laughter and an odd little event.

Each Labour Day, the good folks of Dawson embark on a tradition of merriment, frolic and…ummmmm, privy-riding.

Competitors are tasked with building their own outhouse, or renting one from the Klondike Visitors Association. Next, five-person teams decorate their private privies to perfection, and then race the outhouses around a 3-kilometre course. Four of the team members are involved in the pushing. Of the outhouse, that is. The fifth member of the team is the designated sitter. That's right—sitter! The pushers carry or push the privies up and down hills, through gravel and across paved surfaces, all in the hope of winning a fortune in toilet paper. Actually, there are cash prizes. Not sure about the toilet paper.

Some past innovations in the decorating challenge have included: "The Whizzer of Oz" with Dorothy, Toto and the rest of the gang, and four prison guards pushing an O.J. Simpson look-alike in "Canned Juice." Get it? (O.J. Simpson's nickname used to be Juice.) And when you're a prisoner, you're often said to be in the "can," which is also a term used to describe an outhouse. These people are fun!

~ Big, Gargantuan & Ridiculously Oversized ~

An hour east of Edmonton, on the Yellowhead Highway, you'll discover the town of Vegreville, Alberta. Vegreville is famous for having the "World's Largest Pysanka." A pysanka is, of course, the Ukrainian word for Easter egg. And a large percentage of the population in Vegreville is descended from Ukrainian immigrants. So why not build the world's largest pysanka in 1974 to commemorate the 100th anniversary of the Royal Canadian Mounted Police? Why not, indeed? And why not mount a Mountie atop the egg? Because it's just silly, that's why…and rude! The good people of Vegreville did not add the Mountie, but they did build the pysanka for the RCMP centennial. The giant pysanka is not just famous for being big—though it is 7 metres long and 5.5 metres in diameter and stands 9.4 metres tall from base to top. It's famous also for its beauty and for achieving nine mathematical, architectural and engineering firsts. I won't bore you with those, but suffice it to say a computer scientist from the University of Utah—Ronald Resch—was brought in to design the pysanka and did so by being the first person to do a computer model of an egg. The pysanka rests on a rather heavy base that allows it to turn in the wind like a weather vane. Queen Elizabeth II and the Duke of Edinburgh visited the pysanka on their royal visit in 1978. Prince Philip was heard to say: "I'd like to see the blood sausage that goes with that, eh Liz!" Just kidding. But it does sound like something he'd say, eh?

SNOWKING WINTER FESTIVAL
YELLOWKNIFE, NORTHWEST TERRITORIES

I think when most people in Canada think of Yellowknife they think of cold…of snow…and of ice… Most of us also know that Yellowknife is the capital of the Northwest Territories and the only city in the territory with more than 19,000 residents. Geographically speaking, Yellowknife is situated on the north shore of Great Slave Lake. Something many people may not know is that Yellowknife got its name from the copper knives used by First Nations people who moved into the area in the 1800s. But let's get back to the cold and the ice and the weirdly long winter.

SnowKing says: "Winter is not weird." Okay, but it is damn cold, especially on the ice of Great Slave Lake. But each year for "ought 10 or more" (grizzled 1890s prospector talk for "about 10 or more"), his Majesty SnowKing has built a castle on the ice of Great Slave Lake and celebrated the season in wacky fashion, which makes it all a bit weird, unique, interesting, odd and fun! They start building SnowKing's castle in December or January, even though the festival doesn't start until March. Must be some castle!

I asked SnowKing to give me some details about his castle, but he wasn't giving anything away. "How the castle is built must be a guarded secret, and you can't handle the responsibility until you've spent time in the quarry cutting blocks," his Majesty proclaimed. For more details, SnowKing said I had to convince my publisher to shell out for a return air ticket and hotel for a week so I could be on "ground zero," learning at the elbow of the master—that would be SnowKing. Actually, the whole thing sounds like a hoot, so who knows, I may just show up this year. I mean, if it's good enough for Rick Mercer and the *Monday Report*?

SnowKing's festival includes events like the Royal Puppet Theatre, the annual Peter Gzowski Invitational Golf Tournament, SnowKing's Royal Ball (with orbs, sceptres and ladies-in-parkas-in-waiting, no doubt) and the Frozen Dog Film Festival, which I hope is not a film festival chronicling the freezing of a dog. SnowKing is always looking for sponsors and accepting bookings for the Royal Icy SnowKing Chapel. Indeed, winter is not weird. But I have to say I think SnowKing is a bit. And good for him!

~ Big, Gargantuan & Ridiculously Oversized ~

It's a Bigfoot! It's an ape! It's my uncle Mel in a diaper smoking a cigar?! Well, the pictures of this roadside Sasquatch in Vermilion Bay, Ontario (west of Dryden), could be any of the above. I have no idea who the artist was, and I'm betting he wants to keep it that way. The—for the sake of argument, we'll call it "Bigfoot"—Bigfoot is 5.5 metres tall and sits on the Trans-Canada Highway in front of a gas station. And he looks angry, my friends! His arms are outstretched, and his thumbs reach into the sky. That's why some people think he's hitchhiking. I personally think his hands form a rude gesture, but he's a Bigfoot and has gotten the fingers mixed up. There is apparently a speaker inside the statue that allows the gas station's owners to mess with people's heads by having Bigfoot talk to them. Oh yeah, and I'll bet they're all fooled into thinking the Bigfoot mutant is real!

A Crater, a Ring
or a Glowing Orb

Some of the weirdest places we've ever encountered are, alas, no longer with us. They are relegated to pictures and memories and remembrances of better times. (Cue the violins.)

However, their impact on the weirdness that is Canada is not forgotten. And speaking of forgotten, we mustn't forget those places of folklore, myth and delusion that never were, that might have been or that perhaps were placed on a different plane of existence. Read on...

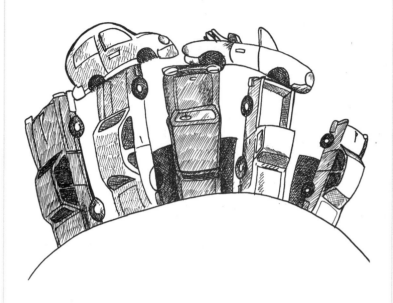

AUTOHENGE
OSHAWA, ONTARIO

Like the dawn of a new age, Autohenge rose on the grassy knoll of a farmer's field one morning back in 1986. It was conceived and built by a then little-known artist, environmentalist and true original, Bill Lishman. A farmer's field north of Oshawa was the setting for the full-scale replica of the infamous Salisbury Plain monument, except that it was built out of partially crushed cars as opposed to the original's sarsen and bluestones.

Chrysler Canada paid for the monument and used it in commercials to illustrate the fate of their rivals' cars. The sculptor used old cars, placed them vertically and crushed them slightly to create the familiar circular ring of Stonehenge. He then used more cars and capped some of the others to create a full-sized copy that included the post and lintel arrangement.

Autohenge existed for five years and attracted tourists from around the world. According to Bill Lishman, an extraordinary number of people experienced a profound sense of déjà vu while visiting Autohenge. Lishman says it happened to him the day they completed the sculpture.

On that same afternoon in 1986 when the structure was completed, Lishman remembers there was an impending electrical storm. He says he looked up at one moment to see that the hair on all four of the people working on the site was "standing straight out like dandelions gone to seed." Frightened by the sight, Lishman and his workers hightailed it out of there in a hurry. A neighbour later reported seeing a lightening strike within Autohenge's ring that very afternoon.

Sadly, Autohenge was dismantled in the early 1990s, and nothing is left except a subtle ring that sometimes shows in the crops that are grown on the knoll. The farmer who owned the land became worried about liability, and according to Bill Lishman: "Autohenge fell to the fear of those dark minions of Satan who might arrange blame on him for some perceived happening." Translation—it had become the site for moonlit teenage druid events, a spot where teenager girls sacrificed their virginity by night and others could supplement their incomes by day picking up empty beer bottles.

Bill Lishman went on to create an ice version of Stonehenge called Icehenge on Lake Scugog and many other sculptures, as well as an underground dwelling.

~ Big, Gargantuan & Ridiculously Oversized ~

The "World's Largest Dinosaur" stands very proud and very tall in Drumheller, Alberta. He's 25 metres tall and 46 metres long from head to tail. An actual T-rex only stood 4.5 metres tall and 12 metres long. Dino 2000, as the T-rex project is called, was built as part of the millennium celebrations. And this isn't just another dinosaur to be viewed from a distance. This one has 106 stairs inside that lead from just behind its right leg up into its mouth and onto a viewing platform. And what an experience it must be for brave tourists who get an insider's view of what it would be like to be one of those human hors d'oeuvres from the *Jurassic Park* films. Family-friendly fun!

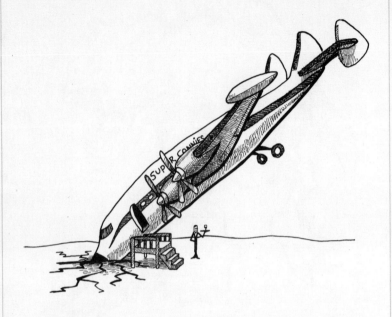

SUPER CONNIE'S AIRPLANE BAR
MISSISSAUGA, ONTARIO

What a concept! You take a beloved old passenger plane, anchor it to the ground, build wooden steps up to it fore and aft, and serve drinks to people inside it. If this isn't the height of kitsch, I don't know what is. And that's what they did at Toronto's Pearson Airport.

The plane in question is a Lockheed Super Constellation, and these planes are beyond beloved. Four propellers, black nose, three rudders…sleek mid-century design. This one previously flew with Trans Canada Airlines (TCA), the forerunner of Air Canada, and is apparently the last of TCA's Super Connies. Howard Hughes more or less designed this plane for TWA, where he was the controlling shareholder from

1939 to 1966. Most of the world's major airlines flew these planes in the 1940s and 1950s. They were also known as Starliners.

URGENT UPDATE: It looks as though Super Connie's Airplane Bar will never fly again as either a bar or a plane or as a Canadian-owned piece of aviation history. At press time, Super Connie's was being dismantled and prepared for shipment to its new owner, the Museum of Flight in Seattle, Washington. Air Canada has promised to paint the Super Connie in its original TCA colours, but many people involved in Canadian aviation are crying foul and hoping the federal government will cancel the sale by not granting an export permit. These people think the last Canadian Super Connie should remain Canadian.

However, whether it stays or goes, the airplane bar concept seems to be sunk. And barring a surprising turn of events, you'll have to visit the United States to see Canada's last Super Connie…

Run quickly if you want to see the Super Connie. Last time I checked, it was in pieces at the intersection of Derry Road East and Torbram Road in Mississauga. Who knows—with enough public outcry (hint, hint), the bar may fly again on Canadian soil…or the plane may bar again!

ESTOTILAND

Estotiland—a strange and wonderful place inhabited by people of European descent who have their own language, Latin books (that they don't know how to read), cities and the requisite New World pile of gold. The island became known in 1558, with the publication of a book and map of the voyages and discoveries of the Venetian brothers Antonio and Nicolo Zeno. The fabled—and lost or missing or never was—island of Estotiland has been pinpointed as being either Nova Scotia or Labrador. That's quite the pinpointing, don't you think! It gets better. The official Zeno documents and map describe Estotiland as being 1600 kilometres west of Frisland. Which is? Well, I guess as Canadians, we should be happy we've been included in the tall, Old World tales of lands that never were.

~ Big, Gargantuan & Ridiculously Oversized ~

"The Village of Glendon would like to welcome you to the home of the World's Largest Pyrogy, which is situated in Pyrogy Park just off Pyrogy Drive." So says the web site for the town of Glendon, Alberta—clearly a proud, proud pyrogy place! The large pyrogy in question is actually hanging off a giant fork stuck in the ground. The community is proud of its Ukrainian heritage, so what could be more appropriate as a tourist attraction than a giant, filled, dumpling-like thing that's an Eastern European staple? And the pyrogy has been worth its weight (2722 kilograms) in publicity gold! Newspapers, magazines and CNN have run stories about the Alberta town with the 8.2-metre-tall pyrogy. Beat that, Mount Rushmore!

ARCTIC OASIS

MYSTERIOUS
TROPICAL VALLEY AND FORESTS
NAHANNI NATIONAL PARK,
NORTHWEST TERRITORIES

Remember that 1970s movie with Doug McClure, where he's among a group of Brits that are captured by a German U-boat. You know, the one where they end up in the Arctic and suddenly discover a tropical valley with dinosaurs and cavemen? Well, since time immemorial, there have been whispers, peeps and crazy legends about just such a tropical oasis in Canada's North. Parks Canada suggests that the most likely spot for such a place is at Kraus Hotsprings in Nahanni National Park in the Northwest Territories. The park is located along the South Nahanni River and a ways north of Fort Nelson, BC. Hang on a second! Kraus is a German name, and that 1970s film, *The Land that Time Forgot*, had Germans and their U-boat running roughshod over just such a valley… Coincidence? I think not!

Kraus Hotsprings is made up of two thermal hotsprings that spout water at 35°C, thus creating a paradise of lush green fields, tropical forests and dinosaurs. Parks Canada won't confirm either the green fields or the tropical forests, and they won't even talk to me about dinosaurs, but I know they're there. All they'll say is that the hotsprings smell of rotten eggs because of sulphur. And by the way, the Kraus Hotsprings are accessible only by boat, plane or on foot. This last piece of information begs the question: Just what is Parks Canada trying to keep secret?

~ Big, Gargantuan & Ridiculously Oversized ~

A potato that is 4.3 metres tall and 2.1 metres in diameter stands at the entrance to the Potato Museum in O'Leary, Prince Edward Island. The giant potato is made of fibreglass and is of the russet variety. Not to be outdone, the town of Vauxhall, Alberta, is known as the "Potato Capital of the West"—I assume they mean western Canada and not the Western Hemisphere. But in the tradition of great potato-growing regions, Sammy and Samantha Spud greet all visitors at the town's entrance with a sign that hangs between them. It appropriately reads: "Welcome to Vauxhall, Potato Capital of the West."

IT'S NOT OVER!

All good things must come to an end…or so they say. Although who "they" are is usually a mystery, in this case it is, in fact, my publisher. And so, it is with mixed emotions—perhaps cramps from sitting at this desk for so many weeks—that I bid a fond farewell to *Weird Canadian Places*.

The most disappointing thing about writing this book is that I had to omit literally thousands of weird things. There is only so much room and so few trees (for paper) since they grow so slowly. Damn them!

And if you've got suggestions, nominations or comments about what you've read, we'd love to hear from you, so write to us at bluebikebooks@yahoo.ca.

And go forth with this thought in mind: Everything is weird to someone!

ABOUT THE AUTHOR

Dan de Figueiredo

Dan de Figueiredo has been a journalist, television writer, filmmaker and playwright. His love for words began when his aunt and uncle gave him a copy of *Robinson Crusoe*, and he has never looked back. After earning his BA in political science at McMaster, followed by a BAA in journalism from Ryerson, Dan worked on the Canadian edition of *Who Wants to Be a Millionaire*, *Reach for the Top*, numerous television and theatre productions and several independent films. He is currently a freelance television writer, producer and researcher.

WEIRD
CANADIAN WORDS
How to Speak Canadian

Edrick Thay

The Publisher: Folklore Publishing
Website: www.folklorepublishing.com

Library and Archives Canada Cataloguing in Publication

Thay, Edrick, 1977–
    Weird Canadian words / by Edrick Thay.

(Great Canadian stories)
Includes bibliographical references.

ISBN 13: 978-1-894864-32-9

    1. Canadianisms (English) 2. English language—Etymology.
    I. Title. II. Series.

PE3231.T48 2004   422   C2004-907020-7

Project Director: Faye Boer
Production: Trina Koscielnuk

We acknowledge the financial support of the Alberta Foundation for
the Arts for our publishing program.

We acknowledge the financial support of the Government of Canada through the Book Publishing Industry Development Program
(BPIDP) for our publishing activities.

Canadian Patrimoine
Heritage canadien

Table of Contents

Dedication

To the boys of the Boxing Day Classic

Acknowledgements

As always, I would like to thank the people at Folklore Publishing for their help on this book, notably. For her sure editing hand, Sandra Bit deserves my gratitude and thanks to Trina Koscielnuk for her work on the layout.

I would also like to extend my thanks to my brother, Eldwin Thay, on whose futon I crashed while researching and writing this book. For bolstering my spirits during the most taxing and stressful of moments, I extend my thanks again to my fellow writer-in-arms, Dan Asfar. I would also like to acknowledge Nick Protti, Bonnie Kar, Michelle Chew and Tessa Kroeker for their ideas and insights.

Introduction

GROWING UP, I'D NEVER really given much thought to words that were distinctly Canadian. I knew that as a Canadian, I was supposed to say "eh" a lot, but that was about it. It wasn't until I lived in the United States that it became quite clear that Canadian English has a vocabulary all its own. Beyond the squeals of delight every time I said "eh" and peals of laughter that erupted every time my friends asked me to say, "out and about in the house," I found that Americans were unfamiliar with many words that I took for granted. Words like tuque, two-four, gaunch and Bloody Caesar only drew confused stares. The words I spoke marked me as foreign, different, and most importantly, like my passport, the words marked me as a Canadian.

When I began research for this book, I started with those words most commonly associated by foreigners with Canadians—words like hoser, Canuck, and of course, the ubiquitous eh. But as I dug deeper, I began uncovering terms whose origins surprised me. I'd little idea that the Bloody Caesar had been invented in my home province of Alberta (I'd always believed that it had been conceived in the Las Vegas casino of the same name) and was stunned to learn that hat trick was a term derived not from hockey, but from that most British of sports, cricket. What became clear to me as I wrote is that Canadian English, like any other language, is a symbol of our history, our past and our identity. And while many believe that little differentiates Canadian culture from American culture (a reasonable assumption since we watch their movies and their television programs, eat at their restaurants, consume their goods and listen to their music), the language of Canadians reveals just how unique a nation we inhabit.

5

Although hat trick may not be uniquely Canadian, many others associated with our national pastime are. Terms like five-hole, puck and even hockey may have murky roots, but they are most certainly Canadian in origin—a reflection of our great national obsession. Our language reveals us to be a great nation of innovators. Canadians invented the snowmobile, the paint roller, the Macintosh apple, Trivial Pursuit and Medicare. Inventions such as Marquis Wheat and the Yukon Gold potato had an indelible impact upon the development, expansion and evolution of our country. Without Marquis Wheat, the western prairies may have remained forever inhospitable to settlers, and Canada would be without its breadbasket.

Canada is a diverse nation that borders three oceans—the Pacific, Atlantic and Arctic. As a result, idioms and terms are specific to each region, from British Columbia (where Chinook jargon has given rise to many terms in common use today) to Ontario (where many of its idioms reflect its strong British heritage) and from Québec (where its love for food and Gallic heritage are mirrored in terms like creton, poutine and cipaille) to the Maritimes (where a host of words, like ballicater and gaspereau, reveal those provinces' close ties to their nautical traditions) and finally, to the north (from where aboriginal words like inuksuk and kayak have entered Canadian English).

Many of these words may be familiar, but I hope that the origins and usage of some few might lead to smiles of surprise and delight, and that this volume gives more than a fleeting glimpse at the sociology of our history and that it deepens an understanding of our culture.

ACADIA and ACADIAN

Historically, an Acadian was a native of the original French colony of Acadia. Today, an Acadian is any French-speaking descendent of the early French settlers of that colony. Those settlers are probably best remembered for being the victims of a nasty and spiteful mass expulsion at the hands of the British in the mid-1700s. Acadia was established by France in 1604, initially at Port Royal, presently Annapolis Royal, Nova Scotia. That colony later grew to encompass all the land between the Atlantic Ocean and the St. Lawrence River, including what is today southeastern Québec, eastern Maine, Nova Scotia, New Brunswick and Prince Edward Island. From the early 1600s to the early 1700s, Acadians lived contentedly under French rule, although the British made noises for years about wanting them gone. Unfortunately, after losing the French and Indian War (1754–63), France surrendered Acadia to Britain in 1763 as part of the Treaty of Paris. But the deportation and exile of many thousands of French Acadians to other parts of North America, France and England had already begun in 1755. When the war ended in 1763, the exile was technically over, after which some Acadians tried to return to their homes. They soon discovered that their land had been settled by others, so there was no going back. Exiled Acadians resettled in various places in the eastern U.S. and Canada and abroad, but perhaps the best known group settled in Louisiana, and their descendants became known as Cajun. In 2004, Acadians around the world celebrated Acadie 2004, the 400th anniversary of the arrival and settlement of the French in Acadia.

ACCLAMATION
From the Latin word *acclamare*, to shout, acclamation has been in use since the mid-16th century. It usually means a shout of enthusiastic approval or a vote taken without a formal ballot. In Canada, acclamation is a political term referring to an unopposed election win; a political victory by default owing to a lack of opposition.

ALBERTA CLIPPER
The Alberta Clipper is reviled through much of the American plains for its high winds, snow and frigid temperatures. It was named for the clipper ship, a very fast sailing vessel—the word clipper itself was derived from the verb *to clip*, or to move quickly. The Alberta Clipper can attain speeds of 60 km/h, with gusts approaching 100 km/h. Born from a low pressure zone that forms over Alberta,

8

A

the Alberta Clipper dives southeast into the Dakotas and Minnesota and then eastward to the Great Lakes, dropping light, powdery snow and temperatures along the way. Should it cross the Appalachians, as it sometimes does, the Alberta Clipper becomes a nor'easter, with winds notorious for their snows and high winds. The Alberta Clipper's effects have been felt as far south as Texas.

ALBERTITE
In the mid-19th century, a black substance with a bright and glassy appearance was discovered in Albert County, New Brunswick. Many disagree on who may have found the mineral first (various accounts credit its discovery to Gould Hoar, or John and Peter Duffy, or Abraham Gesner). It was mined throughout New Brunswick from about 1849 until 1884. When mixed with coal it became a valuable fuel source.

ALBERTOSAURUS
Often overshadowed by its distant relative, the Tyrannosaurus Rex, the Albertosaurus may have been smaller, but it was no less fearsome. Living some 76 to 74 million years ago during the late Cretaceous period, the Albertosaurus was about 9 m long, stood 3 m tall and weighed close to 2.7 tonnes; it was about half the size of the Tyrannosaurus Rex but lived 5 to 10 million years earlier. Albertosaurus had short, stubby arms; long, powerful legs with clawed feet, and a long

9

tail for balance and quick turns. Its teeth were able to punch through marrow, bone and tendon with great ease. Able to attain speeds of up to 40 km/h, the Albertosaurus may also have been one of the fastest predators of its day. Remains of Albertosaurus were discovered along the Red Deer River in Alberta in 1884 by Joseph Tyrrell, who was working for the Geological Survey of Canada. Harry Fairfield Osborn of the Natural History Museum in New York described the great lizard in 1905 (the same year that Alberta became a province), baptising it Albertosaurus or the Alberta lizard.

ALOUETTE

French for skylark, alouette is many things to many Canadians. To sports fans, the name of Montréal's Canadian Football League team is the Alouettes. Founded in 1946, the team gained immediate success but then drifted for years. It was renamed the Concordes in 1983 and folded in 1987, despite four Grey Cup titles. The Alouettes were resurrected in 1996 and won another league title in 2003. Alouette is also the name of a popular French-Canadian folk song that describes the preparation of a skylark for cooking. In Canada, the song is synonymous with Québec, but children sing it across the country. It was even once heard on an episode of The Simpsons. Alouette is also the name of the first Canadian-built satellite, launched into orbit from California on

September 29, 1962, making Canada the third country to build and launch a satellite.

A

AMMOLITE

According to Blackfoot legend, a long, harsh winter once plagued its peoples. Their stores of food were nearly exhausted and could not be replenished. The great herds of bison had already moved on. Starved and cold, the Blackfoot turned to the heavens for assistance. The Great Goddess recognized their plight and, in a dream, she appeared to a young Blackfoot girl and told her to find a brilliantly coloured stone. The stone possessed magical qualities and when brought back to her tribe, the bison would return. The girl did as she was told and set off to find the stone. She wandered for days in the drifting snow but found nothing. Cold, she began looking for firewood when she suddenly heard singing from beneath a cottonwood tree. Curious, she began pawing at the snow and found the magnificent rainbow-coloured stone she had seen in her dreams. With the rock in her hand, she hurried back to her tribe. The next day, the Blackfoot were awakened by the sound of thundering hooves. The buffalo had returned. The stone had done its job and it became known as *Iniskim*, or the buffalo stone, and was used in buffalo-hunting ceremonies. The stone that the girl found may be one of the rarest gemstones in the world. In 1908, engineers with the Canadian Geological Survey reported finding a brilliant gem in the bearspaw shale of southern Alberta, near Lethbridge. It was the fossilized shell of the ammonite, a hard-shelled squid that swarmed the waters of the vast, shallow sea that covered southern Alberta more than 65 million years ago. In 1967, a Calgary rock shop owner dubbed the stone ammolite, though it wouldn't be officially recognized as such until 1981. Also known as "grandmother of pearl," ammolite is extremely rare and highly prized for its use in both jewellery and holistic healing. It has been found in scattered locations across the globe, but its greatest concentration is in southern Alberta.

ANORAK

Ridiculed at length in one memorable episode of *Seinfeld*, the anorak may not be the most fashionable item in a closet, but it wasn't designed with style or aesthetics in mind. The puffy and somewhat chunky lines of the anorak do keep the cold out, which it was designed to do. As with many of Canada's now-common winter garments, the anorak was borrowed from the Inuit. Early Europeans, woefully unprepared for the arctic climate they encountered in North America, eagerly took up the garment and modified it. The anorak, originally made with waterproof sealskin and a hood, draws its name from the Inuit, *annoraqq*. Today, any heavy, hip-length jacket with a hood is referred to as an anorak. If you're shopping for an anorak in the United

Kingdom, however, be aware that there, anorak is also slang for a lover of all things computer.

ARBORITE

Arborite, like Formica, is a brand name that has come to be used to describe all sorts of plastic laminates. In 1942, at the Howard Smith Paper Mills in Cornwall, Ontario, researchers began experimenting with pulp resin in an attempt to develop a new decorative surface that could be used on desktops and countertops. Three years later, the first pressing of their melamine laminate was made. In January 1948, the Arborite Company was formed, and it began producing the thin laminates pasted onto particleboard seen so often on entertainment centres and computer desks today.

ARCTIC CHAR

The arctic char is the most northerly distributed freshwater fish (hence its name, although the etymology of char is unknown) and has been a part of the Inuit diet for centuries. Whether eaten raw, frozen, dried, smoked or cooked, arctic char is a nutritious fish, full of protein, vitamins and calcium. Its bones were used to make sewing needles, and its skins were used in the making of waterproof kayaking coats. It is the dominant species of the Arctic coast, but it wasn't until the 1940s that this northern species was caught commercially. Since then, arctic char has become prized at restaurants throughout Canada and the United States, with a flavour many describe as a cross between brook trout and salmon. Its flesh can be red, pink or white, though red demands the highest price.

BABY BONUS

Introduced in 1944, the Family Allowance Act was Canada's first universal welfare program. It originally provided monthly payments of $5 to $8 to all parents of children under 16; it's little surprise, then, that it became known as the baby bonus. Its introduction was meant to allay fears that six years of war would plunge the country into an economic depression, leaving parents unable to provide the basic needs for their children. The baby bonus was the beginning of social security in Canada, and it was quickly followed by unemployment insurance and a proposal for health insurance. It's known today as the Canada Child Tax Benefit, although only low-income families now qualify for it.

BALLICATTER

Ballicatter describes the ridges of ice formed on and around shores, rocks, vessels and wharves from waves and salt spray. Used most commonly in Newfoundland, ballicatter is an alteration of the word barricade and has been in use since the mid-19th century. It can also be used to describe frozen moisture around the nose and mouth.

B

BAKEAPPLES

Bakeapples, also known as baked-apple berries, as chicoute in Québec, as cloudberries in the United Kingdom, as hjortron in Sweden, as lakka in Finland and as molte in Norway, thrives in the bogs of coastal regions. They are a favourite of many northern cultures where humidity and relatively mild summer temperatures create the perfect conditions for the fruit to thrive. In Canada, they are found throughout Nova Scotia and Newfoundland. In late summer, when the berries are ready for picking, individuals of all ages come out to harvest the fruit. A relative of blackberries and raspberries, bakeapples are generally larger than both and bear an amber hue. They taste like the pulp of a roasted apple, a resemblance reflected in the fruit's name. Rich in flavonols and anthocyans—anti-oxidants that make berries among the most nutritious and healthy of all fruits—bakeapples are eaten either raw or cooked. They are used in recipes for everything from pies and toppings to jams and liqueurs.

BANGBELLY

It may not be the most popular dish in these Atkins-crazy days, but bangbelly has been a staple of Newfoundland cuisine for over a century. In its harsh Atlantic winters, you either ate large or you spent your days shivering beneath your tuque. The word's origins are lost, but it was described in 1896 by a writer in the *Journal of American Folklore* as a "low and coarse word, denoting a boiled pudding consisting of flour, molasses, soda and not uncommonly seal-fat instead of suet." It sounds like pretty heavy, but definitely tasty stuff. Variously a pudding, cake or pancake, bangbelly was originally prepared by fishermen and trappers. They did not use molasses, preferring to mix their bangbellies with pork fat and drop them into pots of thick pea soup.

BEAVERTAILS

In 1978, bolstered by the modest success they'd had selling their pastries throughout the Ottawa Valley, Grant and Pam Hooker opened a permanent stand in Ottawa's Byward Market. They called their venture BeaverTails, and it wasn't long before their creation—a deep-fried, flat pastry shaped like a beavertail and topped with either sweet or savoury flavourings—became more than just a modest success. BeaverTails are now synonymous with Ottawa's outdoor festival, Winterlude, where they are sold in booths along the Rideau Canal. The snack's origins can be traced back to the days of the voyageurs, who often baked quick flatbreads over open fires. It has been adapted slightly, with help from a family recipe that traces its origins to a German pastry called *küchl* (German for little cake). BeaverTails are made from whole wheat flour, then rolled until they're about 30 cm long and 7.6 cm wide. Once cooked, they're topped with everything and anything from cinnamon sugar to maple butter to garlic butter to creamed cheese to salmon. Headquartered in Canada, the Hookers' company has gone global, with BeaverTails franchises located in the United States (one can be found at Walt Disney World in Florida), Costa Rica, Indonesia, the Philippines, Malaysia and Scotland.

BIRD COURSE

No, the term does not describe a class in ornithology. For generations of Canadian university students, a bird course was a gift from the academic gods, a gimme, a class beloved for its promise of an easy A. As with many slang terms, its origins are obscure, but it may have something to do with the slang connotations of the word "bird." In mid-19th century England, to give the bird was to express one's disapproval with a hiss that was meant to resemble the sound of a goose. It was a term of derision and dismissal.

BISCUIT

A euphemism for a hockey puck, biscuit and its cousin, the wafer, came into popular use during the 1940s. Sportswriters worried that they might be using the word puck a little too often and began creating their own words for the rubber disk. Biscuit caught on and is still used today.

BLACK BLIZZARD

Canadians entered the 1930s battered and weary. The Great Depression was still wreaking financial havoc, ravaging the human spirit and will. But for those who thought the dawning of a new decade would provide some relief, they were sorely mistaken. The Great Depression had only been a prelude. In the 1930s, the North American continent experienced one of its worst droughts in history. Between 1933 and 1937, the Prairie provinces received only 60 percent of their normal rainfall. Combined with poor agricultural practices, heat and high winds, the drought crippled the land, devastating and displacing millions of people throughout the United States and Canada. Livestock died in the millions and crops withered in arid fields. Over-ploughed and over-grazed, the parched prairie land was little more than dust. These conditions created a terrifying new phenomenon: the black blizzard, the severest kind of dust storm. When whipped into the air by the strong, dry winds that blew across the plains, black prairie soil rose up like a cloud, blocking out the sun and suffocating anything in its path. To many, it was the hand of God itself, descended from the heavens to bring about the end of the world. And that wouldn't be overstatement: some black blizzards were reported to be over 2400 km long, 1440 km wide and 3.2 km high. A quarter of a million people abandoned the prairies, and when the rains finally came, prairie farmers were

19

left with ruined lives to rebuild and the searing image of the black blizzard.

BLOQUISTE

In 1990, the Meech Lake Accord, which would have recognized Québec as a distinct society, was defeated. Disappointed members of both the Progressive Conservative and Liberal parties, led by Lucien Bouchard, who had been federal Minister of the Environment, left their parties in disgust. Bouchard's band of disgruntled politicians formed the Bloc Québecois, a national political party that, like the Parti Québecois, would dedicate itself to Québec independence. Its members and supporters are sometimes called bloquistes, a derivation of the French word *bloc*, which means coalition. Although the party's support steadily declined during the 1990s, recent scandals involving the ruling Liberals have reinvigorated it.

BLOODY CAESAR

Also known as the Caesar, this drink may sound as if it has Roman origins, but in truth, they are more humble. The Bloody Caesar, which, like the Bloody Mary, incorporates tomato juice, vodka and Worcestershire sauce, was invented in Calgary in the late 1960s. Bartender Walter Chell had long tinkered with the drinks at the restaurant where he worked, wanting to create a savoury accompaniment that would complement the Italian fare that was heavy on tomatoes, spices and seafood. One dish in particular captured his attention: the spaghetti vongele, essentially spaghetti with clams. For months, Chell worked on his concoction, until finally he pressed some clams into a nectar that he then mixed into a Bloody Mary. The drink was a success, with patrons claiming that it was fit for an emperor, and the Bloody Caesar was born. Chell's invention drew the attention of Mott's, a juice company based in California. At the time, Clamato was not as common on grocery store shelves as it is today, so to perfect its recipe, Mott's hired Chell to consult. Clamato became the mix of choice for bartenders all over the country who were looking to make Caesars. The Caesar continues to be popular with Canadians; in 2003, a survey found that more than 310 million Caesars had been sold in Canada alone, making it the country's most popular cocktail. It may have originated in a humble city on the prairies, but the Caesar is now truly worthy of its namesake.

BLUE NOSE

Blue nose is often used to describe people of a puritanical bent, but it also denotes a Nova Scotian. No one really seems to know why, as there are several different etymologies for the word. Bill Casselman, in his book *Casselman's Canadian Words,* writes that "nobody truly knows this [word's] origin," but he does offer a number of hypotheses. Could blue nose have been inspired by the chilled beaks of sailors returning from a journey into the Atlantic?

Or did it draw inspiration from the War of 1812, when a Nova Scotia privateer allegedly painted his cannon bright blue and earned a living harrying and attacking American ships, thus drawing their ire as well as the name The Blue Nose? Or does it have something to do with the *Blue Nose*, the schooner immortalized on the Canadian dime and which was originally built to win the International Prize? Whatever its origins, the word is most likely a source of pride for Nova Scotians. It confers ruggedness, hardiness and durability, qualities anyone living along the Atlantic must surely possess.

BOMBARDIER

Given our snowy climes, it's not surprising that it was a Canadian, James Armand Bombardier, who invented the snowmobile. Widely used today as a recreational vehicle, Bombardier's original snowmobile, created in the 1930s, seated 12 and was used to transport the ill and infirm through heavy snowfalls. It wasn't until the late 1950s, with the advent of lightweight engines, that his brainstorm's recreational potential was fully realized. With skis at the front and caterpillar tracks at the back, the yellow snowmobiles that became synonymous with his name made full use of his patented sprocket-wheel/track traction system. He had realized his boyhood dream to one day "build a little machine that glides over the snow." Today Bombardier Inc., the company that the man from a rural village in Québec started so many years ago, is world famous for its Ski-Doos, Sea-Doos and Lear jets.

THE BRIER

Football has its Grey Cup; hockey has its Stanley Cup. But for Canadian curlers, true greatness can only be attained at the Brier. Known today as the Nokia Brier, the Brier's roots go back to 1927. That year, Macdonald Tobacco sponsored a national men's curling competition and named it after one their most popular products—the Brier, a tobacco pipe made from the woody roots of a small Mediterranean shrub. The word brier came from *bruyere*, the French word for hearth, and it entered the Canadian consciousness, forever transcending its humble origins. When Macdonald Tobacco stopped sponsoring the event in 1979, Labatt retained the competition's moniker. In 2000, Nokia followed suit.

BRIN BAG

In Old English, *brinded* was used to describe fabric that was brown in colour. It evolved into brin, or strong, coarse-woven sacking. In other words, brin is burlap. Brin bags were used to store a wide variety of foodstuffs, including vegetables, animal feeds and breads. They were used to press blubber for its valuable oils. There was also the brin apron that stretched from the neck to the knees, and was worn when a floor needed a good scrubbing.

When a brin bag had outlived its intended purpose, enterprising Newfoundlanders found the fabric particularly useful in the hooking of rugs. The burlap was stretched tightly and nailed to a four-sided wooden frame. A design was then sketched onto the brin with charcoal. With a bent nail, strips of old clothing and fishing nets that had been dyed with vegetable dyes, spruce twigs and powders were then pulled through the burlap. It was arduous work, and some hooked rugs have as many as 200 loops per inch. The completed rugs were used to keep floors warm.

BUCK AND DOE

Stag parties have a long, storied tradition dating back to the days of ancient Sparta. On the night before his wedding, a Spartan would feast and drink with his friends for one last night of carousing before he settled into domesticity with his wife. At the end of the evening, if he and his friends were coherent enough, they would swear undying allegiance to one other. The stagette is a modern variation on the idea, as it seemed wholly unfair that women should be denied the same privilege. In rural Ontario, couples wanting neither the stag nor the stagette party united the two in what has become known as a buck and doe party (other names include a Jack and Jill and a stag and doe). The elements are the same, although there are some differences. A buck and doe is typically held in a hall, and guests are admitted only if they have previously bought a ticket from either the bride or the groom. Drinks are available for a small fee and to further entice guests to attend, prizes are awarded as well. Essentially a fund-raiser for the soon-to-be married couple, buck and doe parties have become increasingly popular throughout Canada and as far away as Alaska.

BUNNYHUG
Known as a kangaroo and a hoodie to some, the bunnyhug is what it's called in Saskatchewan. A bunnyhug is a hooded sweatshirt with a pocket in front to keep your hands warm, or store your keys or perhaps some tissue. Made of fabric that is fleecy on the inside, the bunnyhug has been described as a very warm item, particularly useful in warding off the freezing cold prairie winds of winter. Some even say that when you wear one, it feels a little like a bunny is giving you a hug. Is this the word's etymology? If so, then there must be some gargantuan rabbits in Saskatchewan.

BUSH PILOT
A bush pilot flies small aircraft over rugged, inaccessible terrain to remote areas. In Canada, the northern territories are the bush pilots' arena; for the remote communities they service, they are often the only connection to the outside world, and they bring with them mail, medicine and food supplies. Bush flying began after the First World War when Canadian combat pilots, enraptured

with the idea of flight, sought avenues to put their skills to use. Bush piloting required a breed of individual with both piloting and mechanical skills. One of the earliest bush flights took place in 1920, when a fur buyer entered the Winnipeg offices of Canadian Aircraft and asked for a flight home to The Pas, hundreds of miles away with lakes, bushes, swamps and bogs lying in between. Today, the distance can be covered in 11 hours by automobile; in 1920, the terrain and distance made the journey extremely difficult. An intrepid pilot took the fur buyer home and showed that small planes could access remote areas of the North. Bush pilots continue to fly today, and although the planes they fly have improved vastly over the earliest bush planes, they are still participating in a Canadian tradition.

BUTTER TARTS

The butter tart has been a staple of the Canadian diet since its early days. Scottish immigrants coming to Nova Scotia brought with them a recipe for a particularly runny, gooey and delicious snack they called an Ecclefechan butter tart, named for a Scottish town that is also the birthplace of Thomas Carlyle. With its delicate crust and rich sweet centre, the dessert found a ready following; its ingredients were simple, incorporating items readily available in a settler cook's larder: butter, eggs, brown sugar and raisins. The Ecclefechan recipe differs in one aspect; it calls for the use of vinegar while its Canadian cousin does not. The debate continues about the origins of the butter tart as Canadians know and love it today. Some say that it might have been a take on the pecan pie of the American South (whose taste the butter tart resembles), or adapted from sugar pies or maple syrup pies. Regardless, the butter tart is firmly entrenched within the national identity, as Canadian as the beaver, the maple leaf and the Nanaimo bar.

THE BUTTERFLY

For a long time, hockey goalies were taught to stay on their feet or stack their pads to stop a puck. But in the 1960s and 1970s, two Canadian goalies revolutionized goaltending. Glenn Hall is widely credited with creating the butterfly, a style of goaltending so named for the way a goalie drops to the ice with both pads pushed laterally along the ice, splayed out like the wings of a butterfly. Tony Esposito used a sort of butterfly too, and both goalies had spectacular, Hall of Fame careers. But in its popularity lay its downfall, and while many goalies imitated the method, few knew how to use it properly. By the 1980s, goalies were once again advised to stand in their crease. But that was before Patrick Roy. Roy's recent success as a goalie using the butterfly has influenced generations of goaltenders in his native Québec. The province is often called a goaltending factory, with goalies such as Martin Brodeur, Patrick Lalime, and Marc Andre Fleury all finding success in the National Hockey League using the butterfly.

CABOTEUR

In the late 15th century, Giovanni Caboto, born near Naples, became John Cabot, an early explorer of North America who sailed under the English flag. Like the man who inspired its name, caboteur has gone through centuries of shifting origins. Originally a French word, caboteur was adopted by the English and then Canadians. The word is used throughout the world, although in Canada it very specifically describes a coastal trading ship or boat (or coaster, if you will) sailing the Gulf of Saint Lawrence and the Saint Lawrence River.

CALGARY REDEYE

Although redeye was originally used to describe any number of cheap whiskeys that Canadians might have brewed in their bathtubs or basement stills, in Calgary, redeye is now used to describe a combination of beer and tomato juice. No one knows who came up with the concoction, although perhaps someone looking to make a Bloody Mary had only beer to mix with the tomato juice, and a tasty treat was born. And while some may shudder at the thought of combining tomato juice with beer, the drink has passionate adherents who claim that a Calgary redeye approaches something akin to the sublime.

C

CALLIBOGUS

In the 18th century, many people found the local brews of Newfoundland not particularly strong and not very effective at producing inebriation. To spice up such concoctions as spruce beer (which has a low alcohol content), imbibers began mixing gin, rum and other liquors into their beer. Soon the mixtures contained more liquor than beer, and they came to be called callibogus. Callibogus has been consistently popular in Newfoundland for over two and a half centuries, and the combination of spruce beer, molasses and dark rum has become a drink in its own right.

CALUMET

Early French Canadians encountering the Mi'kmaq of Nova Scotia found that these Natives often carried a pipe festooned with beads, feathers and ribbons. To the French Canadians, the pipe looked very much like a beautiful foreign instrument. They called it the *chalumeau*—reed pipe. Later, they discovered that the reed pipe was not an instrument at all, but was a tobacco pipe of sacred and religious significance. To smoke from the pipe was to share in a communion with the animate powers of the world; it was used at the conclusion of peace treaties and at adoption ceremonies. Aboriginal ambassadors carried these pipes as proof of their identity. The pipe protected them from harm. *Chalumeau* was eventually anglicized into calumet.

CANADA DRY

In 1890, pharmacist and chemist John J. McLaughlin, a graduate of the University of Toronto, opened a small plant in Toronto to make soda water—a common mixer for fruit juices and extracts. In 1904, after years of work, McLaughlin unveiled a drink that would become known throughout the world as Canada Dry Pale Dry Ginger Ale. He wanted to duplicate the dry champagnes of France. McLaughlin revolutionized the carbonated beverage industry, taking it out of the corner drug store and to the public by mass bottling and distributing the drink in ballparks and at beaches. During Prohibition, Canada Dry's popularity soared, as many found the sweet, brown liquid the perfect mask for foul-tasting bathtub hooch. By 1938, Canada Dry was being produced in 14 countries and as far away as New Zealand. In 1986, Cadbury Schweppes, based in London, England, purchased Canada Dry and today, it is a part of Dr. Pepper/Seven Up Incorporated, itself the largest subsidiary of Cadbury Schweppes.

CANADA TEA

Also known as wintergreen (*Gaultheria procumbens*), Canada tea grows in the sandy and acid soils of eastern North America and has long been used in the folk medicine of the aboriginal tribes of North America. Early French explorers noticed how the Inuit of Labrador used the plant's glossy oval leaves and crimson fruits to treat a wide variety of ailments, including headaches, muscle aches and sore throats. The Delaware and Mohican used the plant to treat kidney disorders, while the Great Lakes and Eastern Woodlands tribes used poultices of Canada tea to treat arthritic and rheumatic pains. The Algonquin, Cherokee, Chippewa and Iroquois all used the plant as a herbal remedy. The explorers followed suit and took to steeping the leaves in boiling water. Today, herbalists use Canada tea to treat ailments because modern science has discovered that the plant produces a compound closely related to aspirin. It must be used in moderation. In high doses, it can aggravate both the stomach and the kidney.

CANADA THISTLE

Canada thistle (*Cirsium arvense*) is pretty notorious, even for a weed. Aggressive and hardy, Canada thistle is the bane of many a farmer's and gardener's existence, although it didn't originate in Canada at all. It was probably introduced into North America in the early 17th century, a contaminant in the crop seeds brought over by the settlers of New France. The weed took root and became so prevalent throughout eastern Canada

31

that aboriginal tribes had enough time to actually develop medicinal uses for the plant, using it to treat a wide range of stomach illnesses before it spread throughout the continent. It's unknown how the thistle came to be named after Canada.

CANADARM

In 1981, the American space shuttle *Columbia* rocketed into orbit, bearing with it the Shuttle Remote Manipulator System. The SRMS is known more familiarly as the Canadarm, Canada's first contribution to NASA's space shuttle program. NASA was so impressed with the Canadarm's performance that it has, over the years, ordered four of them, resulting in $900 million in export sales. The Canadarm was the brainchild of MD Robotics, which had been hired by the National Research Council of Canada. The Canadarm's main duty is to place satellites into orbit and retrieve them for any necessary repairs. Most notably, it played a crucial role in the repair of NASA's Hubble Space Telescope, which could have been a costly and crippling embarrassment for the beleaguered agency. It is currently being used to help build the International Space Station.

CANADIAN WHISKEY

Canadian whiskey trails only vodka in distilled spirits consumed in the United States, accounting for 11.5 percent of the market. Although Canadian whiskey is commonly called rye, the latter is a bit of a misnomer. Canadian whiskey is typically a blend of corn, rye and barley, with corn being the principle ingredient. However, rye, even in the smallest amounts, can influence the flavour of the drink, giving it a spicy flavour. Canadian whiskey has its roots in the 19th century, when rum, which was easily and widely available, was mixed with high wine, a whiskey spirit made from grains, to add flavour. It was also widely used in trade with aboriginals, who found the "fire-water" of the Europeans addictive as well as intoxicating. Canadian whiskey's popularity south of the border can be directly attributed to American Prohibition in the 1920s. In 1924, two-thirds of whiskey imported into the United States came from Canadian distilleries, which had built factories all along the Great Lakes near Detroit to serve the American market. Seagram's and Hiram Walker both made fortunes from this illicit trade. After Prohibition was repealed, Canadian whiskey continued to be popular as American distillers scrambled to rebuild their dismantled operations.

CANDU REACTOR
Designed and developed in the late 1950s through a cooperative effort between the Canadian government and the private sector, the CANDU nuclear reactor is a pressurized heavy water, natural uranium power reactor. It was first used in 1962, at Rolphton, Ontario, and began providing

power to thousands of homes and families. Using technology that had been developed for the construction of the atomic bomb, Canadian scientists hoped that they had created something that could bring safe and inexpensive power to the world. Standing for Canada Deuterium Uranium and not the can-do attitude of the researchers and scientists who built it, the CANDU reactor had many advantages over other nuclear generators. Running on unenriched uranium, it could be operated without expensive fuel enrichment facilities, and it needed no large pressure vessels. It was highly efficient too, even if it did use the purest and most expensive grade of heavy water ever developed. Unfortunately, its strengths turned out to be weaknesses, and while the CANDU reactor continues to be sold across the globe, many people see these sales as a potential threat to world security. Theoretically, the reactor and its unenriched uranium fuel could be used to produce plutonium for nuclear weapons. Still, in 1987, the CANDU reactor was named one of the top 10 Canadian engineering achievements on a list that included the CN Tower, the Bombardier snowmobile and the St. Lawrence Seaway.

CANOLA

Known for its brilliant yellow flowers that can make a field look like a bright golden carpet, canola is a modified member of the rapeseed

34

family. Before the Second World War, rape-seed oil was used commonly in kitchens and as an engine lubricant. In Asia, it has been used as a cooking oil for over 4000 years. But following the Second World War, concerns were raised about the high levels of both erucic acid and glucosinates in rapeseed oil. Heart disease was blamed on erucic acid, while glucosinate proved toxic to animals when it began to break down. Canadian planters began experimenting with the rapeseed to create a "double-low" variety: low in erucic acid and low in glucosinates. In 1974, Baldur Stefansson at the University of Manitoba crossbred the first variety, which he called Tower. In 1979, the name was changed to canola by the Western Canadian Oilseed Crushers Association, shorthand for Canadian oil low acid. Its health claims are disputed by conspiracy-minded theorists, who believe Canada is on a mission to grow wealthy off the peddling of its "industrial oil." Detractors cite canola's associations with the rapeseed, which is erroneously believed to have been used in the manufacture of mustard gas, and the incorrect belief that canola was genetically engineered. Canola has even somehow managed to be blamed for mad cow disease. Regardless, canola oil's popularity is growing, and Canada now accounts for 15 percent of the world's production.

CANUCK

Originally used by northeastern Americans as a derogatory term for French Canadians following the American Revolution, Canuck has become a name of pride for both francophones and anglophones, although foreigners are advised not to use the word liberally. The origins of Canuck are not clear, and there are many theories about the word's origins. One suggests that it originated from a combination of the French expression *quelle canule* and cold weather. In 1776, during a siege on Québec, American troops, under the command of Benedict Arnold, heard *quelle canule* repeated often among the French enemy, so they began repeating it, too. But unaccustomed to the cold, the Americans couldn't stop shivering when they spoke, and they ended their *canules* with a "k" sound. Another theory offers the idea that it may have originated with German mercenaries captured at Saratoga from Burgoyne's army. When given the opportunity to return to Canada, they allegedly replied, "Nien! Nien! Genug vun Kanada." Unsure of what they said, their captors instead took to repeating "Genug vun Kanada" over and over again, until they decided finally to drop the "vun." Genug Kanada could have become Canuck. Still another theory says that Canuck is derived from the Iroquoian word for hut: *kanuscha*. Or maybe it came from *Connaught*, a popular Irish surname that early French Canadians mistook for a nickname for

Irish Canadians. Regardless, the word Canuck appears as early as the mid-19th century. Johnny Canuck appeared shortly thereafter and became as synonymous with Canada as John Bull with Britain and Uncle Sam with the United States. Today, it is more familiarly associated with the perennially disappointing Vancouver Canucks hockey team of the NHL and with the very brief period when the Crazy Canucks of Canada competed with the likes of Austria and Germany for skiing supremacy.

CAPLIN

Newfoundland has always been closely tied to the ocean and has a proud fishing heritage. It was the abundant cod that brought fishermen from France, England and Spain to the area in the 16th century. The silvery caplin (*Mallotus villosus*) may be small—no more than 17–19 cm long—but they loom large in the Newfoundland consciousness. The word, derived from the French word *capelan*, meaning "codfish," has been in use since the early 17th century. A close relative of freshwater smelt, caplin is one of the most important forage species in the Northwest Atlantic. Preying upon plankton, caplin is a favoured prey of flounder, whales, seals and cod. Recognizing this relationship, early Newfoundland fishermen looked forward each year to early summer, when schools of caplin would come ashore during the caplin scull to breed.

There was a time when entire villages would turn out for the caplin scull. Armed with buckets and dip nets, the people gathered up the spawning caplin for use not just as bait for cod, but as fertilizers for gardens, as feed for sled dogs and, when dried and salted, as a tasty and welcome alternative to salt beef. The caplin scull no longer inspires the fervour and excitement as it once did, and it's a loss that many Newfoundlanders still lament.

CARIBOU

The caribou is a kind of deer native to northern Canada's tundra regions. It has large antlers that are present in both sexes, though female antlers are significantly smaller and simpler. In Europe, caribou are known as reindeer, the very same that pull Santa's sleigh every Christmas Eve. For centuries, the caribou has played a prominent role in the aboriginal cultures of Canada's north as a source of food, fuel and clothing in an environment sorely lacking all three. Its name is a corruption of the Mi'kmaq word *xalibu* or *xalipu,* meaning "one who paws," and has been in use since the mid-17th century. According to Bill Casselman, aboriginals often observed the *xalibu* pawing its way through the snow to get to the grass below. The word has new meaning in Québec, where caribou has become the name of a particularly potent and mind-numbing alcoholic drink. Also known as caribou juice, caribou is made of one part red wine and six parts grain alcohol. One variation substitutes dandelion wine for the red wine and gin for the grain alcohol.

CATTALO

The Boyds of Bobcageyon, Ontario, were an entrepreneurial lot. In 1844, Mossom Boyd built Bobcageyon's first sawmill and was soon running the third largest lumber operation in Ontario. When Boyd died in 1883, it was turned over to his two sons, Mossom Martin and Willie. They formed the MM Boyd Lumber Company and expanded their timber limits from Ontario into Québec and as far away as the Northwest Territories and British Columbia. Mossom Martin had other interests as well. Cattle brought into the West from Eastern Canada were ill equipped to deal with the extremes of the prairie climates. Settlers there quickly learned that cattle from the western United States, like the bison that once roamed the vast plains of North America in great numbers, were hardier and sturdier creatures, better adapted to long, harsh winters. It seemed that some of these durable creatures were the progeny of natural crossbreeding between bison and cattle. By 1885, ranchers were deliberately mating the two. In 1894, Mossom Martin began his own crossbreeding program and called his resultant hybrid the cattalo, a cross of the words cattle and buffalo. None of his animals produced offspring, as the males were usually sterile while the females possessed underdeveloped reproductive organs.

Nor did they possess any pronounced advantage in growth or carcass performance. Yet, others picked up the work he began. Agriculture Canada experimented with the breed from 1916 until 1965. Researchers at the University of Guelph produced some cattalo in the 1970s for a study on the genetic aspects of crossbreeding. Cattalo meat is said to be low in both fat and cholesterol, but higher in protein and iron. In the United States, the hybrid is known as the beefalo.

CHEECHAKO

A word that has its origins in both the Yukon and Alaska, cheechako is a combination of two Indian words: the Chinook word *chee*, meaning "new and fresh," and the Nootka word, *chako*, meaning "to approach or to come." Used as long ago as the early 19th century by traders of the Hudson's Bay Company, cheechako was used to describe immigrants newly arrived to the Yukon. They might also have been called Outsiders. It has a slightly pejorative meaning and is used in much the same way as city slicker, tenderfoot and greenhorn are. *Ballads of Cheechako* was a poem written in the early 20th century by Robert W. Service.

CHIMO

First recorded in 1748, although probably much older, chimo is the Inuit equivalent of hello or greetings. It also means friendship. According to some accounts, when meeting in the North, people would rub their chests in a circular motion and then say, "Chimo?" to which the other person would respond in kind. In that context, chimo was being used to ask, "Are you friendly?"

CHINOOK

A Chinook is a warm, dry easterly wind that sweeps down the eastern slopes of the Rocky Mountains and often brings a welcome, though all too brief, respite from the polar temperatures of a long winter. It is aptly described in this passage from a 1900 edition of the *Calgary Weekly Herald*:
"Those who have not the warm, invigorating Chinook winds of this country, cannot well comprehend what a blessing they are. The icy clutch of winter is lessened, the earth throws off its winding sheet of snow. Humanity ventures forth to inhale the balmy spring-like air. Animated nature rejoices."
A Chinook can cause great changes in weather; one dramatic transformation occurred in Calgary on January 11, 1983, when the temperature rose by 30 degrees, from −17° C to +13° C, in four hours. Also known as a snow-eater, a Chinook thaws snowbanks and can melt as much as 2.5 cm of ice from frozen ponds and lakes in just one hour. Its name is taken from a Pacific Northwest Coast tribe that once lived along the banks of the lower Columbia River. Although the Chinook has been blamed recently on the high incidence of

migraines and allergies among those living in its path, most people welcome its arrival and speak warmly of the wind that has "chinooked them."

CHINOOK JARGON
The early 19th century in British Columbia was the heyday of Chinook Jargon, the trade language of the Pacific Northwest. The region was a melting pot, with traders from France and England working closely with aboriginals such as the Salish and the Nootka. It's not surprising that they created their own common, yet multicultural, mosaic of a language. English fur traders were known as *kin chotsch-men*, or King George Men. The French were *passioks*, a word meaning "blanket-men," while Americans were called *Boston-men*. Many Chinook Jargon words are still in use in western Canada, and it is still spoken as a first language among some residents of Oregon. Linguists believe that a trade language, the forerunner of Chinook Jargon, existed before the late 17th century.

CIPAILLE
A layered meat pie, the cipaille is a traditional French Canadian dish that was cited at least as early as 1747, when it appeared in a cookbook. A typical cipaille consists of three layers of meat, spices and potato, separated by pastry, baked in a cast-iron pot. At one time, there may have been as many as six layers, which led to the name, *six-pâtes*,

and the eventual corruption of that word into cipaille or cipâte. In Ontario, the dish is known as sea pie, an anglicized pronunciation of the French word.

COADY

Popular in Newfoundland, especially to pour over boiled pudding, coady is a sweet sauce of boiled molasses mixed with butter. It has also been made with milk, sugar and vinegar and thickened with cornstarch. According to Bill Casselman, the word may have been derived from *coaty* or *coatie*, a coating on food.

COHO SALMON

Also known as silver salmon, hooknose and sea trout, the Coho salmon (*Oncorhynchus kisutch*) is native to the Pacific coast of Canada and has long been part of the diet of aboriginals such as the Salish. Its name is an alteration of the Salish word *cohose*, and so important was this fish to Salish society that the month of September was called *chen'thaw'en*, or the time of the Coho. The Coho is a small fish, with an average weight of 2.3–2.7 kg, and though it is native to the north Pacific, it has been introduced with great success into the Great Lakes. The Coho is a dark metallic blue colour, with tints of green on its back and upper sides.

COPY

With the popularity of extreme sports these days, one wonders why copy, a game and pastime popular in Newfoundland, has yet to acquire the same popularity as street luging or base jumping. Originating in the late 19th century, copy draws its name from the childhood game of follow or copy the leader. Usually played in spring, copy began when children, in imitation of sealers, began jumping from one piece of floating ice to another. Not exactly the safest of pastimes, the game courted danger, as not every ice pan was buoyant enough to support the weight of the jumpers. Leaping from one large floe of ice to another was considered too safe and not in keeping with the spirit of copying. The term now applies to anyone crossing any pan of ice, even if there is no game involved. But there are days in spring when people can be heard fondly recalling, as they did to the *Canadian Journal of Linguistics* in 1964, that "we were so busy catching tomcods, copying pans in the spring that we didn't have time to chase all our vitamins" and that "the minute school was out we ran helter-skelter to one of the coves to copy pans."

COULEE

Though the word has spread to the south and is used throughout the western United States, coulee's origins lie in the French Canadian language.

Meaning "a deep gulch or ravine," usually with inclined sides and dry in the summer, coulee is a French Canadian word whose origins lie in the French verb *courir*, meaning "to run or to flow."

CRETONS

Not to be confused with a cretin, cretons is a pâté-like, highly seasoned pork spread popular throughout Québec. Spread on toast, cretons is a favourite breakfast item. It has its origins in medieval France and a coarse pâté of ground pork and pork fat. Creton was originally used in Old French to describe a piece of fried pork fat.

DAMPER DOGS

A sort of pancake, damper dogs (other names include damper boy, damper cake and damper devil) are small pieces of dough that have been fried atop a stove's damper, an adjustable plate used to control the draft on a woodstove or coalstove. Harold Horwood recalled in his 1969 book, *Newfoundland*, that his grandmother often made damper dogs to tide her grandchildren over until she could make a new batch of bread.

DEKE

Deke, as both a verb and noun, first entered Canadian English usage in the 1960s. An abbreviation of the word decoy, deke was used to describe a fake or feint used to fool a defender or a goalie on an opposing hockey team. The word was just too good to be limited to the sport of ice hockey and can now be employed in a variety of contexts, including deking your way out of something you don't want to do.

DÉPANNEUR

In France, a dépanneur is usually a repairman who specializes in electronics or automobiles, or someone who helps you out of a tough spot. It's this philanthropic flavour of the word that's at the root of the Québecois version of the word. In Québec, a dépanneur is not a repairman; it's not a man at all. The dépanneur is a convenience store, usually open from 7:00 in the morning until 11:00 at night, able to provide all sorts of items and typically family owned and operated. In previous decades, dépanneurs were the only stores in the province permitted to sell beer and other alcoholic beverages. The word was once used strictly by francophones, although it is now a part of Québecois English as well. It's also known as the dep.

DIGBY CHICKEN

The word gained some notoriety in 2001 when it tripped up mathematics student Shannon Patrick Sullivan of Memorial University of Newfoundland on the Canadian edition of *Who Wants to be a Millionaire?* The question was worth $16,000, but Sullivan guessed incorrectly that in Nova Scotia, digby chicken refers to smoked lobster. Nova Scotians know that digby chicken refers to smoked and salted herring. The tiny fish are a popular snack in Digby, the fishing port from which it draws its name. Digby itself was named for Admiral Robert Digby, who brought Loyalists from America to Nova Scotia aboard the H.M.S. *Atlanta* in 1783.

DULSE

D

Originally popular in Ireland, the purply-red sea-weed known as dulse was also found to thrive along the North Atlantic coast of Canada. Settlers of New Brunswick found the edible seaweed as tasty and appetizing as it had been in Europe, and it is now commonly used throughout the Maritimes as a condiment in both soups and stews. Found on rocks, fronds of dulse can vary in colour, from a pink to purple, and is picked by hand between the months of June and September. The fronds are spread on netting to dry, for eager and health-conscious consumers to eat either as is (pan frying them is common, as is baking them in the oven) or to add to doughs, sandwiches and chowders. High in vitamins, potassium and fluoride, dulse is treasured throughout Canada for both its taste and nutrition. Nova Scotia markets its dulse as sea parsley. The word dulse itself is Gaelic in origin; its root word is *duileask*, which means, appropriately, "sea bits."

EAGER BEAVER

The beaver, industrious and hard-working, is our national animal, a source of pride and patriotism. Coined by the Canadian army in the mid-20th century, eager beaver is an offshoot of other expressions, such as "busy as a beaver," that play off the beaver's hardy reputation. Eager beaver is commonly used as a term of derision, applied to anyone demonstrating excessive zeal or enthusiasm.

EH

Perhaps no word is considered as distinctly Canadian as eh. The word has been in use for well over 1000 years, with roots in both Latin, Old English and Middle English. In Latin, it was derived from the word *interiectio*, which means "something thrown in between." In Middle English, the word was *ey*, an interjection common in Geoffrey Chaucer's *Canterbury Tales*. Even then, the word was considered slang, and little has changed over the centuries. In Canada, eh is used at the end of a statement, basically turning the statement into a rhetorical question and tacitly assuming the other person's agreement—"It's cold in Canada, eh? I sure could go for a beer, eh?" and so forth. It's not exactly clear how the expression became so popular in Canada and how it became so closely identified with the country. Even in 1959, the *Journal of Canadian Linguistic Association* was reporting that "eh is so exclusively a Canadian feature that immigration officials use it as an identifying clue."

ERMITE CHEESE

First produced by the monks of Saint-Benoît Abbey in eastern Québec in 1943 with the opening of the Fromagerie de L'Abbaye, ermite is a semi-soft, blue cheese. Rindless with a bluish vein and an aroma resembling mushrooms, ermite was named after the French word *l'ermite*, meaning "hermit." The Saint-Benoît Abbey is a popular Roman Catholic retreat.

ESKIMO

For years, the native inhabitants of the Arctic and subarctic regions of North American and Siberia were known collectively as the Eskimo. And, for years, people believed that the term was derived from the Algonquin word for "eater of raw flesh." Living in a harsh environment with few trees and resources for cooking fuel, the northern Natives did often eat their meat raw, a habit that appalled the supposedly more civilized and more cultured European explorers. But it was the Europeans who suffered from scurvy in great numbers, while the Eskimos thrived and, until recently, suffered little from typically Western ailments such as heart disease. In the 1970s, the term Eskimo was replaced with Inuit in Canadian governmental and scientific publications. In recent years, however, linguists have begun to argue that the basis for the word Eskimo may not have been "eater of raw flesh" at all, but may, in fact, have come from a Montagnais word that described the lacing of a snowshoe. The matter remains unsettled. It should be noted that the word that has come to replace Eskimo, Inuit, refers only to the Inuit-speaking people of northern Canada and some parts of Greenland. The northern Indians of Alaska and Arctic Siberia are known, respectively, as the *Inupiaq* and the *Yupik*.

FIDDLEHEADS

Popular in spring throughout Québec and the Maritimes, fiddleheads are the croziers or tightly curled, young and edible tips of the ostrich fern. When boiled or steamed, fiddleheads lose their natural bitter taste and acquire a flavour that many say is uniquely earthy, grassy and nutty, similar only to the flavour of cooked asparagus or artichoke. Rich in vitamins A and C, fiddleheads have been a food staple for centuries, figuring prominently in the diets of early Natives, especially New Brunswick's Maliseet. Maliseet clothing, canoes and wigwams were often decorated with a fiddlehead motif, reflecting its prominence in Maliseet culture. It was from the Natives that early French explorers learned of the fiddlehead. It acquired its name from English traders and trappers, who thought that the spiral shape of the frond resembled the scroll found at the head of a violin or fiddle. In other parts of the country, fiddleheads are available fresh for a short time in June and frozen year-round.

FIRST NATIONS

The term First Nations was popularized in the 1970s as a welcome alternative to the term Indian, which many Canadians aboriginals found insulting and offensive (it is a term based, after all, on an assumption made by Christopher Columbus). First Nations has come to refer to the tribes of six major cultural regions across Canada: the Woodland First Nations, the Iroquois First Nations, the Plains First Nations, the Plateau First Nations, the First Nations of the Pacific Coast and the First Nations of the Mackenzie and Yukon River basins.

FIVE-HOLE

According to hockey tradition, there are five holes that a goalie typically leaves exposed. The one-hole is found in the upper left corner, the two-hole in the upper right, the three-hole in the lower left and the four-hole in the lower right. To increase the area of the net that the goalie covers, he or she typically crouches, with the legs splayed out. The space thus created between the legs is referred to as the five-hole. People rarely talk about the other holes, but to be beaten through the five-hole is a great source of embarrassment for a goalie. Some hockey historians claim that the five-hole's origins may also lie in the Roman numeral for five: V. When a goalie is in his crouch, the area between his legs looks similar to an inverted V.

FOG-EATER

The term has many definitions. In the United States, a fog-eater is a coastal inhabitant. For rail-waymen, the fog-eater is an engineer. But in most ocean regions, a fog-eater, a term that has been in use since at least the 19th century by seamen and those accustomed to fog, refers to either a rainbow or a white bow in the clouds seen in heavy fog that usually precedes the fog's lifting. In Canada's North, the term is used frequently, a remnant of the first European settlers, and it doesn't take great imagination to realize the term's etymology.

FOUR-POINTER

During the 1690s, French fur traders were scouring the North American wilderness for the beaver and mink furs so popular in Europe. They also relied heavily upon aboriginal tribes for pelts, and traded goods such as alcohol, trinkets and blankets for the pelts. A four-pointer was a large, thick and heavy blanket, durable and compact enough to fight back the Canadian cold. Noted for its warmth and versatility, this blanket could be adapted for use as clothing. Trade blankets were made under a point system, a point being a unit of measurement. One-pointers were the smallest, also called "cradle blankets." The largest were five-pointers, although French traders were outfitted most often with the four-pointer.

FOX 40

To referees everywhere, the Fox 40 was and is a lifesaver. The Fox 40 is a whistle, invented and developed by Canadian referee Ron Foxcroft in the late 1980s. Prior to the Fox 40, most whistles used by referees in leagues such as the National Basketball Association and the National Hockey League were cork-pea whistles. They usually did their job, but cork-pea whistles are notoriously temperamental and finicky. If blown too hard, they make no sound. If they get dirty or wet, they make no sound. If a crowd is particularly loud, and the cork-pea whistle does work, no one can hear its feeble tone. And if a whistle makes no sound or is inaudible when it does, how is a referee to do his job? Foxcroft finally decided to make a change after the 1976 Montréal Olympics. Before a crowd of 18,000 fans gathered to watch the basketball final game between the United States and Yugoslavia, Foxcroft saw a Yugoslav player elbow an American player. He blew his whistle. There was no sound. Play went on, and Foxcroft found himself the object of a chorus of boos and hisses. After working on 14 prototypes, Foxcroft finally perfected his pea-less whistle, which had no moving parts to malfunction and a loud, ear-splitting tone that could be heard above the rowdiest of crowds. The Fox 40, named after Foxcroft and for the age he was on the day he patented his invention, was used professionally for the first time at the Pan-Am Games in Indianapolis, Indiana, in 1987. Its success and efficiency had the Indianapolis Police Department asking for Fox 40 whistles. In 1990, the whistle was being used by the National Basketball Association, the National Collegiate Athletic Association and the Canadian Football League. It has been used in the World Cup of soccer. The Fox 40 may just very well be the referee's new best friend.

FRANCOPHONE, ALLOPHONE, ANGLOPHONE

Francophone, allophone and anglophone are french terms that have migrated to Canadian English from Québecois French. *Phone* comes from the Greek phônê, meaning "voice/sound." These words reflect Canada's cultural diversity, its aboriginal heritage and its two official languages. A francophone is one who claims French as a mother tongue and primary language; an anglophone claims English as a mother tongue; and an allophone is usually an immigrant or an aboriginal person whose native tongue is something other than English or French. In 2001, the Canada Census found that 59.1% of Canadians are anglophones, 22.9% are francophones, and 18% are allophones. Chinese is the third most common language spoken in Canada.

FRAZIL

Derived from the French word *frasil*, frazil is a French Canadian term for fine individual ice crystals that appear either as spicules (long and needle-like splinters of ice) or as plates suspended in water. Frazil is often found in waters too turbulent for pack ice to form and in icebanks along shorelines. *Frasil* is French for cinder, which French Canadians felt the ice resembled. The term has been in use since the late 19th century.

GARBURATOR

Although the origins of this word are lost (linguists believe that it may have once been a Canadian trade name for a garbage disposal unit—probably a hybrid of garbage and incinerator), garburator has become the Canadian term to describe an under-the-sink garbage disposal unit. First invented by Racine architect John W. Hammes in 1927, the garburator gained widespread popularity and acclaim in the 1970s and 1980s. Environmental concerns curbed its use for a while, but it remains a staple of Canadian kitchens everywhere, ready to consume all food waste and mangle the occasional stray utensil.

GASPEREAU

In Nova Scotia, there is a town called Gaspereau, a Gaspereau Valley, a Gaspereau Mountain and a Gaspereau River. In a province so closely tied with the ocean and its bounty, it's not surprising that so many places have been named after a fish. Known to the English as alewife, gaspereau is an Acadian French word for a small, herring-like fish that has been a staple of Nova Scotia's economy since its earliest days. Gaspereau is fished in spring with traps, gill nets and dip nets when it enters freshwater rivers such as the Saint John in New Brunswick and the Gaspereau in Nova Scotia to spawn, and is used as bait in lobster and snow crab traps. It can also be found on local menus fresh, dried, smoked or salted, its roe is sold as a delicacy and it is used in the making of pet foods. No wonder that the versatile fish, also known as kiack in Nova Scotia, is in danger of being over-fished. In 1958, North Atlantic fisheries caught 75 million pounds of gaspereau. In recent years, the catch has dropped to less than 5 million.

G

GAUNCH, GINCH, GONCH or GITCH

Why are there so many different terms for underwear in Canada? It's a mystery, although gaunch is a term that appears to be specific to British Columbia and Alberta while gitch seems to be a favourite among Ontarians. No one knows why, but perhaps the difference may be tied to western alienation; Ontario has its term, so the West must have its own. It's important to note that the terms don't just describe any sort of undergarment; to qualify as a gaunch, ginch, gonch or gitch, an undergarment must be a little worn, dirty and malodorous.

GOOEYDUCK

Slang for geoduck, gooeyduck might have come about because people couldn't pronounce the word correctly. The geo in the word isn't pronounced like the geo in geography, but like the slang—gooey. The pronunciation of the word is based in Nisqually and Chinook Jargon, which are old trader languages of southern British Columbia. The gooeyduck is the largest burrowing clam in the world. It is found deep beneath the sands of ocean beaches along British Columbia's coast. The Nisqually tribe found the clam particularly tasty but difficult to harvest. They called it the *go-duk*, meaning "dig-deep." The name carried over into English, and traders found the clam quite appetizing as well. Harvesting the geoduck is more than a little tricky, but given that the geoduck can live for as long as 146 years, harvesters have time on their side.

GOPHER

When French explorers arrived in North America, they noticed a short-tailed, burrowing rodent that plagued crops. They discovered that the animal lived beneath the ground in a honeycomb-like network of carefully constructed tunnels. To this animal with its cute, fur-lined cheeks, French explorers gave the name *gaufre gris*. In French, *gaufre* means "honeycomb." English settlers adopted the word but not the spelling.

GREY CUP

The Grey Cup, which has been associated with Canadian football excellence for almost a century, was intended to be a trophy for Canada's senior amateur hockey champion. Unfortunately, Governor General Lord Albert Henry Earl Grey was unable to bequeath his gift; in 1910, banking mogul Sir Hugh Andrew Montagu Allan donated his own championship hockey trophy, the Allan Cup, making Lord Grey's cup unnecessary. Undaunted, Lord Grey decided to donate the trophy to the champions of amateur football. The Grey Cup was contested for years by amateur Canadian teams, but in 1958, professional football emerged in Canada with the creation of the Canadian Football League, and the Grey Cup has been coveted by CFL teams ever since.

GRITS

Grits, the nickname for members of the Liberal Party and not the food so popular in the American south, was first popularized in the mid-19th century. Editor and political reformer George Brown used the phrase "Clear Grit" often to describe members of his wing of the Reform party, a group of rural Presbyterian and Methodist farmers unhappy with the ruling political parties. Clear Grit was a highly symbolic term. In the United States, someone having clear grit was said to be unflinching and obstinate, qualities Brown believed reformers needed to possess, but it also referred to the first-grade sand that Scottish stonemasons of Upper Canada used in making mortar. After Confederation, Brown's Reform party disappeared; the Liberal Party, which also represented disenchanted rural Protestant farmers, was given the mantle instead.

GST

Although many initially considered GST an acronym for the Gouge and Screw Tax, GST is really an acronym for the Goods and Services Tax. In 1989, Brian Mulroney and his Progressive Conservative government proposed the creation of a national sales tax and though opposition was fierce, it came into being on January 1, 1991. The tax, a 7 percent charge on goods and services, ruined the Progressive Conservative Party, and in 1993, Jean Chretien and the Liberal Party were elected with a strong majority. Chretien's promise to repeal the GST never happened because the much-maligned tax was a great source of federal revenue. Canadians today have accepted the GST, although people in Alberta long for the days when they paid no taxes at all on any goods and services—Alberta is the only province in Canada without a provincial sales tax.

GTA

GTA is an acronym used for decades to describe the Greater Toronto Area. Taken together, the GTA and Toronto make up the largest metropolitan area in Canada and fourth largest in North America, with a population of over 5 million. The GTA includes cities such as Barrie, Burlington and

Mississauga and towns such as Markham and Oakville. The area is so large that it uses six distinct area codes, which has led to the creation of an area code aristocracy. The 416s are for those living in Toronto and are the most coveted; everything outside is known as The 905s, even though there are four other area codes within the GTA.

H

HABS

Habs is the nickname for one of Québec's most
beloved institutions, the Montréal Canadiens,
and is short for *habitants*, the name given to early
French settlers. The term was at one time pejorative, akin to redneck or yokel, and came to include
not just a farmer, but anyone from rural Québec.
The H and the C that form the Montréal Canadiens' logo actually stand for "Club de Hockey
Canadien," but in 1924, American reporter Tex
Rickard was mistakenly told that the H stood for
habitants and the team's French farmer hockey
players. Rickard passed the information on, and
the name stuck.

HAT TRICK

Although the hat trick is strongly associated with
scoring three goals in a hockey game (at which
point fans throw their hats and caps onto the
ice), its origins rest not in hockey, but in cricket.
Dating back to the late 1800s, a hat trick was
achieved when a bowler took three wickets off
with three successive balls, a rare and celebrated

feat. The bowler was usually given a hat as a reward for his efforts, although some say the term may have originated with the tradition of the bowler passing his cap through the crowd to collect tips after completing a hat trick. It is believed that hockey's version of the hat trick may have started in the 1940s, when a Toronto hat maker promised free hats to any player scoring three goals in a game. The first hat trick in hockey history has been lost to time, although some claim that Joe Malone was the first to score three goals in a game. Wayne Gretzky owns the record for most hat tricks with 50. A hat trick is increasingly rare in the goal-stingy NHL of today, and rarer still is the natural hat trick: three consecutive goals scored by one player.

HIGH MUCKAMUCK

In Chinook Jargon, *hyas muckamuck* meant "big food" and "plenty to eat." It could also be used to describe a feast. Guests often found the local aristocracy, who were invited to sit at the head table, arrogant and overbearing, and soon the corrupted term high muckamuck entered Canadian English slang to describe such folk. A derogatory term, it was applied to any important yet overbearing person and was first cited in 1856.

HOCKEY

As Canada's national sport and favourite pastime, hockey inspires much debate and passion; the word itself inspires almost as much as the game. It may have been a derivation of the word hurley. It may have been coined in Halifax, Nova Scotia, in the 1860s. Or it may have been derived from the French word *hoquet* meaning "a shepherd's crooked staff or stick." It spread eastward from the Maritimes, through to Québec and Ontario. By the end of the 19th century, the game had become a national phenomenon, and hockey, regardless of its origins, had become shorthand for Canadian nationality and pride, as well as a boon for beer manufacturers such as Labatt and Molson.

H

HOOTCH

Hootch is fairly common throughout Canada and is used to describe any kind of homebrew liquor. The word originated in the Yukon and British Columbia and was borrowed from the Tlingit word, *khutsnuwa*, meaning "grizzly bear fort," and the name of a Native village on Admiralty Island that was famed for its homegrown whiskey. On English tongues, *khutsnuwa* became *hootchinoo*, which was eventually shortened to just hootch or hooch.

HOSER

First popularized in the early 1980s on the Canadian sketch comedy show, SCTV, by Rick Moranis and Dave Thomas, who gleefully embraced the Canadian stereotype, the term hoser describes a particular sort of Canadian. Hosers are clumsy and oafish, presumably because they are constantly drinking beer, and noticeably Canadian, because they wear tuques. As a verb, to hose first entered common Canadian English usage during the 1960s. To hose a hockey team was to soundly beat them; to hose an individual was to interfere with his or her plans. Although often used in a derogatory manner, hoser can be a term of endearment as well.

HOUND POUNDER

As in most Canadian cities, hockey is almost a religion in Sault Ste. Marie, where the Greyhounds of the Ontario Hockey League come to play. Among their many fans are the hound pounders, so named because they really, really, really love the Greyhound players.

HYDRO

Though most people know it as electricity or a utility, to many Canadians, it's hydro. An informal shortening of the Hydro-Electric Commission of Ontario, which was formed in 1906, hydro has become shorthand for the actual power or electricity distributed by a corporation. There's BC Hydro, Ontario Hydro and Québec Hydro, to name just a few power corporations whose governments have adopted the name. So instead of an electrical bill, Canadians pay a hydro bill. When caught in a blackout, they'll say, "hydro's out."

Those unfamiliar with the term can be forgiven for thinking that it's their taps, and not their refrigerators that have stopped running.

ICE-POOL

A spring event, an ice-pool is a sweepstakes in which the winner is the one who most accurately predicts when the ice will move during the spring break-up. In the days of the Klondike Gold Rush, spring break-up meant much-needed supplies from the south could arrive. A pool describes all the money bet on a particular event by a number of individuals.

ICEWORM

According to the South Tuchone people of the southern Yukon, on winter nights and on days when the sun never rises, the iceworm emerges from its habitat to terrorize trespassing humans. Should a human come near one, the creature attaches itself like a leech to any area of exposed flesh, sucking out all a person's body heat and leaving nothing but dead skin behind. The legend of the iceworm was popularized during the Klondike Gold Rush of the 1890s. Elmer "Stroller" White, a writer with the *Whitehorse Star*, wrote an imaginary tale about the giant iceworm.

The creature had a head on either end of its long, slippery body and came out when the temperature dropped below −60° C. Its smaller brethren, resembling earthworms, were said to be the main component of the iceworm cocktail, a practical joke played on new prospectors by grizzled veterans and immortalized by Robert Service in his poem *The Ballad of the Ice-Worm Cocktail.* There actually is a creature called the ice worm that lives its entire life within glacial ice, in small water pockets near the surface. Ranging from a few millimetres to centimetres in size, the tiny iceworm is a close relative of the earthworm and cannot tolerate temperatures of more than 4° C.

IMAX

In 1970, Canadians Graeme Ferguson, Robert Kerr and Roman Kroitor (with the help of friend William Shaw) premiered the film *Tiger Child* at the Fuji Pavilion of the 1970 World's Exposition in Japan. Audiences were stunned to see images splashed across an eight-storey screen so large that it felt as if they had been immersed in the very images themselves. The film had been presented in the newly invented IMAX format. Ferguson, Kerr and Koitor had established themselves with their films *Polar Life* and *Labyrinth*, which debuted at Expo '67 in Montréal. They were multiscreen spectacles that floored audiences and left them wanting more. The problem was that to show these films, multiple cumbersome projectors had to be used. When they were approached by the Japanese to develop a film for their Expo, Kroitor turned to friends Ferguson and Kerr, and with Shaw's engineering assistance, they invented the IMAX projector. An entirely new genre of film was born. While IMAX has become a popular format today to screen blockbusters such as *The Matrix* and the *Harry Potter* films, Ferguson, Kerr and Koitor developed their device to reduce the number of slide and film projectors required to exhibit audio-visual and multimedia presentations.

INCONNU

When Alexander Mackenzie was exploring the Northwest Territories, his team of voyageurs encountered a fish the likes of which they had never seen before. They called it simply the *poisson inconnu*, the unknown fish. Today it is known as the largest member of the whitefish family. Although its Latin name is *Stenodus leucichthys*, which means narrow-toothed whitefish, it is still called inconnu. From inconnu comes the corruption *conny* or *connie*, by which the inconnu is also known. The Inuit call the fish *shees*, from which yet another name is drawn: sheefish. Not a bad assortment of names for a fish that was once unknown. The inconnu is found throughout the Northwest Territories and the Yukon. It is a long fish with a wide mouth of small, densely packed teeth. Before 1945, the fish was not caught commercially, although it is now popular in the United States, where its high oil content makes it perfect for the smoked fish industry. It is caught principally in Great Slave Lake.

INUKSUK

In the barren landscapes of the North, eerie and stoic figures rise up from the land, stony, lumbering sentinels that look as old as time. These are the Inuksuit of the Canadian Arctic. Meaning "to act in the capacity of a human being," an Inuksuk is a large figure made of rocks that resembles a human with outstretched arms. Occupying a place in Inuit folklore, these Inuksuit also served a very practical and very basic need. In a landscape of few natural landmarks, the Inuksuit serve as navigational markers, coordination points, message centres and indicators of good hunting and fishing grounds. Inuit hunters often hide behind an Inuksuk to better ambush a herd of caribou.

JOE LOUIS CAKES

To those unfamiliar with these best-selling cakes made in Québec, one might ask why a French Canadian dessert was named after American boxer Joe Louis. It wasn't. In 1923, Arcade Vachon and his wife Rose-Anna moved to Saint-Marie-de-Beauce in Québec to start their own bakery. Initially, they sold just breads, but in 1928, the couple began experimenting with cakes as well. Among these was the Gateau Jos. Louis, named after their two sons, Joseph and Louis. It was anglicized into Joe Louis cakes, confusing generations of Canadians. Joe Louis cakes consist of a layer of vanilla sandwiched between two layers of chocolate cake and then covered with yet more chocolate; the number of recipes available for these snacks testifies to the Joe Louis cakes' continuing popularity.

KAYAK

From the Inuit word for "man's boat," a kayak was originally used by the indigenous peoples of the North and Greenland to hunt on the Arctic Ocean. Made from a light wooden frame and rendered waterproof with a tightly stretched membrane of sealskin, the kayak is a small, one-man canoe steered and propelled with a double-bladed paddle. The paddler sits amidships, feet forward, and is protected from the water by a sprayskirt. Modern versions are used mainly for recreation and come in a host of materials such as plastic, fibreglass and Kevlar.

KEENER

Usually found sitting in the front row of a classroom and fond of asking questions of great irrelevance, keeners have been reviled in Canadian university classrooms for decades. They are known elsewhere as suck-ups, boot-licks and kiss-asses. Overly enthusiastic, eager and intense, keeners make a habit of trying to impress people in authority to further their own ambitions and thereby earn the ire of those around them. While they may be called keeners (after the adjective meaning "intellectually alert"), the term is used ironically and may have, in fact, been derived from another meaning of the word keen. From the Middle English *kene*, keen can also mean pungent and offensive to the nose, which keeners most certainly are. A popular game in university classrooms is Keener Bingo. In Ireland, a keener is a professional funeral mourner.

KEROSENE

Distilled from petroleum in a method invented by Canadian doctor Abraham Gesner, kerosene is a thin, colourless fuel that was once widely used in cooking stoves and hand-held lamps. Gesner first exhibited his discovery in Prince Edward Island in 1846, although he didn't get around to naming it until 1854. He combined the Greek word for wax, *keros*, with the common chemical ending *ene*, to get kerosene. It makes sense, really, because the fuel was used in lamps, replacing the finicky wax candles popular at the time. Today, a variant of high-grade kerosene is used as fuel for jet engines.

KLONDIKE

On July 14, 1897, the steamship *Excelsior* sailed into San Francisco bearing a precious cargo of more than $500,000 in gold that had been panned in the Klondike region of Canada's Yukon Territory. With a severe recession crippling both the United States and Canada, the press fell upon the story like wolves, writing sensational articles about the vast stores of gold just waiting to be panned in the Klondike. The gold rush was on. Prior to 1896, the Yukon was a frontier land, sparsely populated by aborginals, fur traders, prospectors and a few members of the North-West Mounted Police. The territory had a total population of just under 5000 people. The Klondike Gold Rush pushed that number to over 30,000 in just two short years. Dawson City was transformed from a sleepy fishing village into the most cosmopolitan city west of Winnipeg, with stores offering French champagnes, oysters and the latest fashions from Paris. Fortunes were made. In 1897, $2.5 million dollars worth of gold was extracted. A year later, it was $10 million. But as quickly as the rush had begun, it ended. With the discovery of gold at Nome, Alaska in 1899, prospectors fled the Yukon to test their fortunes there. Still, in 1900, over $22 million in gold was extracted from the Yukon. The Klondike itself is a tributary of the Yukon River and is an anglicized version of the Gwich'in word, *tron-duik*, meaning "hammer river."

KOKANEE AND SOCKEYE SALMON
Although kokanee for many people will be nothing but a beer pitched by a man dressed in a Sasquatch costume, it is originally a Kutenai word that translated means "red fish." The Kutenai lived in the Kootenay region of southeastern

British Columbia and southwestern Alberta and often fished the kokanee salmon. Along the Pacific coast, the Salish also had a word for red fish, "suk-kegh," which has been turned into sockeye, of the famous sockeye salmon. Although the fish are not usually red, when the sockeye salmon turns upstream to spawn, its back takes on a brilliant red hue that contrasts sharply with its green head. The sockeye and the kokanee are actually the same fish, although the kokanee may be slightly smaller. The only difference between the two fish is that the kokanee is a land-locked, freshwater sockeye salmon. And seeing as it is a sockeye, the kokanee also turns a bright red colour when spawning, which explains how one fish could have two names.

LABRADOR TEA

Labrador tea is the name of both a small aromatic shrub (*Ledum groenlandicum*) common throughout northeastern North America and the hot beverage made from its narrow, leathery leaves. The shrub is a plant of many uses. For centuries, it was used by North American Indians, such as the Cree, to treat skin ailments and, considering its high content of vitamin C, to prevent scurvy. When Hudson Bay's Company traders began exploring the continent, they too realized its usefulness, finding it particularly effective in treating arthritis, dizziness, stomach troubles, heartburn, colds and tuberculosis. Little surprise then, that Labrador tea is also known as Hudson Bay tea. It thrives in cold bogs and mountain woods and is grazed upon by both caribou and moose. But as effective as the plant can be in treating ailments, use it in small doses. Excessive consumption of Labrador tea can cause blistering headaches and even intoxication, and may be why Laplanders place the bush's leaves in their grain to keep mice away. Placed in clothing, the leaves deter moths. In Russia, the leaves are used in the leather tanning process. Newfound-land and Labrador's coat of arms features a small field of Labrador tea.

LABRADORITE

Named after the Labrador Peninsula where it was first discovered by missionaries in 1770, labrador-ite is the provincial mineral of Newfoundland. A feldspar, it's a stone composed of silica, alumina, iron, lime, soda and potash, and is deceptively plain. Viewed from one angle, it may appear grey-green. From another, the stone's iridescence, so strong and remarkable that it has become known as labradorescence, reveals itself in a dazzling dis-play of blues, and in rarer cases, yellows, reds and golds. Though used primarily today in jewellery, it was for a time ground and used as an additive in washing powder and a polishing agent in toothpaste. Labradorite has a long and sometimes mystical his-tory. Native American Indians who encountered the stone called it firestone and powdered it for use in potions and magic. Modern-day mystics still ascribe magical qualities to the stone, believ-ing that it can unleash the power of the imagi-nation, amplify a person's strengths, aid in sleep and foster empathy. In Inuit folklore, the North-ern Lights were imprisoned within labradorite. An Inuit warrior found them, and with a stab of a mighty spear, freed most of them. The rest remain trapped in labradorite, destined to forever shimmer and dazzle.

LACROSSE

The oldest organized sport in North America, lacrosse was first played by aboriginal peoples, including the Iroquois and Cherokee. For them, it was far more than just a sport. Called baggataway or teewaraathon, it was a sacred ritual and was viewed as the Creator's Game. Hundreds or even thousands of people would spend days at the game, running across fields that spanned as much as 24 km to lob a clay or stone ball at a tree marker. People viewed the game as a training ground for war; the Cherokee called it "the little brother of war." Early French explorers who witnessed these events saw something familiar. The sticks, they felt, resembled a bishop's crozier, which they called *la crosse*. The game itself may have resembled a field hockey game called *jeu de la crosse* that the French often played. Modern lacrosse embodies elements of basketball, soccer and hockey, and the rules for the modern game were laid down in the late 19th century by Dr. William George Peers, a Montréal-based dentist.

LATEER

An anglicized version of the French Canadian word *la tire*, lateer is what you get when you pour hot maple syrup into the snow: brittle shards of sugary goodness popular throughout Québec with all ages (though they call it *tire sur la neige*). *La tire* is French Canadian for toffee, and it was derived from the French verb, *tirer*, to pull, a literal description of how toffee is made.

LCBO

In 1927, after an 11-year experiment, the Ontario Temperance Act was repealed. Prohibition was over. With the province wet again, the government, still concerned about people's consumption of alcohol, created the Liquor Control Board of Ontario—the LCBO. Established by the Liquor Control Act, the LCBO would control the sale, transportation and delivery of alcoholic beverages in Ontario and would regulate the availability and consumption of alcohol. In 1927, the first LCBO stores opened in Toronto, and soon there were 80 across the province. Sales were over $12.3 million. Today, the LCBO has over 600 stores, employs about 5000 people and generates sales of $2 billion. It is one of the largest single purchasers of alcohol in the world. In 1997, consumers were allowed to buy alcohol on Sundays. In Ontario, LCBO has become synonymous for the liquor store, and people can often be heard in Toronto's downtown core saying, "I can't believe this LCBO closes at 6 on a Saturday." In recent years, the Ontario government has flirted with the idea of privatizing the sale of liquor, meaning that the LCBO may soon be nothing but a memory.

LOBSTICK

The northern Cree used a lobstick as a living landmark: a tribute or a monument to a friend, perhaps, or as a personal talisman or a geographic marker in a land that could swallow up even the hardiest and knowledgeable of explorers. The lobstick itself was a conspicuous thing, a spruce or pine tree that had been denuded of all its branches save for the topmost and two bottom ones. The earliest voyageurs used lobsticks as trailmarkers over 200 years ago. The great explorer Alexander Mackenzie coined the name for these strange and eerie monuments in his 1789 book, *Voyage from Montréal*.

LOONIE

In May 1987, the Canadian government, in an attempt to cut costs, introduced an 11-sided, gold-coloured coin to replace the one-dollar bill. The move wasn't a popular one and in jest, Canadians took to calling the coin "Mulroney's Loonie," after then Prime Minister Brian Mulroney. Not only did the term rhyme, but loonie perfectly described the new coin. Made of aureate bronze plated onto pure nickel, the loonie depicts on its reverse side a loon drifting lazily through a lake. On the obverse is a portrait of Queen Elizabeth II. The loon was designed by famed wildlife artist Robert-Ralph Carmichael, but it was not the original intended design. The plan was to have a voyageur, but he got lost during his portage to the Royal Canadian Mint in Winnipeg. No matter. The loon is Canada's national bird and while it didn't gain popularity until 1989 when the Royal Canadian Bank stopped producing one-dollar bills, the coin quickly became common, weighing down the pockets and purses of Canadians everywhere. The name loonie stuck.

LOTUS LAND

It's not clear when Canadians began referring to British Columbia as Lotus Land, but it probably has something to do with the province's laid-back, relaxed and easy-going attitude. With a temperate climate, beautiful beaches and proximity to both the ocean and the Rockies, British Columbians are able to enjoy their leisure and care little if stressed easterners cluck their tongues and turn their noses up. Lotus Land as a term for a land of dreamy and languid contentment is drawn from Homer's *The Odyssey*, in which Odysseus journeyed to the land of the Lotus-Eaters, where people lived in a blissful, drugged and indolent state. While British Columbians use the term with pride, the term Lotus Land does have pejorative overtones, associated as it is with laziness and lives devoted to little else besides pleasure and luxury.

MAL DE RAQUETTE

Mal de raquette, or snowshoe sickness, was the bane of many of Canada's earliest explorers. Aboriginals used snowshoes with the greatest of ease, but the coureurs de bois, often found that the muscles of their legs and feet were ill-prepared for the rigours of tramping across the snow on the raquette, or snowshoe. Novice users of snowshoes are advised today to tread lightly and avoid the mal de raquette.

MALPEQUE OYSTERS

Although just a tiny province, Prince Edward Island looms large in the culinary world because in Malpeque Bay, PEI, Malpeque oysters are grown. Prized for their buttery texture and sharp-sweet, briny flavour, Malpeques can fetch as much as $3 per single oyster at some restaurants in New York, arguably the culinary capital of North America. The first Prince Edward Island product to be widely exported, Malpeques are still harvested by fishermen using traditional hand-held rakes. When the winter ice begins to break up, fishermen head out in 16-foot long dories to rake the mud to expose the oysters that are just beginning to feed again after a long winter's hibernation. Malpeque Bay is an Acadian French translation of the Mi'kmaq word, *Mak Paak*, meaning "large bay."

MAPLE SYRUP AND ITS TERMS

As the world's leading producer of maple syrup, Québec has developed a language all its own to describe the various aspects of the maple syrup industry. It produces close to 90 percent of Canada's maple syrup and sells its product all around the globe. A lot of maple syrup terms revolve around the word sugar, which is the main component of maple syrup and why consumers love the stuff so much. Native peoples, especially those living in the St. Lawrence and Great Lakes regions, have been drawing syrup from maple trees for centuries. They used an innovative and practical method of boiling down the sap. The Algonquin called the sap *sinzibuckwud*, meaning "drawn from wood." Legend has it that the syrup was discovered by the Iroquois, who often cooked their meat in maple sap. At some point, they began collecting sap in hollowed-out logs they called *mococks.* Stones were then heated and tossed into the logs, boiling the water off. French explorers sampled the product and quickly fell in love with it. In 1690, a Frenchman is believed to have been the first European to make maple syrup, and with so many stands of maple native throughout the

Maritimes, southern Ontario and Québec (and as the only source of sugar available to settlers), the industry flourished. *Maple sugaring,* the harvesting and processing of maple syrup, had become a community event by the 18th century. The sap was collected during three runs: *the robin run, the frog run* and *the bud run.* The *sugarshack* became the building where water from the sap, collected in stands of maple trees called a *sugarbush,* was boiled off under the watchful eye of the *sugarmaster.* The maple leaf has adorned our national flag since it was first unveiled on February 15, 1965, and on April 25, 1996, it became Canada's national arboreal emblem.

MARQUIS WHEAT

In the mid- to late 19th century, settlers were beginning to populate the vast prairies of the Canadian West, lured there by the cheap land and the convenience and ease of the railway. But the prairie weather was harsh, and farming proved difficult in the short growing season. The Red Fife wheat that was grown, while hardy, was easily damaged by frost. William Saunders, working at Ottawa's Central Experiment Farm, decided to rectify the problem. Along with his son Charles, Saunders spent almost 10 years cross-breeding countless wheat varieties in the hopes of creating a durable wheat that matured quickly. In 1909, the Saunders unveiled the fruit of their labours: Marquis wheat, a cross between Red Fife and Hard Red Calcutta. Introduced to the

West in 1910, it proved hardy, had high yields and matured three to ten days faster than the Red Fife, and could therefore be harvested before the onset of frost. Marquis wheat opened the prairies, doubling the amount of land that could be farmed. By 1920, 90 percent of Canadian wheat being grown was of the Marquis variety. William Saunders and his son were single-handedly responsible for turning the Canadian West into the breadbasket of the world. When Sir Charles Saunders died in 1937, the *London Daily Express* wrote in his obituary that "he added more wealth to his country than any other man. Marconi gave power. Saunders gave abundance. Great lives, these."

MARSH PEGS

He may not have ever fulfilled his dream of playing in the National Hockey League, but Fred Marsh can claim something that not even the greatest hockey players such as Wayne Gretzky or Bobby Orr can. Since 1991, a part of Fred Marsh has been at every NHL game, every playoff game and every Stanley Cup final game. He's even been to the Olympics twice and to the World Cup. How has he accomplished this feat? Marsh's story begins in British Columbia, where he worked in arenas for four decades. In 1984, the community of Kitimat was concerned about the injuries hockey players were sustaining after crashing into the metal posts of the goalie's net. Anchored by rigid metal rods, the nets had little give. Legs were broken and careers were aborted. Marsh set about creating Marsh Pegs, which would allow the net to move but not enough to dislodge it during play. If a player crashes into it, the net comes loose, thereby decreasing the chances of injury. In 1991, the National Hockey League began using Marsh Pegs, too, and at long last, at the age of 56, Fred Marsh had made it to the big show.

MCINTOSH APPLES

If it weren't for a family squabble and an unfortunate love, the world might never have known the pleasures and delights of eating the sweet, red, crisp fruit known as the McIntosh. In 1796, John McIntosh was living in the Mohawk Valley of New York state with his Scottish parents. But, after a family feud over a girl McIntosh had fallen in love with, he headed north to meet his love, whom he planned to marry in secret. But when he arrived, he discovered that she had passed away, the victim of a sudden and unexpected illness. Distraught and heartbroken, McIntosh settled near Prescott, Ontario, in a little farming community named Dundela. While clearing his land in 1811, McIntosh made a serendipitous discovery. Several young apple trees were growing on his land; McIntosh transplanted them to a garden near his home. One tree in particular bore an apple of such sweetness and crispness that family and friends clamoured for more. They even wanted their own trees, but unfortunately, McIntosh and others could not replicate nature's work. Finally in 1835, McIntosh, on the advice of a farmhand, succeeded when he tried the techniques of grafting and budding. From that one tree came millions of others, each bearing apples that became known as McIntosh Reds. Today, there are over three million McIntosh trees throughout North America, and the McIntosh comprises almost half of Canada's annual apple crop.

MEDICARE

On July 1, 1962, the Co-operative Commonwealth Federation government of Saskatchewan finally introduced its Medical Care Act. It was the realization of a dream that had begun when Premier Tommy Douglas, widely acknowledged as the "Father of Medicare," had been first elected in 1944. As early as 1933, the CCF's *Regina Manifesto* stated that "health services should be made at least as freely available as are educational services today...under this system that is namely a private enterprise...costs of proper medical care are prohibitive to the great masses of the people." Ironically, those words are relevant today. The act's passage introduced a new word to Canadians: Medicare, defined as publicly funded and universal health care. It's also a word charged with political and social significance. From its inception, the Medical Care Act was wildly unpopular with Saskatchewan doctors, who staged a 23-day strike in protest. They feared that it would threaten their livelihoods and destroy the patient-doctor relationship. The great experiment turned out to be a great success and, in 1967, Medicare went national with the passage of the Canada Health Act.

MEMORIAL CUP

In March 1919, the Ontario Hockey Association donated a trophy called the OHA Memorial Cup, so named to honour the fallen Canadian soldiers of the First World War. It would be awarded to the top junior hockey team in Canada. From 1919 to 1928, two teams, one from eastern Canada and one from western Canada, met in a two-game, total-goals series to determine the recipient of the Memorial Cup. From 1929 to 1971, the championship was decided in a best-of-three series. In 1972, the commissioners of the Canadian Hockey League decided that the three champions of its three leagues, the Western Hockey League, the Québec Major Junior Hockey League and the Ontario Hockey League, met in a round-robin tournament to determine the cup winner. In 1983, a fourth team, the host team, was added.

MÉTIS

The Métis are Canadian aboriginals of First Nation and European ancestry. The term has been in use since the earliest days of the fur trade to describe the offspring of French and Scottish traders and their Cree, Ojibwa, Saulteaux and Assiniboine wives. The Métis evolved into their own peoples in the historic northwest, with their own customs and language, *Michif*, a mixture of French and Cree that employed French nouns and noun phrases within the Cree verb system. Their culture reflects the diversity of their origins, incorporating Scottish, French, Ojibway and Cree traditions. The annexation of their land by Canada in 1869 crippled their economy, and for years afterwards, they became known as Canada's forgotten people. It wasn't until 1982 that they were officially recognized as an aboriginal people in the Canadian Constitution. Estimates place today's Métis population at anywhere between 300,000 and 800,000 people, most of whom live in western Canada. The word Métis is drawn from the French word for mixed, which itself is derived from the Latin word *miscellus*. Famous Métis heroes include Louis Riel and Gabriel Dumont.

MICKEY or MICKY

Usually found shoved down pants, a mickey, or micky, refers to a 384 ml bottle of liquor, usually whiskey, and often shaped to fit, conveniently, in a pocket. The term gained popularity in the middle of the 19th century, when the bottles became popular with those looking to hide their prodigious drinking. Although it seems only Canadians use the term in this way, the mickey's origins are Irish and American. In the late 19th century, New York City's Irish immigrant population was exploding, and with bigotry hounding their every step, many Irishmen turned to the bars for comfort. Mickey Finn became slang for a rowdy and drunk Irishman. It was first applied to liquor itself in the early 20th century. According to legend, a Chicago bar named Mickey Finn gained great notoriety for its drink specials. Spiked, the drinks contained chloral hydrate, rendering unconscious anyone who drank them. Once knocked out, unsuspecting patrons were taken to a back room, robbed and then dumped in an alley. Other bars adopted this sort of Mickey Finn, but instead of chloral hydrate, they used laxatives, dropping them only into the drinks of the most unruly and belligerent customers. It was the easiest way of getting the overly inebriated to leave in a hurry.

MINTY

Just so there's no confusion, when a person from Winnipeg calls something minty, he isn't saying that it smells like peppermint or that it's fragrant. Minty is a catch-all expression in Winnipeg. It means cool or fantastic or, in some cases, it just means something is mint, as in mint condition. The origins of the term are unknown, though perhaps it relates to the Royal Canadian Mint being headquartered there.

MOLSON MUSCLE

Although its origins are obscure, Molson muscle is a distinctly Canadian term used to describe the pot belly, the beer belly or the spare tire, essentially, an enlarged gut resulting from the consumption of too many Molson Canadians. The alliterative term is much more flattering—it almost sounds like something you could and should be proud of.

MUKLUK

Originally made from the skins of the bearded seal or the reindeer, the mukluk was a knee-high boot, soft, warm and waterproof. Within the etymology of the word lies the mukluk's origin; mukluk is derived from the Yupik word *maklak*, meaning "bearded seal." Yupik was a language of the Inuit of the western Arctic. The word has entered Canadian English and is now applied to any slipper with a soft sole resembling the mukluk. Today mukluks are made from all sorts of synthetic materials.

M

MUSKELLUNGE

Prized by anglers for its ferocity and tenacity, the muskellunge (or musky, as it's also known) is a powerful predator closely related to the northern pike. It is the largest of Canada's freshwater game fish, and though most caught today weigh just between 2.3 and 16.3 kilograms, some have been known to exceed 45 kilograms. Found throughout the St. Lawrence River, the Great Lakes and some inland waters in Ontario and Québec, the muskellunge derives its name from the Ojibwa word, *maskingonge*, meaning "ugly fish" and *lunge*, or "lake trout." Some linguists have also offered the idea that muskellunge may be a corruption of the French *maggue allongee*, or "long face," which is what early French explorers may have called this fighting fish.

MUSKOX

To the northern Indians, it is known as *omingmak*—the animal with skin like a beard. Given its woolly appearance and long skirt of fur that hangs to the ground, it's easy to see why it was given such a name. But early Canadian fur traders, who prized the muskox for its fur, called it something else entirely. They named the creature the muskox, because of its resemblance to the ox and because of the musky smell of its urine, especially during mating season. One of Canada's oldest mammals, the muskox is uniquely adapted to life in the arctic tundra. Its coat is made of two layers, one hairy and one woolly. Its wool, known as *qiviut* to the Inuit, is stronger than sheep's wool, and finer and eight times warmer than cashmere. Not surprisingly, the muskox was prized for its coat and its meat. Its horns were used for Inuit tools and crafts. Often seen standing in outward facing circles to harness their warmth and to protect their young, muskoxen can survive temperatures of −40° C, high winds and blowing snow. Human hunters exploited the muskoxen's defensive circles, using dogs to act as arctic wolves, the muskox's only natural predator, and then using spears and arrows to slay the massed animals.

In 1917, the Canadian government brought the muskox under its protection, and the animal now roams in great numbers across the Banks and Victoria Islands of Canada's North.

NANAIMO BAR

The origins of the Nanaimo bar are unclear. According to one account, the Nanaimo bar was first created about 35 years ago when a Nanaimo housewife decided to enter a magazine cooking contest. She dubbed her entry—a sweet chocolate and buttercream concoction—Nanaimo bars. The treat won raves and a prize, forever linking that Vancouver Island community with the dessert. It proved so popular that it wasn't long before the recipe was made available as a handout, printed onto tea towels and souvenir aprons for Canadians from all over the country eager to duplicate the confection in their own kitchens. However, northeastern Americans claim that the Nanaimo bar has its roots in New York, where it has been known for years as a New York Slice. Still others claim that the Nanaimo bar became popular during that community's mining heydays in the 19th century. Many of the miners who flocked to Nanaimo to plumb its coal-rich depths had come from the United Kingdom. Far removed from their homes and families, they often asked their distant relatives to send them care packages. Nestled among their boxes of tea and biscuits were chocolate squares. These proved popular not just with the miners, but with the locals too, and eventually, they became known as Nanaimo bars. Regardless of its origins, the Nanaimo bar is firmly entrenched as a much-beloved item on the Canadian menu. At its most basic, it consists of a base of chocolate and coconut, a buttercream centre and a chocolate glaze. There are count-less variations, with some recipes incorporating whole nuts, peanut butter and other items, all deliciously addictive.

OKA CHEESE

Oka was first made in 1893 in the little Québec village of Oka. It was first produced by French Trappist monks and was a variation of a Port Salut recipe that had come from Brittany. Monks still oversee the cheese's production, ensuring that the semi-soft cheese with the pungent aroma and creamy taste will continue to reach standards of excellence.

OOLICHAN

To the aboriginals of Canada's northern coasts, the arrival of the oolichan often signalled the end of yet another long, harsh winter. Known as the "salvation fish," the oolichan was the first fish to arrive in the rivers of spring, a welcome sight for the early people whose food stores had almost been depleted. A small, silvery fish, the oolichan (*Thaleichthys pacificus*) is a member of the smelt family, usually growing between 15 and 20 cm long and weighing between 40 and 60 gr. The flesh was sometimes eaten, but the fish was and is prized more for its oil. Northern First Nations all have different methods of obtaining oolichan grease, with each producing slightly different flavours. Typically the oolichan are allowed to ripen under evergreen branches for two weeks and then are cooked in fresh water. The oil is then skimmed from the top to be used, like butter, on salmon, halibut or berries. The grease trails of British Columbia derive their name from the oolichan grease trade.

PABLUM

In 1931, after two years of research at the Hospital for Sick Children in Toronto, three doctors, Frederick Tisdall, Theodore Drake and Alan Brown, unveiled the fruit of their labours. It was called Pablum, derived from the Latin *pabulum*, which means food or animal feed. The doctors' mixture of wheat, oats, corn, bone meal, wheat germ, dried brewer's yeast and alfalfa gave to the world its very first thoroughly cooked, dried and nutritious cereal for infants. Although it tasted terribly bland, the concoction was packed full of five vitamins: A, B_1, B_2, D and E. It was the vitamin D that was most important; the doctors were intent on preventing rickets, a disease that develops in early childhood owing to a lack of that particular vitamin. Free of eggs, dairy and nuts, it was also unlikely to cause allergic reactions. Given its simple, bland flavour and its place as a staple of any infant's diet, the term pablum has also become slang for oversimplified ideas.

PAINT ROLLER

In the 1930s, Norman Breakey of Toronto decided to change the world of painting and design, and to get rich doing it, too. In 1940, he unveiled his idea: the paint roller. People loved the t-shaped device for its simplicity and the way in which it chopped hours off of the arduous task of painting with a brush. Unfortunately, its very simplicity proved to be Breakey's undoing. Imitations of his device popped up everywhere, and though Breakey had patented his invention, he couldn't afford to legally defend it, so the riches that he had envisioned never did materialize. Breakey is credited with revolutionizing the painting and design industry and for ushering in a whole new do-it-yourself movement, but it was of little comfort to him.

PEAMEAL BACON

To most Americans, Canadian bacon is what we call back bacon, a smoked pork product that tastes and looks a lot like ham. But many Canadians (at least those in Ontario), will tell you that real Canadian bacon is actually peameal bacon. Peameal bacon consists of a boneless pork loin, cured in pickle brine, and then rolled in ground yellow peas. The ground yellow peas helped cure the pork and added vastly to its shelf life. The yellow peas are no longer used (they've been replaced by cornmeal), but the name has stuck. How did Canadian bacon become Canadian bacon? According to Ken Haviland, who was born in Ontario but who now lives in Wisconsin, a pork shortage in England at the end of the 19th century led to the importing of side bacon from Canada. The English smoked the meat, and Americans who sampled the product were told that it had come from Canada. Peameal bacon was left for Canadians to savour.

PEMMICAN

From the Abnaki word *pemikan* and the Cree word *pimikan* (meaning "prepared fat"), pemmican was the food upon which Canada was built. Nutritious, hearty and durable, pemmican was prized by North American Indians and fur traders. Fatty buffalo meat provided both iron and energy, while the berries proved especially useful at warding off scurvy. Pemmican was the major food staple of Alexander Mackenzie when he became the first European to cross the North American continent in 1793. To make pemmican, dried strips of meat from animals such as bison, moose, elk or deer were ground and pounded between stones. To the meat, ground berries were added along with the melted fat, suet and bone marrow grease. The mixture was then stored in bags made of bison skin, called *parfleches*, which were sealed with melted tallow. As the bison skins dried, they shrank, compressing the meat and creating an airtight container that preserved the pemmican for years. There are records of traders consuming pemmican that had kept for four years. They are said to have recorded no noticeable difference in taste or texture.

PENGUIN

The original penguin was not the breed with which we are familiar today. The term penguin was first used to describe a large, flightless, short-necked diving seabird known as the great auk (*Pinguinus impennis*), which could be found in great abundance on Newfoundland's Funk Island, far removed from Antarctica and the Southern Hemisphere. In the 16th century, the birds were so numerous that they formed a black mass large and distinct enough that early explorers, including Jacques Cartier, used it as a navigational marker. Funk Island became known as the Island of Penguins. The bird itself was valued as a food source, rich in proteins and nutritious fats and oils. Its distinctive feathers were prized for clothing. The word penguin has many origins; some believe that it is a derivation of pen-winged or pinioned. Still others say that it has Welsh roots, from the phrase *pen gwyn*, meaning "white head." The penguin did, after all, have distinctive white patches in front of its eyes. European explorers in the Southern Hemisphere, glimpsing a bird that looked very much like the penguin they had seen in the north, transferred the name to the flightless birds we know today as penguins. The name might have survived, but the bird did not. By 1844, the great auk had been hunted into extinction.

PÉQUISTE

Formed in 1968, the Parti Québecois is a provincial political party dedicated to obtaining independence for Québec. In 1976, under the leadership of René Lévesque, the Parti Québecois gained control of the provincial assembly and quickly passed Bill 101, making French the province's only official language, requiring the French words to be bigger than any other language on signs. However, in 1980, a provincial referendum rejected plans to open talks with the federal government to negotiate Québec independence. When Lévesque left the party in 1985, the party struggled, returning to power only in 1994. A year later, the party stumbled again when plans for independence were narrowly rejected in a hotly contested referendum. In the 2003 election, the Parti Québecois, led by Bernard Landry, lost to Jean Charest's Liberal Party. The party's tenacious supporters and members are known as péquistes, a derivation of the French pronunciation of the party's initials.

PINGO

From the Inuit word *pingu*, which means "ice-lens," a pingo is an ice-cored hill, typically conical in shape. Water and ice that has accumulated underground is pushed upward, breaking through the surface. Exposed, it begins to collect peat and soil, thus creating the pingo. A pingo is a naturally occurring topographical formation found commonly in areas of permafrost, notably the

Canadian Arctic. In the Mackenzie Delta region there are at least 1450 pingos.

PLOYES

A ploye is the Acadian version of a pancake, but unlike the pancake, a ploye uses no milk or eggs in its preparation. It's a versatile item that is often substituted for bread. In some Maritime provinces and Québec, the ploye is eaten at breakfast with cretons, at lunch with some butter and after dinner with berries and whipping cream. Little wonder that it was once a staple of the loggers' diet and continues to be a staple today. Made of buckwheat flour, which was a common, cheap and hardy crop, ployes are cooked on one side only, on a sizzling hot skillet known as a *poëlonne*. The etymology of ploye is not completely clear; some linguists theorize that the word came from the French verb *plier*, "to bend or to fold," which many people do with their ployes. Others speculate that it may have come from the sound of the ploye batter being mixed—ploye, ploye, ploye. Regardless, it is a popular dish throughout eastern Canada, the northeastern United States and Louisiana.

POGEY

When the Great Depression swept through Canada in the 1930s, millions of people found themselves without a job and without an income. The federal government began offering financial assistance for the most distressed of its citizens. Canadians began referring to the money meted out as pogey. Originally used to describe a workhouse, a poor-house or a prison near the end of the 19th century, pogey has entered Canadian English vernacular. Like the dole in the United Kingdom, pogey is a mildly insulting term for what were once known as unemployment benefits, but which, in this time of overwhelming political correctness, is now known as EI or Employment Insurance.

POT-EN-POT

When the Acadians were expelled from their homes in the Maritimes in 1755, many of them settled in the Magdelan Islands, a crescent-shaped group of islands in the Gulf of St. Lawrence. They brought with them their culture and their foods and even today, centuries later, their influence can be felt in all aspects of life on the islands. One regional specialty is the pot-en-pot, a dish consisting of seafood and potatoes baked in a flaky crust. Its name was derived from the preparation of the dish—two pots were used, the contents of one poured into the other. In Québec, the pot-en-pot is also a meat dish, usually made with chicken and hare, although beef, pork, duck and goose are also used.

POTLATCH

From Chinook Jargon comes the word potlatch, meaning "to give." It is used to describe a ceremonial feast among aboriginal peoples of the north-west Pacific coast given to celebrate the occasion of a marriage or an accession. Historically, the host of a potlatch distributed gifts according to a guest's rank and status, with the implicit understanding that the host would be treated in kind. Gifts ranged from foods, slaves and copper plates to things less material, such as names, songs or dances. It became popular at potlatches for hosts, desperate to maintain some semblance of nobility and status within a society that could not possibly compete with the industrialized world, to destroy property in an extravagant display, as if to say, "I'll just get another." The Government of Canada banned potlatches in 1884 but eventually lifted the ban in 1951.

POUTINE

Like many inventions, poutine was conceived through an act of serendipity. In 1957, to satisfy a customer's craving for both French fries and cheese curds, Québec restaurateur Fernand Lachance put both in the same bag. Lachance called the sticky, oozing mess that he had created poutine, which was an early French Canadian derivation of the English word *pudding*, used originally to describe a mish-mash of cookies, custard and fruit. A phenomenon was born. Eventually, gravy was added to the combination of fries and curds, rendering it even more irresistible. Poutine has become a food staple beyond Québec. Countries such as Italy have even cooked up their own versions, serving the snack with a meat sauce instead of gravy. Even fast food chains such as McDonald's and Burger King have offered their own versions of the snack.

POVERTY PACK

Perhaps this term, describing a six-pack of beer, originated during the Great Depression. With limited funds and little else to do but drink and escape their numbing realities, the unemployed could only afford the six-pack. Whatever its origins, the poverty pack can be used to describe any six-pack of beer.

PRAIRIE

Prairie is used to refer to the great expanse of mostly flat, rolling and usually treeless grassland covering much of western Canada east of the Rockies and west of the Ontario border. The word prairie comes to Canadian English from the Old French word *praierie*, itself derived from the Latin *pratu*, meaning "meadow," used by French Canadian trappers exploring the continent for pelts.

PUCK

A frozen disc, 7.6 cm in diameter, and made of vulcanized rubber, the puck is the hotly contested object lying at the heart of hockey. It was first used during a hockey game in 1860, at Kingston Harbor, Ontario, replacing the India-rubber ball. How the rubber disc got its name is a mystery.

Most believe that it is a derivation of the British dialectical verb, to puck (poke), meaning "to hit or to strike" as in "he pucked the ball." Puck is no longer a verb but a noun; now, people shout "shoot the puck" or "stop the puck!"

QUÉBECOIS

When Champlain built a blockhouse on Cape Diamond in 1608 overlooking the St. Lawrence River, it was hard not to notice that the river narrowed at the point. The Mi'kmaqs called the area *Gepeeg*, or "where the river narrows." From that word, came Québec, and subsequently, Québecois. Although Québecois, at its simplest, refers to a resident of Québec, especially one who speaks French, it is a word fraught with meaning and significance. For many Anglophones, Québecois symbolizes those agitating for political and social independence in Québec, an association no doubt born out of the 1976 election in which the Parti Québecois ran and won on a platform of sovereignty.

RED ROSE TEA

Who can forget the television ads for Red Rose tea, in which a stuffy British gentleman sniffs, "Only in Canada, you say? Pity?" Red Rose, the tea available only in Canada, has its beginnings with Theodore Estabrooks. In 1894, Estabrooks, who worked as an importer and exporter, decided to specialize in tea. From the start, it looked as if Estabrooks had made a terrible decision. He sold only just $166 dollars worth of his product in his first year. But, in 1899, Estabrooks teamed with a friend, M.R. Miles, to create something new and different. Teas at the time were usually a blend of Chinese and Japanese teas. Estabrooks and Miles looked south, to India and Sri Lanka, and created a blend of tea that they called Red Rose Tea. The blend met with great success and by 1900, Estabrooks' company was selling over 1000 tons of tea a year. Headquartered in St. John, New Brunswick, Red Rose found fans throughout that province and Nova Scotia, and eventually the rest of the country.

REEVE

Common in Ontario and some parts of western Canada, a reeve is the elected head of a township council or a rural municipal council. Derived from Middle and Old English, a reeve, in Anglo-Saxon times, was a high administrative officer appointed by a king. Later, the term also came to apply to manor officers who overlooked feudal discharges.

REGALE

As a noun, regale can mean a great feast, or a great delicacy, or some sort of refreshment. Whatever its definition, it's clear that a regale appeals to both the appetite and desire. It's no wonder then, that the fur-traders and trappers of the Hudson's Bay Company used the French word to describe the special ration of rum they received on festive occasions and after a long and tortuous journey. The word survives today in Canadian English, but has come to encompass any handout or favour given at a party.

ROUGHRIDER

Originally a British term used to describe a non-commissioned officer of the British Cavalry and assistant to the riding master, a roughrider became something else during the settlement of the West. Horses were crucial to survival on the open prairies, and men who could break wild steeds for domestic use were rare and therefore prized. Accustomed to the rough and hard riding of a wild horse, these men became known as roughriders. They shouldn't be confused with Canadian Football League teams in Saskatchewan or Ottawa, or with the members of the Rough Riders cavalry regiment that fought under U.S. President Theodore Roosevelt during the Spanish-American War.

SAQ

In 1898, a Canada-wide referendum on Prohibition was held. Given its Catholic heritage (wine was used for communion services) and Gallic love of the drink, most Québec voters response was resoundingly negative. Still, in 1918, the Québec government passed Prohibition legislation. Just a year later, in a province-wide referendum, Québecers voted to exclude beer, wine and cider from the Prohibition law, and Québec became the only jurisdiction in both Canada and the United States not to have total Prohibition. To regulate the sale of wine and spirits, the Québec government passed the Alcoholic Beverages Act in 1921, creating the Commission des Liqueurs du Québec. It opened 64 stories, employed 415 people and, in a testament to the unpopularity of temperance, recorded $15 million in sales. These first stores were nothing but counters set behind a metal grid where only the price list was available for viewing. Patrons could buy only one bottle of spirits a time, and the bottles were wrapped in nondescript paper. In 1941, purchase limits on spirits were abolished, and in 1961, under the newly created Régis des alcohols du Québec, the first partial self-serve stores were opened. In 1971, the Régis des alcohols du Québec was split into two separate entities: the Commission de contrôle des permis d'alcool and the Société des alcools du Québec, which would become more familiarly and fondly known as the SAQ (pronounced sack). Much like the LCBO in Ontario, SAQ in Québec has become slang for the liquor store.

SASHAY

Sashay is an anglicized version of the French word *chasser*, meaning "to chase," and has been in use since the mid-19th century. Brought to Canadian shores by early French explorers, a sashay is a gliding step used in both ballet and square dancing. Informally, it is used, often with derogatory overtones, to describe an effeminate stride.

SCREECH

Screech is short for Newfoundland screech, a particularly potent brand of rum and a traditional drink in the province. Demerara rum from the West Indies was often traded in exchange for Newfoundland salt fish. The rum was a drink with no name and was served in a simple, unlabelled glass bottle. During World War II, the United States established bases throughout Newfoundland. One evening, an American serviceman was out drinking and was tempted to try the shots of liquor that the locals downed in great numbers and with great ease. The American serviceman followed suit, throwing back his drink in one gulp. It didn't agree with him and he let out such a scream that people came running from blocks around to see what the commotion was about. An American sergeant entered the bar, demanding to know what was the reason behind such a "horrible screech." The Newfoundlander who greeted the sergeant at the door simply replied, "The screech? It was the rum." The name stuck, and the government began calling its rum Newfoundland screech. Demerara rum is no longer used; Newfoundland screech is now Jamaica rum, which is far less likely to induce fits of screeching.

SCREECH-IN CEREMONY

For non-native Newfoundlanders who are dying to become Newfoundlanders, there's only one way to go about it: take part in a screech-in ceremony. Performed under the watch of a native New-foundlander, the screech-in ceremony involves kissing an actual fish (usually a cod, but any other fish will do) on the lips. Then, a shot of screech is lifted high, and just before drinking, the words, "Long may your long jib draw" are uttered. Those successfully completing a screech-in ceremony are forever honorary Newfoundlanders.

SHANTY

A shanty, a roughly and crudely built cabin, may have had its origins in French Canada. Loggers working in the woods often lived in meager, austere conditions, in ramshackle huts they called *chantiers* (which is French for lumberyard). The term had become generalized by, at the latest, the early 19th century. Others hypothesize that the term may have come from Irish immigrants. The Irish Gaelic for old hut is *sean tigh*, and many Irish Canadians worked in the woods of Upper Canada, where the word shanty is believed to have originated.

SHEBANG

Since the mid-19th century, a shebang has been used to describe a hut or shed. It can also be a tavern in the bush, a place for weary trappers and traders to rest and carouse. Its origins are Canadian French from the word *cabane* (meaning "hut") but may also have roots in the Irish Gaelic *shebeen*, which also means hut.

SHIVAREE

A Latin custom, and practised for centuries in France, a shivaree is a custom that was brought to Acadia by the French and then transplanted throughout the continent, notably into Louisiana and Mississippi when the Acadians were expelled. Originally known in French as a *charivari*, shivaree is the French-Canadian form of the word. A shivaree is described as a noisy mock serenade given to newlywed couples. In more superstitious times, it was believed that evil spirits would bring harm to newlyweds. To drive

117

these evil spirits away, guests would bang pans and kettles together, driving the spirits (and presumably anyone within earshot) away.

SIEVE

Heard often in Canada, especially during the hockey season, the word sieve is usually uttered with great frustration and consternation. It's not uncommon to walk through a sports bar and hear, and hear often, "He's such a sieve!" The fans are not referring to the kitchen utensil, but to the goalie. It's not much of a compliment. A sieve, in hockey slang, is a lousy goalie, one prone to letting in too many goals. Sieve, as a word, has its roots in Old and Middle English, from the words *sife* and *sive*. In all likelihood, some kitchen-savvy hockey broadcaster, perhaps Foster Hewitt (who uttered the immortal words, "He shoots, he scores!"), probably gave the word its slang definition.

SIR LAURIER D'ARTHABASKA

Sir Wilfrid Laurier was the first French Canadian prime minister of Canada; elected in 1896, he served until 1911. He lived in Arthabaska, Québec, from 1876 until 1919. The Kingsey Dairy in Québec created a cheese in his honour and named it Sir Laurier d'Arthabaska. A soft, washed-rind cheese with a copper-orange rind and an ivory, creamy interior, it has won numerous awards and is quickly becoming a favourite of many Canadian cheese connoisseurs.

SKOOKUM

A holdover from Chinook Jargon, skookum is perhaps the most common and popular Jargon word still in common use in British Columbia. Originally, skookum meant big, strong and good. It came from the Chehalis language, in which *skukm* denoted power and bravery. Today, skookum is used in a number of ways. If something "looks pretty skookum," then it looks solid and indestructible. If "that's skookum," it means you've done a good job. On its own, "Skookum!" is Chinook Jargon's very own cool, or awesome or excellent. Not surprisingly, a jail along the Pacific coast is sometimes referred to as the skookum box or skookum-house.

SLOB ICE

Slob ice is a term that originated in Newfoundland, but has since spread throughout Canada. Originally it referred to heavy masses of slushy or broken ice, snow and freezing water floating out at sea; slob ice was notoriously difficult to pass through, as it was often a tacky mess. Throughout Canada, it refers to the slush that forms when snow melts upon roadways. The origins of the term are Scandinavian and Irish Gaelic. At one time the word slob was used to describe muddy land, and that term came from the Gaelic *slab*, for mud, and the Swedish *slabb*, for slack. Muddy land would have been just as difficult for horses and wagons to navigate as the heavy masses of floating ice, so the use of this term expanded onshore to refer to any sloppy, difficult conditions.

SNOOSE

Also known as chewing tobacco, snooze is a variety of moist snuff, the finely ground, smokeless tobacco that attained popularity during the 18th century. The origins of moist snuff can be traced to Scandinavia, notably Finland and Sweden, where it is still consumed in great amounts and is known as *snus*. Snoose, the anglicized version of that word, entered Canadian English in the late 19th century, when the first great wave of Scandinavian immigration to Canada occurred. Many came to work in the coalmines of British Columbia and to help build railways such as the Grand Trunk. Snoose was so prized and valued among these workers that in 1898, when Canadian railway builder Mike Heney was told that it was would be impossible to construct the White Pass and Yukon Railway to open up the gold fields of the Klondike, he simply said, "Give me Swedes and enough snoose, and I'll build a railway to hell." He did. He constructed one of the steepest narrow-gauge railways in the world, a line that climbs 873 m in just 32 km. In the 1920s, Finnish loggers at Red Lake, Ontario, refused to continue working when they learned that their supply of snoose had been depleted. "No snoose, no wood," is all they would say. Snoose is still a popular tobacco product in Canada today.

SNOWBLOWER

Arthur Simcard knew all too well the problems of navigating through large, snow-clogged routes. He grew up on a dairy farm and on days when snowdrifts were simply too large to surmount, he and his family would lose money as their milk sat, unsold and trapped, in the snow. Simcard began to look for a solution and remembered the wheat threshers he had seen, with their rotating blades that threw wheat into the machine itself. He began experimenting with various designs, and though he failed miserably a number of times, he persevered. In 1925, he unveiled his snowblowing device in Montréal, a four-wheel truck chassis with a snow scooper and a blower with two adjustable chutes that could toss snow 27 m. He called it the Simcard Snow Remover Snowblower, and in 1927 he sold a model to Outremont, a town near Montréal. Communities throughout Québec followed suit, as did Ottawa. Simcard, who had been previously dismissed as a hopeless dreamer, revolutionized the snow-removal industry, allowing cities to clear roads quickly and efficiently.

SPUD ISLAND

As Canada's largest supplier of potatoes, Prince Edward Island is known affectionately to many as Spud Island. With its rich sandy soil and long winters that refresh the earth, Prince Edward Island is uniquely suited to the growing of the tuber, producing 1.5 billion kg of potatoes a year, or one-third of all potatoes grown in Canada. Potatoes from Prince Edward Island are exported throughout North America and also to Venezuela, Italy, Ukraine, Portugal and Thailand. Of the $317 million dollars the island grossed in 2000, over $150 million was from potatoes. The most popular tuber on the island is the Russet Burbank, ideally suited for the production of French fries. The word spud has been in use since the 15th century, originally to describe a sharp, narrow blade used to cut through roots and dig up weeds. As a verb, a plant spuds when it produces new buds or branches. Its origins as slang for potato are not definitive, though many believe it originated in New Zealand English.

STANFIELD'S

Synonymous now with winter and long underwear, Stanfield's got its start in 1866 when Charles E. Stanfield sold his interests in the Tryon Woollen Mills in Tryon, Prince Edward Island, to his brother, so that four years later, he could open the Truro Woollen Mills in Truro, Nova Scotia. There, Stanfield produced woollen underwear of all sorts. He also developed and manufactured the first cardigan jackets and stockinettes in Canada, and he introduced heavy rib underwear to Canadians. In 1896 he sold the company to his two sons, who proceeded to streamline the operation by focusing solely upon knitted merchandise. Stanfield's sons developed the shrinkproof process for which Stanfield's would become famous. By then, the company, known formerly as Truro Knitting Mills Limited, became known as Stanfield's. In the 1950s, it introduced its signature thermal underwear, which made the family millions. Later, when they entered politics, the Stanfields became known as a sort of homebred version of the Kennedys in America. The under-wear was, and is, immensely popular.

STANLEY CUP
In 1893, Frederick Arthur, Lord Stanley of Pres-ton, Canada's governor general and son of the Earl of Derby, purchased a $50 silver punch-bowl to be awarded to the top amateur Canadian hockey team. Lord Stanley had bought the tro-phy with the hopes of increasing hockey's popu-larity, which at the time was limited mostly to Ontario and Québec. The trophy was christened the Dominion Challenge Cup, though it would be remembered for its informal name, the Stanley Cup. It was first awarded to the Montréal Ama-teur Athletic Association in 1893, making it North America's oldest professional sporting trophy. It quickly became the symbol of hockey excel-lence and supremacy, and in what must surely have delighted Lord Stanley, hockey clubs sprang up all across the country. In 1910, the National Hockey Association, which was the forerunner to the National Hockey League, took possession of the cup, and in 1926, it was decided that the cup would be awarded only to National Hockey

League teams. The original cup was retired to the Hockey Hall of Fame in 1969, but its traditions continue. On the Stanley Cup are etched the names of every member of the winning team, and it is still given, for a day, to every member of that team. Lord Stanley never did see a championship hockey game—he returned to England in 1893.

STREET NURSE

In 1987, Vancouver began an outreach program designed to promote AIDS awareness and prevention among the drug users, prostitutes and homeless of its city streets. To do so, nurses were sent into the streets in mobile clinics to exchange needles and distribute condoms. Their jobs also entailed walking inner city neighbourhoods and interviewing street people to learn their sexual histories. If one happened to be HIV-positive, street nurses turned to the bars and motels in the area in an effort to find and convince former sex partners to get tested. Although labour-intensive, the work of the street nurses of Vancouver has become an indispensable part of the city's health care system.

STUBBLE JUMPER

Slang for a Canadian prairie farmer, stubble jumper is a term most commonly associated, negatively in some cases, with farmers from Saskatchewan. The term's origins are murky, but one assumes that it was borne out of the popular and unfortunate misconception that Saskatchewan is nothing but an agonizingly flat prairie, full of wheat, stubble and little else. Some Saskatchewanites consider it a term of pride.

STUBBY
Between 1961 and 1986, Canadian beer was bottled in a short, neckless bottle that became known as the stubby. It was eventually phased out in favour of the longneck bottles with twist-off caps that were so popular in the United States. Many Canadians still yearn for the stubby, and some breweries, recognizing this nostalgic longing, are re-introducing it.

STUPID LINE
Coined by the Canadian Injury Prevention Foundation (now known as SMARTRISK) on January 6, 1994, for a campaign aimed at helping people re-think risky behaviour, the stupid line is the metaphorical boundary distinguishing a smart risk from a stupid risk. The campaign used this tagline to spread its message: "We each have a line of choice that separates a smart risk from a stupid risk. The Stupid Line. Where will you draw yours?" It might be used, for example, when an individual in a drunken stupor phones a former girlfriend and proposes. He has crossed the stupid line.

SWISH

Its origins are unclear, but one can reasonably assume that for as long as whiskey and rum have been produced in Canada, so too has swish. When a rum or whiskey barrel had outlived its usefulness, distillers either tossed the barrels away or sold them to gardeners to use as planters. It wasn't long before some enterprising soul realized that by swishing boiling water in the barrel, alcohol could be extracted from the liquor-soaked wood. Some barrels could produce as many as 22 litres of hootch, with an alcohol content of anywhere from 12 percent to 40 percent. It certainly wasn't the best-tasting stuff around, but swish did the job of rum and whiskey on the cheap. The practice is still common today, and although it's not illegal, its sale is unlicensed and untaxed. In fact, the Alberta Gaming and Liquor Commission recently asked distillers to poison barrels sold to the public so that swish cannot be made.

TO GO OUTSIDE

For a long time, Canada's North lay relatively empty, with scattered communities of traders, hunters and First Nations eking out a hardscrabble existence. Communication was slow and inefficient. Little has changed, and much of the English slang from the North reflects this sense of alienation and isolation. In the North, the outside refers to civilization; to go outside isn't just to step outside the front door, but to go from the Arctic to the more densely settled areas of the country. Not surprisingly, the North is referred to as "the inside."

TOBOGGAN

A toboggan refers to a long and narrow sled, made of thin boards curled upwards at one end. The word is derived from the Algonquin word, *odabaggan*, which originally described a sled made of bark used to drag game through the snow. One assumes that when they came to a hill, they hopped aboard the sled with their game. The Mi'kmaq called their version a *topaghan*, which early French Canadian explorers translated into *tobagan*. The early Inuit made theirs out of whalebone.

TOGGY

Although not the most politically correct garment (it is made of beaverskin, after all), the toggy was popular at a time when keeping warm superceded all other concerns. Early Canada was built from the fur trade. Trappers and traders from the Hudson's Bay Company worked in the North, seeking the pelts and furs in demand throughout Europe. One of their favourite garments was the toggy, a calf-length coat made of either beaver or caribou skin. Its design was influenced by the Cree, who called their version the *misotaki*. Trappers and fur traders shortened it to toggy. The coats themselves were in much demand; after having been worn for a year, human body oils rendered the beaver skin rich and supple, the sort of skin popular with British hatmakers.

TOONIE

In February 1996, a new Canadian coin went into circulation. Like the loonie before it, the coin was designed to eliminate a paper bill. This time, the two-dollar bill was being taken out of circulation. Its replacement was a bimetallic coin, with an outer ring of mostly nickel and an inner ring of mostly copper. The inner ring depicts a polar bear crossing an ice floe in early summer; the image is meant to illustrate the diversity of geography and weather in Canada. The process by which the bimetallic coin is joined together was patented by the Royal Canadian Mint, and while some of the earliest two-dollar coins were flawed (the inner copper ring could be easily dislodged), the errors have been corrected. Among the nicknames for the coin were the *bearly* and the *doubloonie.* One terrible punster came up with *The Queen with the Bear Behind...*quite a mouthful and sure to induce groaning. The name that stuck was toonie, a combination of two and loonie, the coin that preceded the toonie's introduction. This name did elicit groans of its own, but it has become a part of Canadian English.

TOONIK TYME

Since 1965, Iqaluit has celebrated the coming of spring and the return of the sun annually with its Toonik Tyme Festival. For a week, people gather to take part in a wide variety of events, old and new, including igloo-building, ice golf, drum dancing, throat singing, hockey and hunting events involving rabbits, seals and ptarmigans. Its name is derived from the Inuit word *tuniq,* given to the legendary giants of Cape Dorset in the southwest corner of Baffin Island who were said to have preceded the Inuit ancestors. An honorary tuniq roams Iqaluit each year during the festival dressed in an all-caribou outfit and mask. Those who spot him call the local CBC television station for a chance to win prizes.

TOURTIÈRE

Served at either Christmas Eve (usually at the Christmas feast, or reveillon, held the morning after midnight Mass) or on New Year's Eve, a tourtière is a traditional Québec meat pie dish. The tourtière, brought to New France by French explorers, draws its name from a medieval French pie dish used for cooking pigeons and other birds. The contents within were known as the *piece tourtière*; eventually, the name came to describe the meal as well. The tourtière can be made with a combination of beef, pork, lamb, veal or venison and a mixture of different spices, usually including cinnamon and cloves. Each region of Québec has its own special interpretations of this favourite dish.

TOUTIN

A popular breakfast item in Newfoundland, toutin is a sort of dough cake or flapjack. The dough is usually made the night before and then allowed to rest and rise. Cut into bite-sized pieces, the dough is fried in pork fat and then covered liberally with molasses and bits of pork. It was a favourite of woodsmen, who found that the toutin's high levels of fat prevented it from freezing as other foods might. There are almost as many variations on this dish as there are spellings for it: toutan, touten, touton, and towtent. One recipe calls for wrapping the dough pancake around a piece of bologna. Although some might find the dish a little fatty in these weight-conscious days, the meal still warms bellies on those frigid Atlantic coast days.

TRIVIAL PURSUIT

On December 15, 1979, *Montréal Gazette* photo editor Chris Haney and *Canadian Press* sportswriter Scott Abbott got together to play a game of Scrabble. Their set was missing pieces, so they decided to invent a game of their own. They eventually called the new game Trivial Pursuit, a board game that *Time* magazine called the "biggest phenomenon in game history." The first set of Trivial Pursuit, issued under the Horn Abbot Company, was sold in 1981. Although all 1100 copies sold out, toy buyers at the Montréal and New York toy fairs of 1982 seemed less than enthusiastic, placing orders for just 400 games. The company pressed on, finally garnering the attention of Chieftain Products, a Canadian subsidiary of a major American games company. In 1983, 2.3 million sets were sold in Canada, and a million sold in the United States. In 1984, Trivial Pursuit sales topped one billion dollars. Today, Trivial Pursuit continues to be one of the world's most popular board games. It is played in 19 languages in 33 different countries.

TULLIBEE

Early French Canadian fur traders named this small, delicately flavoured fish *toubibi*, a corruption of the Ojibwa *oto-lipi*. *Toubibi* was anglicized into tullibee, a relative of the whitefish that bears a striking resemblance to the sea herring. Used either as bait for lake trout or as food, tullibee is widely distributed throughout Canada, from the Mackenzie River to the Great Lakes and into Labrador. Also known as the cisco (*Coregonus artedii*) or the lake herring, the tullibee is often smoked for consumption.

TUQUE

As Canadian as maple syrup and Canada Day, this knitted, sock-like cap is said to have been the invention of cold European sailors, who created it to keep their heads warm on long ocean voyages. A little controversy surrounds the origins of this word. Some believe that *tuque* is a variant of the Québec French word *toque*, which is supposedly derived from the French verb *toquer*, meaning "to knock" (the original tuque had a long, drooping end that tended to knock its wearer on the back of the neck.) Other sources suggest the word is based on the word *tukka*, a pre-Latin word meaning "gourd or hill," presumably because of the tuque's conical shape. Still others claim the word is a shortened, anglicized version of the Chinook Jargon word *latuk*, which means "woollen cap." However you wear it, the tuque is a practical, if not always aesthetically pleasing, winter garment that no Canadian closet should be without.

VICO

Like Ovaltine and Horlick's, Vico made its name producing and selling a chocolate malted drink. Although few have probably heard of the stuff, it has found a huge number of fans in Saskatchewan, where Vico is a generic term that refers to all chocolate milk.

WHISKEY-JACK

Also called the moose bird, the camp robber or the Canada jay, the whiskey-jack (*Perisoreus canadensis*) is a grey bird common throughout the coniferous forests of Canada. It is known as a voracious eater, fond of almost everything edible and some things not so edible. It is often spotted near campgrounds, where its habit of stealing food has earned it its not-so-flattering nickname. Its name is derived from a mispronunciation of the Cree name for the bird, *weskuchanis*, meaning "little blacksmith." Early English trappers heard whiskey-jack and the name stuck. The bird tends to use its saliva to glue meat, suet and whatever else it can find from a campsite into balls, which it then hides among pine needles near its nest.

WHOOP-UP

The whoop-up has its origins in southern Alberta where, near Lethbridge, there once stood a notorious fort. Since 1832, it had been illegal to sell alcohol to aboriginals in the United States. Undeterred, whiskey traders from Montana headed north to Canada. In 1869, using Fort Benton as a supply post, two men, John Healy and Alfred Hamilton, built Fort Hamilton in southern Alberta. From there, they traded whiskey to the Natives. The liquor proved especially popular after the great herds of buffalo had been decimated. Ingredients such as soap, red ink and tobacco went into the brews, which acquired names such as "fire water," "red eye," "bug juice" and "whoop-up wallop." The fort burned to the ground in 1870, but was rebuilt that same year and rechristened Fort Whoop-Up to continue its business. Fort Whoop-Up was a plague upon the land until Canadian Prime Minister John A. Macdonald sent the North-West Mounted Police to bring order to the prairies. After 1875, Fort Whoop-Up was used only as an outpost, but its reputation survived.

WINNIPEG GOLDEYE

A freshwater fish, the Winnipeg goldeye (*Hiodon alosoides*) was named for its gold-coloured eyes and because Lake Winnipeg was the largest producer of the fish. Long a part of the diet of the Cree and other First Nations tribes, European explorers found the goldeye flesh soft and tasteless. But sometime in the late 19th century, someone noticed that Natives often smoked and cured the fish before consuming it, and an industry was born. For a time, smoked Winnipeg goldeye became a popular luxury item, with demand far exceeding supply. But by the 1920s, stocks of the fish in Lake Winnipeg dwindled to almost nothing as a result of overfishing. Today, Winnipeg goldeye is fished mainly in the North and South Saskatchewan rivers, although the fish is still processed and smoked over oak fires almost exclusively in Winnipeg. The Winnipeg goldeye is a small fish, just 30.5 cm long, with a dark-blue to blue-green back, silver sides and a white belly. Like those of a cat, the goldeye's eyes reflect light.

WOBBLY WOBBLY

Established in 1905, Industrial Workers of the World, or the IWW, is also known as the Wobbly Wobbly. Although the union was created in Chicago, its nickname has distinctly Canadian roots. In 1912, railway workers and members of the IWW went on strike. Up until that time, they had been called everything from International Wonder Workers to I Won't Works. As the IWW was one of the first unions that didn't deny membership to Chinese Canadians or Chinese Americans, the IWW had much support among Vancouver's Chinese population. Among them was a restaurateur who, legend has it, offered free food and credit to members of the striking IWW. He asked strikers coming into his restaurant, in thickly accented English, if they were in the "I Wobbly Wobbly." The name struck a chord with the strikers, who adopted it as their own. Mortimer Downing, an IWW member, stated in a 1923 letter, perhaps with a little overstatement, that the nickname "hints of a fine, practical international-ism, a human brotherhood based on a commu-nity of interests and of understanding." Not bad for a simple mispronunciation.

WONDERBRA

The Wonderbra, like the Canadarm, revolution-ized the world—a Wonderbra is sold every 15 sec-onds. Canadian designer Louise Poirier invented it in 1964; the etymology of the word should be obvious. It had 54 design elements, all working to validate the bra's full name: The Wonderbra Push-up Plunge Bra. Poirier fashioned the device for the Canadian lingerie company Canadelle, which became a part of the Playtex family, itself a subsidiary of Sara Lee. Sara Lee introduced the Wonderbra to the United States in 1994 to great acclaim and popularity; it appeared on year-end Top 10 Product lists in *Newsweek, Fortune, Time* and *USA Today*. Who says Canadians are known just for maple syrup and hockey? We can add The Wonderbra Push-Up Plunge Bra to the list.

XY COMPANY

With the signing of the Treaty of Paris in 1763, the French fur traders of Montréal found their practice and business choked off by the newly emboldened Hudson's Bay Company and the burgeoning ranks of Scottish businessmen in the city. Their livelihood threatened, Montréal fur traders realized that solidarity was critical and made several aborted attempts to form a company of their own. Finally, in the winter of 1783, a group of traders, led by Simon McTavish, created the North West Company, beginning a period of intense rivalry and bitter competition that lasted almost forty years. But while its main competitor was the Hudson's Bay Company, the North West Company faced foment from within. In 1795, a reorganization of the company created dissension and resentment between North West Company agents and its winterers—the men who braved harsh conditions to trade with the Native population. In 1798, embittered and disillusioned, the alienated winterers created the New North West Company. To distinguish their goods from those of the

North West Company, the New North West Company marked its bales with an XY. The business became known as the XY Company. Although the XY Company did reach as far as the Athabasca in 1798, the competition was devastating for both. Liquor use among agents and winterers skyrocketed, as did wages. In 1804, McTavish, the man many held responsible for the necessity of the XY Company, died and tensions between the two gradually dissolved. In November, the two companies merged, and the XY Company receded into history. The North West Company shared a similar fate in 1821 when the British government, embarrassed and at the end of its patience following the fighting at the Red River Colony, forced the squabbling North West Company and Hudson's Bay Company to merge.

YUKON GOLD

The Yukon Gold potato was the first Canadian potato to be marketed and bred by name, and it is truly a potato of the people. Before the introduction of the Yukon Gold, Canada's potatoes usually had a white flesh that was unfamiliar to new arrivals, who much preferred the yellow-fleshed tubers of their homelands. The only problem was that no one had managed to create an enhanced, disease-resistant, gold variety potato that could prosper in the North American climate. At least, not until Dr. Gary Johnston set about finding a solution. Beginning in the late 1960s, Johnston, with funding from Agriculture and Agri-Food Canada, began work on developing a gold potato at the University of Guelph. For 13 years Johnston toiled. Finally, in 1980, he succeeded with a crossbreed of a North American white potato and a wild South American yellow potato. He called it the Yukon Gold, and it soon became the favourite potato of chefs and gourmets. Although the white potato of North America still remains the most popular tuber sold, the Yukon Gold is quickly gaining popularity.

ZIPPER

Some may argue that Swedish-born Canadian immigrant Gideon Sundback is not the true father of the zipper. After all, Elias Howe and Whitcomb Judson, both Americans, had patented fastening devices to replace the inefficient buttons that were used to close pants and jackets. But the inventions of Howe and Judson proved wildly unpopular. Howe chose not to market his device, and when Judson unveiled his "Clasp Locker" to the public at the 1893 Chicago World's Fair, he sold only 20 to the United States Postal Service. It took a marriage and Gideon Sundback to usher the zipper into the modern age. At Judson's Universal Fastener Company, Sundback's design skills came to the attention of the factory foreman, who was Sundback's father-in-law. Sundback became Universal's head designer, responsible for improving the design of its Clasp Locker. After his wife's untimely death in 1911, Sundback channelled his grief into his work, and in 1913, unveiled his "Separate Fastener." He had increased the number of fasteners from four per inch to 10 or 11 and widened the opening for the glider's teeth. Although his design wasn't perfect (the fastener tended to rust), Sundback had created something unique and was issued a patent for his design in 1917. The initial reaction to the zipper was tepid, and almost 20 years passed before the zipper would become commonplace. In 1923, B.F. Goodrich ordered 150,000 of Sundback's devices for use in his new product: the rubber galosh. Goodrich loved the hookless fasteners, and even more, loved the sound they made. He began calling them zippers, and the name stuck. In the 1930s, zippers in children's clothing were promoted as a means of helping children become more independent; the fashion industry took notice and began using the device. By the late 1930s, French clothing designers were raving about Sundback's invention. *Esquire* magazine called it the "Newest Tailoring Idea for Men." Today, Sundback's "Separate Fastener" is found everywhere with thousands of zipper miles produced each day.

Z

Notes on Sources

Casselman, Bill. *Canadian Food Words*. Toronto: McArthur & Company, 1998.

Casselman, Bill. *Casselman's Canadian Words*. Toronto: Copp Clark, 1995.

McConnell, Ruth E. *Our Own Voice: Canadian English and How it Came to Be.* Toronto: Gage, 1978.

Orkin, Mark M. *Speaking Canadian English: An Informal Account of the English Language in Canada*. Toronto: General Publishing, 1970.

Story, G.M., W.J. Kirwin and J.D. Widdowson (Eds.). *Dictionary of Newfoundland English*. Toronto: University of Toronto Press, 1990.

FOLK LORE PUBLISHING

CANADIAN SPIES & SPIES IN CANADA
Undercover at Home & Abroad
by Peter Boer

Did you know that James Bond creator Ian Fleming learned how to be a spy at a top-secret Canadian training camp? That's just one of the fascinating stories you'll find in this entertaining book about Canada's world of undercover. Shaken, not stirred.

$9.95 CDN • ISBN 13: 978-1-894864-29-9 • 5.25" x 8.25" • 128 pages

CANADIAN WAR HEROES
Ten Profiles in Courage
by Giancarlo La Giorgia

From the battles of the great warrior Tecumseh to the escapades of flying ace Billy Bishop to the heroism of Princess Patricia's Canadian Light Infantry in Afghanistan, this book traces the Canadian experience of war through the centuries.

$9.95 CDN • ISBN 13: 978-1-894864-35-0 • 5.25" x 8.25" • 128 pages

CANADIAN INVENTIONS
Fantastic Feats & Quirky Contraptions
by Lisa Wojna

What do *Pictionary*, five-pin bowling, and the electric light bulb have in common? They were all invented by Canadians! This book will give you newfound respect for both the ingenuity of your countrymen and dozens of objects that you use every day.

$9.95 CDN • ISBN 13: 978-1-894864-31-2 • 5.25" x 8.25" • 128 pages

CANADIAN WOMEN EXPLORERS
Stories of daring or courage
by Tamela Georgi

This entertaining and informative book chronicles the fascinating exploits of strong Canadian women who influenced the course of Canada's history. Read about mountaineers Sharon Wood and Marcella Nordegg, astronaut Roberta Bondar, explorer Mary Schaeffer, artists Emily Carr and Frances Anne Hopkins and many others who have pioneered new horizons for women.

$9.95 CDN • ISBN 13: 978-1-894864-39-8 • 5.25" x 8.25" • 128 pages

CANADIAN CRIMES & CAPERS
A Rogue's Gallery of Notorious Escapades
by Angela Murphy

This book chronicles exciting and little-known accounts of murder and mayhem from across the country, revealing the dark underbelly of Canadian society.

$9.95 CDN • ISBN 13: 978-1-894864-30-5 • 5.25" x 8.25" • 128 pages

Look for books in the *Great Canadian Stories* series at your local bookseller and newsstand or contact the distributor, Lone Pine Publishing, directly. In Canada, call 1-800-661-9017.